LAND OF BONDAGE LAND OF THE FREE

RAUL S. MANGLAPUS

Original Edition, 1967
Re-issue, 2017

Social Revolution in the Philippines

DEDICATED TO THE
MEMORY OF
JOSEPH MULRY, S.J.,
WHO FIRST SENT THE AUTHOR
IN QUEST
OF SOCIAL JUSTICE

PREFACE

The Publishers have decided in lieu of a regular preface, to reprint in the following pages, the first public utterance by Raul S. Manglapus on social revolution and land reform.

He delivered his oration "Land of Bondage, Land of the Free" (which we have adopted as the title of this hook) as a student in Decemher, 1939 at the Ateneo Auditorium. He was representing the Ateneo de Manila in a national inter-university oratorical contest sponsored by the Civil Liberties Union of the Philippines. President Manuel L. Quezon was guest of honor and Senator Lorenzo M. Tanada then president, of the CLU, was chairman.

Mr. Quezon was so impressed by the oration that thereafter he called upon the young orator to give him advice whenever he was to deliver an important speech before young audiences, He was particularly pleased that a young student from a religious college should speak on this favorite Quezonian subject — social justice.

LAND OF BONDAGE, LAND OF THE FREE
(Oration)

UNITED STATES OF AMERICA

Commonwealth of the Philippines

IN THE HIGH TRIBUNAL OF CIVIL LIBERTIES
MIGUEL LOPEZ DE LEGAZPI, adelantado of Spain, 1565,
SINIBALDO DE MAS, secret investigador for the Spanish
THEODORE JAGOR, archaeologist for the Berlin Museum, 1859,
JOHN FORMAN, American trader, 1924,
KATHERINE MAYO, volunteer American investigator, 1925, and
JIM MARSHALL, correspondent-atlarge, 1938 PLAINTIFFS,

VS.

The TAO of the Philippines, DEFENDANT.

COMPLAINT

Come now the plaintiffs in the above entitled case and to this honorable tribunal of civil liberties respectfully allege

That the said TAO is guilty of ignorance, improvidence, refusal to comply with health regulations, non-support of family, gambling, indolence, vice, non-cooperation with the government.

Contrary to temporal and eternal laws.

Wherefore, we respectfully pray that the said TAO be condemned to loss of citizenship and be deprived of the rights enumerated in Article Three of the Constitution.

Your Excellency,
Mr. Chairman,
Fellow Speakers,
Ladies and Gentlemen,

My client, the defendant in this case, has admitted that the charges in the complaint just read against him are in great part true. But before you pass judgment upon him, I pray you hear his story:

Once upon a time, the TAO owned a piece of land. It was all he owned, but he cherished it, for it gave him three things, having which he was content: life, first of all, and liberty, and happiness.

Then one day the Spaniard came and commanded him to pay tribute to the Crown of Spain. The TAO paid tribute. And he was silent — because in his simple but passionate trust in the promise of the *informacion posesoria*, he was certain that he was still master of his land.

Now the Spaniard did not send the tribute to his kin, but kept it for himself; and in this way he became rich. And with riches evil entered into him, and he came to the TAO a second time with a formidable document, and said: According to this *decreto real*, which unfortunately you cannot read, this that you have been paying me is not tribute but rent, *not tributo* but *canon*, for the land is not yours but mine. The TAO paid the *canon* and said nothing. . .He ceased to be a freeman. He became a serf. Still the TAD held his peace. The *canon* went up and up. The TAO starved.

And this time at last he spoke. Not in words, but with that rustic instrument with which he cleared the land once his own — the halo. He transformed it from an instrument of tillage to an instrument of death, and with it he drove out the stranger. Then he returned to his field saying: "Now, indeed, shall I again be master of this land, once my own, but stolen from me by the trickery of quicker wits than mine."

But the TAO was wrong. For the land indeed had another master; but it was not he.

And the new master was not a stranger, but his own countryman grown rich. And the TAO had a new name, *kasama,* which to us means partner but which to the TAO meant still a slave, for once more he suffered from his countryman the same things he had suffered from the stranger: the rents, the usury, and all the rest of it. And so he remains today; for this story has no happy ending, or if it has, that ending is not yet.

Yes, the TAO returned to his field thinking that he was free. So did you, ladies and gentlemen, so did every one of us think that the TAO was free, when he was given a Constitution, when he Was given a Bill of Rights to guarantee his freedom dearly won!

You are familiar, I am sure with the provisions of the BILL OF RIGHTS?

NO PERSON SHALL BE IMPRISONED FOR DEBT;

NO LAW SHALL BE PASSED ABRIDGING THE FREE-DOM OF SPEECH.

THE LIBERTY OF ABODE AND OF CHANGING THE SAME WITHIN THE LIMITS PRESCRIBED BY LAW SHALL NOT BE IMPAIRED. '~

NO LAW GRANTING A TITLE OF N OBILITY SHALL BE ENACTED... '

By the way, you are acquainted also, I imagine, with that equally interesting document — I mean, the Bill of Wrongs? It is the obverse, I believe, the rather disreputable unwritten rider to the Constitution, which renders the Bill of Rights nugatory with regard to the TAO. For instance:

NO PERSON SHALL BE IMPRISONED FOR DEBT.

That depends on what you mean by a prison. If you mean by a prison those comfortable apartments of temporary detention now so much the fashion, where a man for the trifling cost of performing some misdemeanor (for instance, murder) is guaranteed a bed to sleep in, regular meals, band concerts, the movies, the radio — if you mean by a prison all this — then I regretfully admit that the TAO is free. But I mean by a prison no such palatial residence. I mean by a prison something very different — a two-room shack, rent by every wind, without any *comforts*, except that three families have there the privilege to starve. That is the TAO's prison. Its doors, if you can call them such, are wide open. It is a prison none the less. For the TAO is bound to it, not with chains of steel, with a stronger chain than that — this honor. No man knows this better than the man who put him in that prison — the usurer. To the TAO who comes to the, usurer for money, the usurer says: "Here is money. But after the harvest you must pay me double and in kind." And then the harvest comes. The usurer takes it all for he fixes the price of the harvest. It is a beautiful system, ladies and gentlemen. It is called *takipan.* — its most beautiful virtue being that it keeps the TAO in perpetual debt. There is on record in the Bureau of Lands the example of a man who borrowed ninety pesos from a usurer. Having in the interval of nine years paid one thousand four hundred pesos on the debt, he still owed at the end of nine years one thousand six hundred pesos! What a pity, ladies and gentlemen, that the TAO is an honorable man. I have no doubt at all that that man continued to pay his debt — and that his children, still imprisoned in the same shack where their father starved and died, are paying that debt to this day.

And yet, ladies and gentlemen, the TAO is constitutionally free.

NO LAW SHALL BE PASSED ABRIDGING THE FREEDOM OF SPEECH.

If you mean by law, the statutes officially passed by an officially powered assembly representing the TAO then I say we have no law abridging the freedom of speech. But there is another kind of law — a statute unofficially passed by an official assembly, a one—man assembly, where the *hacendero*, representing himself, proposes the law to himself, and approves it; a statute, not promulgated in the Official Gazette, but-secretly in the barrios, before election time, a statute not sanctioned by the courts of justice, but by the swift injustice of ejection and starvation in the streets. This law has only one provision:

"I have a candidate. He has little faults (for instance, embezzlement), but see that you speak well of him. See that you say nothing evil of him — that you vote for him, or else. . ."

The TAO complies. So would you, ladies and gentlemen, if the penalty was destitution.

And yet, this man is "constitutionally" free!

THE LIBERTY OF ABODE AND CHANGING THE SAME WITHIN THE LIMITS PRESCRIBED BY LAW SHALL NOT BE IMPAIRED. And what are the limits prescribed by law? A line running from west to east along or near the twentieth parallel of north latitude, and through the middle of the navigable channel of Bachi, and thence a line enclosing these seven thousand pearls set on a silver sea, these seven thousand spots of earth, these Isles of the Philippines, the habitation of a free people, blessed by a kindly sun, this demi-paradise swept by the very winds of Eden, and thence along the one hundred and eighteenth degree meridian of longitude east of Greenwich to the point of beginning. Nay, more than that, — the TAO may go beyond this imaginary enclosure — the world is his — and if he should decide to pack up his belongings and settle on the moon — the law of the nation cannot stop him! But the law of the *hacendero* can and does stop him — that law by which he is tied like an animal by the chain of indebtedness to two hectares of unproductive earth— — enclosed by a line running from one *mojon* of the last cadastral survey to another, a spot of earth, a very little spot of earth — the habitation of a slave! Can he leave it? Certainly he can. He can cast off this debt, this usurious debt, this debt saddled on him from time immemorial. He can do this and then sneak away into exterior darkness, dragging his carabao with his children on his back. But will he? No, ladies and gentlemen, he will not, because the TAO is an honorable man.

And yet, this is "constitutionally" free!

NO LAW GRANTING A TITLE OF NOBILITY SHALL BE ENACTED.

Of course not. Why should the *hacendero* come crawling to the national Assembly for titles of nobility? He is a noble—— by his own decree. He can step into his carriage — super-charged — and be conveyed to his ducal castle in Pampanga and there mete iron justice to five hundred slaves. You are acquainted with his coat-of— arms — a vulture, couching on a scarlet field, with the motto — *OMNES PROPTER UNUM* —all for one —— and by the way, that one is I! You will not find this escutcheon engraven in any wall. You will find it engraven by the brand of perpetual serfdom in the heart of the hacendero's slave .— your brother in blood — the TAO! Is this not the part of a noble — that while the Conde de Negros, Duque of Muscovado, Baron von Coprax is flicking up a richly-liveried foot to the mad boom of the Conga in some air-conditioned pavilion, the slaves of his feudal household broils in the blistering sun that he may have money to squander! Is this not the part of a noble to inveigle a freeman into his service with golden promises; to call him friend, compadre, partner, KASAMA; and then with a wave of the magic wand of usury, to transform him into a slave?

And yet, ladies and gentlemen, the TAO is constitutionally free!

No wonder, then that the TAO, being a slave, has acquired the habits of a slave. No wonder that after three centuries in chains, without freedom, without a hope, he should lose the erect and fearless posture of the freeman, and become the bent, misshappen, indolent, vicious pitiful thing he is! Who dares accuse him, who dares rise up in judgment against this man, reduced to this subhuman level by three centuries of oppression? Ladies and gentlemen, the TAO does not come here tonight to be judged — but to judge! Hear then his accusation and his sentence!

I indict the Spanish *encomendero* for inventing taxes impossible to bear!

I indict the usurer for saddling me with debts impossible to pay!

I indict the irresponsible radical leaders who undermine with insidious eloquence the confidence of my kind in our government.

I indict the *hacendero* for seizing my lands :by subtle trickery and reducing me to peonage! I indict him for sacrificing the honest efforts of an honest government on the altar of his illimitable greed!

You accuse me of not supporting my family. Free me from bondage and I shall prove you false!

You accuse me of ignorance. But I am ignorant because my master finds it profitable to keep me ignorant. Free me from bondage, and I shall prove you false!

You accuse me of indolence. But I am indolent not because I have no will, but because I have no hope. Why should I labor, if all the fruits of my labor go to extinguish an unextinguishable debt! Free me from bondage, and I shall prove you false!

Give me land. Land to own. Land unbeholden to any tyrant. Land that will be free. Give me land for I am starving. Give me land that my children may not die. Sell it to me, sell it to me at a fair price, as one freeman sells to another and not as a usurer sells to a slave. I am poor. But I will pay it! I will work, work until I fall with weariness for my privilege, for my inalienable right to be free.

But if you will not grant me this last request, this ultimate demand, then build a wall around your homes... build it high!... build it strong!. .. place a sentry on every parapet. . . for I who have been silent these three hundred years will come in the night when you are feasting, with my cry and my bolo at your door. And may God have mercy on your soul!

CONTENTS

LAND REFORM

INTRODUCTION

The Agricultural Land Reform Code is a revolutionary piece of legislation that responds to the imperatives of social justice. The record of deliberations over it is more than usually lengthy. The passages selected are brief in comparison; but they may help to give some indication of the climate of social opinion as it manifested itself in the Senate debate in 1963.

The first selection, which is the sponsorship speech delivered by Senator Manglapus, gives a general description and initial justification of the contents of the bill. This is followed by three selections which record the debate on the essential features of the bill — the abolition of share tenancy, the expropriation of land, and the compensation for land expropriated. The last selection, on the feasibility of the land reform program, may soon be rendered academic by events; but it has been included for what it can add to the portrayal of a social question.

1 - Appointment with History.

MR. PRESIDENT: I rise this morning to keep an appointment with history.

Most of us here, Mr. President, have had in early days an academic brushing with the subject of land reform.

I myself recall an evening in 1939 when I participated in an oratorical contest presided over by the distinguished gentleman from Quezon, who was then the president of the Civil Liberties Union. The title of my speech was "Land of Bondage, Land of the Free," and making up for youthful naiveté with the consuming fire that 1s only to be seen in collegiate oratory, I indicated a social and economic system which kept the *tao* paradoxically in bondage 1n a land of constitutionally free men.

I remember that I was privileged to hear two great Filipinos express approval of my impertinent demand that the tiller be given the opportunity to acquire the land which he and his ancestors centuries before him had worked with their hands. One was the chairman himself, a distinguished constitutional lawyer by the name of Lorenzo M. Tanada; the other was the guest of honor — President Manuel L Quezon.

At about the same time, in anothe1 part of the world, there was one nation that. was undergoing the procedure of land reform. Let me read to you what one account has to say about that social revolution:

"On the other hand, in certain areas, mainly in the South, much of the land was concentrated in large estates where the field work was done by excessively ill-paid workers. A typical estate would have a large number of "sharecroppers" who received a share of the crop in place of wages. The owner also operated a store where the sharecroppers had to buy their food and other supplies, and where they were usually deep in debt. Interest charged on these debts were high. The worker's share of the crop went to the store in payment for his debts, and usually failed to clear it all.

"The sharecropping and the farm-tenancy systems were closely similar in their effects to those commonly found in many developing countries throughout the world. Largely because of the widespread poverty of the mass of the farm population, and the unproductive luxury of the land-owning class, the southeastern region of the country was underdeveloped in 1933.

People called the region the nation's number one economic problem, and many different development programs were launched after 1933 to cure this condition.

"Land reform was one of the chief instruments of modernization. Through a 'Farm Security Administration' the government bought large tracts of land, divided them into family-sized farms, and sold the farms to the sharecroppers and tenant farmers on easy terms of payment.

"Not all the troubles of that region have been cured, but by 1945, it was clearly no longer underdeveloped. It had taken off into the modern world."

(Modernization in the U. S. A. by David Cushman Coyle)

Which country was this, Mr. President? Destitute, sprawling underdeveloped India? Poor, struggling, peon—worked Mexico?

No, Mr. President, this was the rich, the powerful United States of America.

Even that country, of all countries of the world the most advanced, found it necessary, if it was to maintain its pace of modernization and live up to its constitutional pledge to offer equal opportunity to all, to undertake, at that late stage in its march to progress, the painful but rewarding process of land reform.

Mr. President, I said that I rise today to keep an appointment with history, because what I academically advocated 24 years ago, I am now privileged :to advocate on the floor of this august body, seeking new not just the applause of a collegiate audience and the nod of a board of judges, but the passage of a bill that will actually make possible this transformation of our traditional society. And it is perhaps by express edict of the goddess of history that I should have been chosen to be a co-chairman of the Land Reform Committee, and therefore co-sponsor of this bill, mainly at the instance of the man who first approved of my speech 24 years ago — the Hon. Lorenzo M. Tanada.

Mr. President, the explanatory brochure prepared by the Presidential Committee that drafted the original bill which was the basis of this committee bill, lists down the following four objectives of the Land Tenancy Reform Program:

  a) To abolish tenancy in the Philippines;
  b) To establish owner-operated, family-size farms as the
     foundation of Philippine agriculture;
  c) To increase the farmer's productivity and income; and
  d) To enhance the relationship between agricultural and
     industrial productivity.

To this I would add a fifth — to make of farmers independent, useful, self—reliant and spontaneous members of our democratic society.

It would be an error to judge this program purely in economic terms. It is possible to debate indefinitely on whether its immediate effect will be the increased productivity of the farmer. The overwhelming indications are that this productivity will indeed increase. But I doubt if it is debatable at all that ownership of land in an agricultural society is the first badge of dignity and that dignity is the first condition for productivity.

I have been the first to admit, nay assert, that ownership, while being a condition for productivity, is not a guarantee for productivity. I have said that ultimately it is the mind, the personal philosophy, that is the key to the spontaneous contribution to progress by the individual citizen.

In Cotabato, there are many independent farmers who refuse to kill the rats that are destroying their crops because of superstition. In India, millions of small landowners continue to be poor —they are victims not of landlords or money lenders, but of their own beliefs. A recognized sociologist has concluded from the experience of reform in the Indian state of Uttar Pradesh that "Land Reform does not make new men; new men make land reform."

But while we cannot legislate the transformation of the people's minds, we can legislate those conditions which will facilitate this change.

An independent landowner may continue to be locked in the prison of his own mind, but at least he is free to take those steps and absorb that advice that will lead him to his ultimate liberation.

But a tenant is not free to do that. He is not free because he lives in a paternalistic *ambiance* and makes a minimum of decisions for himself and his family. And he is unproductive because he is without incentive, since he only gets a part of the increase in his production.

The Land Reform Program seeks to make the tiller free and productive by making him the ultimate owner of the land. Having set him free, it will not abandon him. It will continue the process of his liberation by providing him assistance, by improving his farm methods, by giving him loans for the purchase of farm implements, by marketing his goods effectively and profitably and settling his legal problems.

It seeks to provide opportunities for big landowners desirous of becoming professional farmers who can develop large-scale plantations in new areas that are now public land.

What happens once the Land Reform Bill is approved into law?

Once the Land Reform Council declares that the government agencies organized in this bill for assistance to the farmers are ready to operate in a region, share-tenancy becomes illegal and at this point the landlord may either:

a) lease his land to the tenant for a fixed rent; or

b) sell his land to the tiller.

Under the first alternative, the tenant becomes a lease-holder and works for himself and his family. He becomes his own manager and worker, free to farm the land as he sees best. His obligation to the former landlord is confined only to the payment of the fixed rental of the land even though he may increase his production.

Thus, the leaseholder-tiller, with due regard to the rights of the former landlord, becomes a dignified participant in production with real incentive to increase his harvests, income and purchasing power.

After share-tenancy becomes illegal, farms being tilled by the leaseholder—farmer may sooner or later be declared by the government as open for purchase by the leaseholder.

Purchase will be made after the government declares certain farm regions as suitable for acquisition and a fair purchase price is fixed.

A Land Bank is to finance the purchase of land from land-lords and the resale of the same land to tenants.

The land is bought by the Land Bank in the following manner:

The price of the land is agreed upon by both the landlord and the government, if the landlord voluntarily sells his land. Should the government initiate the purchase of the land, and the landlord does not offer a price, the government estimates a fair price through a systematic classification and evaluation scheme. Thus, a basis for just compensation is established.

The Land Bank then pays the landlord for his land, 10 percent in cash, at least 60 per cent in land bonds. and the balance in shares of stock of the Bank. These last two have at least the same security and rate of growth as the land purchased.

The land bonds are negotiable and acceptable as collateral for loans if the landlord wishes, say, to invest in industry. If the landlord wishes to keep the bonds, he will earn six per cent interest a year, income-tax—free. He can also use the bonds to buy public land and start a plantation.

The shares of stock given the landlords entitle them to elect one member of the Board of Trustees of the Land Bank. This Will keep control of the Land Bank in the hands of those working for the interest of both the tenant and the landlord.

The Bank is to use the P400 million capital to invest in private corporate securities that have proven stable earnings and reasonable records of growth and to pay the 10 per cent portion of the compensation for lands acquired by the Bank. All earnings of the Bank's investments will accrue to the Bank's shares of stock. Thus, shares held by the landlord will increase in value as the value of private corporate securities increases.

There will be an Investment Committee which will decide in which corporations the Land Bank is to invest its funds. Of the Investment Committee's three members, the chairman and one member is to be elected by private shareholders.

The tenant can be helped by the Land Bank to purchase the land he tills.

The Land Bank will pay a fair price to the landowner for his land and keep the title to the land. The tenant will work the land and pay the Bank in small amounts every month until such time as he can pay for the full cost of the land, and become a true and full owner of the land he tills.

Meanwhile, the Agricultural Productivity Commission and the Agricultural Credit Administration will provide financing and technical assistance to tenants to make the land they till more productive. Eventually this will enable the owner-cultivator to pay for the land out of the increases of his income over a reasonable period of time.

The Bank is authorized to issue and pay the landowner land bonds and its own shares of stock for the land which the government will acquire.

The title to the land bought for the farmer will be held by the Bank until such time as the farmer can pay the Bank the entire cost of the land he tills.

There are government lands available for clearing and sale to tenants. The Land Reform Program intends to resettle tenants in these regions if there are not enough family-size farms available for all the tenants of one area.

It may cost the government P10,000 to resettle a family in new lands, but the cost 1s well worth it if the farmer can finally get his own farm, work for himself and his family, and thereby increase his income.

A Magna Carta of Agricultural Labor defines the rights of the agricultural wage laborer as follows:

a) Right of self—organization;

b) Right to engage in concerted activities;

c) Right to a minimum wage;

d) Right to work for not more than eight hours a day;

e) Right to claim for damages in the event of death or injuries suffered while at work;

f) Right to compensation for personal injuries, death, etc.;

g) Right against suspension or lay—off from work;

h) All other rights of industrial workers applicable to agricultural laborers.

In this manner, farmers working for wages will have similar rights as those working in factories.

The Court of Agrarian Relations, as reorganized and expanded to expeditiously handle all court suits involving land reform, will specialize in the resolution of disputes involving the rights of land-owners and tenants.

If the disputants wish to appeal the decision of the Court of Agrarian Relations, they may go up to the Court of Appeals or to the Supreme Court, depending upon the nature of the issue involved.

The Office of Agrarian Counsel, consisting of lawyers specializing in counselling agricultural lessees and agricultural owner-cultivators, will provide legal help for free if the tiller is unable to afford private counsel.

The Land Reform Council is the organization that coordinates the functions of all the agencies under the Land Reform Program in respect of any particular land reform project.

It determines the particular area where land reform is to be instituted and develops for such. area a coordinated work program for all the agencies under the proposed Land Reform Act. The work program will be based on public hearings, interviews, and other data gathered and analyzed by Project Teams which the Council will send to the area for which the land reform is proposed.

Once the Committee approves such a program, all agencies, particularly the Land Authority, the Land Bank, the Agricultural Productivity Commission, and the Agricultural Credit Administration, will be bound to follow, implement and execute it in full.

Mr. President, I would like to end this sponsorship speech by quoting from the pages of a book written by the distinguished gentleman from La Union, Senator Camilo Osias. In this book, Mr. Osias quotes the words of an early Filipino land reformer who, although not a lawyer, wrote in 1887 a brilliant brief for the distribution of land in his hometown.

"The town leaves its case in the government's hands, hoping for either a formal and equitable contract between the estate and the planters or the sale of these tracts of land to those who have brought them under cultivation, under the auspices of the government, and title-deeds which the estate may bring forward ought not to be more valid in the judgment of the nation than the remonstrances of a town which has always been submissive but which is now weary of so much injustice."

That land reformer was Jose Rizal.

Mr. President, mine is no brief against landowners. Heaven knows most landowners have contributed by work and investment to the economic and industrial development of this land.

This is a brief against a system — a system that retards, that kills initiative and makes bondsmen of them who should be free.

In presenting it before you, I would like to execute a salute to the man who, whatever faults some here may find in him, has had the courage and the vision to insist that it be presented— President Diosdado Macapagal.

I would also add that I am proud to be a co-sponsor with such men as the distinguished gentleman from Tarlac, Senator Jose Roy, whose devotion to the cause of the farmer has moved him to be intimately associated with the most worthy bills on tenancy in this Congress for the past fifteen years, and the distinguished gentleman from Zambales, Senator Genaro Magsaysay, who has shared with his immortal brother a consuming love for the millions who till the soil.

Mr. President, I ask that this bill be approved and the ceremonial ribbon be cut at the opening of the road to progress.

2 - The Abolition of Share Tenancy

(The following are excerpts from the speeches delivered in the Senate on June 13, 14, 1963.)

SENATOR TANADA: Before I discuss these defects permit me to say it clearly and categorically here and now that I am not against land reform as such. On the contrary, I will be the first one to support a land reform measure which is practical, constitutional and productive of calculable improvements in the lives of our peasants and in the conditions of our economy as a whole. But, to my mind, with due respect to the brilliant minds who worked out the present Land Reform Bill that is now before us, this positively is not the kind of reform measure that I can support. And there is to begin with —— the obvious unconstitutionality of the bill in many of its provisions.

Section 4 which is one of the basic sections of the bill provides:

"Any agricultural share tenancy in whatever form shall be abolished in any region or locality upon proclamation by the Land Reform Committee that all the government machineries and agencies in that region or locality relating to leasehold, envisioned in this Act, are operating. Thenceforth, all relationship between landowners and tenants in the region or locality with respect to agricultural land shall be governed by a system of leasehold provided for in this Act: Provided, however, that the conversion to leasehold in the proclaimed area shall become effective at the beginning of the next agricultural year after the proclamation. Any person establishing or maintaining, or causing the establishment or maintenance of, a system of share tenancy other than leasehold or labor administration shall be subject to the civil and criminal sanctions imposed by this Act."

In other words, upon the effectivity of the Act, any agricultural share tenancy in whatever form whether oppressive to the tenants or not shall be abolished. This particular provision of Section 4 is unconstitutional because it impairs the obligation of contracts insofar as existing share tenancy agreements entered into pursuant to the provisions of Republic Act No. 1199 are concerned, and because it curtails the freedom of the landowner and the tenant to enter into an agreement provided it is not contrary to law, morals and public policy.

Share tenancy is not per so an evil and Congress has, therefore, no power to abolish or totally prohibit it. Congress may only regulate it insofar as its terms are concerned to» prevent the exploitation of the tenants by the owner. But the share tenancy whose terms are reasonable and not oppressive and that the tenant is even given a fair share of the produce to enable him and his family to live in relative comfort and security, cannot be prohibited or abolished. To hold otherwise is to disregard the freedom of contract that is guaranteed by the Constitution. It is true that that freedom is not absolute. But it is likewise true that the State can restrict that freedom only when its exercise is prejudicial to public interest.

According to Section 4, upon the effectivity of the law the landowners and the tenants become lessors and lessees whether they like it or not. In other words, the relationship of lessor and lessee is by operation of law imposed upon them even if the tenants, because of financial reason, prefer share tenancy to leasehold. I contend that while the State may prohibit certain kinds of contracts, it may not, however, impose a relationship or a contract upon the parties. This portion of Section 4 is, therefore, clearly unconstitutional because, besides being dictatorial and arbitrary, it deprives the landowner of his liberty and property without due process of law.

Another import of Section 4 is that upon the effectivity of the law, the establishment or maintenance of share tenancy becomes *ipso facto* an offense, a crime, and shall be subject to the civil and criminal sanctions imposed by the law. The original bill, the one that came from Malacanang, did not define share tenancy. And I contended during the Committee hearing that a definition of the term must be made, otherwise, Section 4 will be unconstitutional for it is well settled that no one may be required at the peril of life, property and liberty to speculate as to the meaning of penal statutes. Under the due process clause of the Constitution, all are entitled to be informed as to what the State commands or forbids. As a consequence, the present bill now defines "share tenancy" as follows:

"Share tenancy" as used in this Act means the relationship which exists whenever two persons agree on a joint undertaking for agricultural production wherein one party furnishes the land and the other his labor, with either or both contributing any one or several of the items of production, the tenant cultivating the land personally with the aid of labor available from members of his immediate farm household, and the produce thereof to be divided between the landholder and the tenant in proportion to their respective contributions." (Sec. 198, par. 25)

It is submitted, Mr. President, that the maintenance and establishment of share tenancy as thus defined cannot by legislative fiat be made a crime. For is it immoral or prejudicial to public welfare for a landowner and a tenant to agree on a joint undertaking for agricultural production wherein the landowner furnishes the land and the tenant his labor and the produce thereof to be divided between them in proportion to their respective contributions? Is it immoral to enter into such an agreement? Certainly, Mr. President, where the division of the produce is, according to the definition and I am quoting: "in proportion to their respective contributions," Congress is without power to outlaw such an agreement.

The Courts have held that while it is true that acting within constitutional bounds the Legislature is clothed with unlimited and absolute power to define statutory offenses or prescribe punishment for their violations, a statute enacted for the prevention of such offenses which the Legislature deems as essential to declare to promote public good must be reasonably adopted to attain that end without unnecessarily invading personal or property rights before it can be held a valid exercise of police power.

And it is now well settled, Mr. President, that the Legislature cannot in defining crimes or in prescribing their punishment take away or impair inalienable rights secured to the citizens by the Constitution. There is nothing in the share tenancy as defined in the bill that in any way threatens or endangers the public health, safety, morals 'or order. On the contrary the undertaking or agreement between the landowner and the tenant for agricultural production under the terms prescribed in the definition which includes the sharing in the produce "in proportion to their respective contributions" is not only innocent or innocuous, but is also beneficial. And the Legislature may not declare that to be a crime which in its nature is and must be under all circumstances innocent. (Felton v. U. S. 699, 24. L.ed. 875).

The precept of police power may not be validly raised to justify the abolition of share tenancy by making contracts of such nature criminal, for as aptly stated in a Philippine case, "The State, under the police power, is possessed with plenary power to deal with all matters relating to the general health, morals, and safety of the people, so long as it does not contravene any positive inhibition of the organic law and provided that such power is not exercised in such a manner as to justify the interference of the courts to prevent wrong and oppression." (Case V. Board of Health & Heiser, 24 Phil. 250. (Italics supplied).

SENATOR SUMULONG: I should like to compare the land reform under Magsaysay and the present bill, because to me there is an ocean of difference, there is a very material difference between the two. Under Magsaysay, more specifically under RA 1199, otherwise known as the Agricultural Tenancy Act of 1954, we in Congress, and there are many here. I see here faces who participated actively in the enactment of that Agricultural Tenancy Act of 1954, thoroughly discussed and considered that measure here in the Senate as well as in the House of Representatives, and the philosophy of that Agricultural Tenancy Act of 1954 to respect the right of civil determination of our peasants, of our landless farmers, those who cultivate and till the land the legal possession of which belongs to another. It does not impose, there is no compulsion in that bill. That Agricultural Tenancy Act of 1954 spells out the rights and regulations of the owner of the land and of the crop-sharing tenant in a way by which the tenant is assured of a fair deal, a fair share in the produce of the land.

We also spelled out in that Act the rights and obligations of the owner and of the lessee under a leasehold system. We spelled out the rights and obligations of each to make sure that the tenant is not exploited and that he receives a fair and reasonable share of the produce of the land. And after spelling out the conditions of its systems, the system of share tenancy and the leasehold system, then we say in the Act that the tenant is given full liberty to choose what system to adopt. If he wants share-tenancy system, let him have it; if he wants leasehold system, let him have it; if he wants one-fourth crop-share arrangement, that is, if he wants 70—30 or he wants. to provide himself with farm implements and working animals; so that the crop—share arrangement is different. He is free to do it. Why should he not be the one? Since he is the one concerned, he should know what is best for him, or do we think that we know more of what a tenant needs than the tenant himself? That is the/philosophy of the Magsaysay Agricultural Tenancy Act— to give the freedom of choice to the workingman, to the farm laborer. We talk so much when it comes to nations; we talk so much about the right of self-determination; we talk so much about fundamental human rights. If we are so concerned about the right of self-determination and fundamental human rights for nations, we must also give that right of self-determination to our workingmen, to our farm laborers, to our landless farmers. So, under that Agricultural Tenancy Act of 1954, it is the tenant that has freedom of choice. Under the present bill, that freedom, that liberty, that right of self-determination, is taken 'away from him and he is being told by the government through this bill: "Whether you like it or not, we want you 'to adopt leasehold."

I do not deny that there was a time, there were times, not only in the history of the Philippines but in the history of all, nations, when share tenancy was exploitive and oppressive. It was used as a system to exploit by the owners of the land — to engage in usurious practices in exploiting the farmers. But when you make a general and sweeping accusation that share tenancy — even the share tenancy that we embodied in the Agricultural Tenancy Act of 1954 —— is evil, feudal and anachronistic, you are not only insulting the members of Congress who approved that Act. You are also insulting Magsaysay. We have done our best to weed out the evil aspects of the share— tenancy system; and the gentleman from Tarlac, Senator Roy, was largely instrumental in that move, I know, from the time we were congressmen and even here in the halls of the Senate. During Roxas' time we changed the tenancy system. Again, we changed it and we amended it until, finally, it was embodied in a clearly spelled-out manner in the Agricultural Tenancy Act of 1954. So that even if a tenant should opt and elect share tenancy, we want to make sure that he will not be exploited, he will be fairly treated, and he will be given a fair and reasonable share of the produce of the land. But evidently, the proponents of the measure would like to impose on the tenant the leasehold system on that premise. SO, I ask each and every member of the Senate: Having given to the tenant the right of choice under Republic Act No. 1199, whereby he can shift to leasehold if really — if really — share tenancy is evil and feudalistic, whereby the tenant under Republic Act No. 1199 can leave share tenancy and immediately make it his intention under that law to' shift .to the leasehold system, why, why are there many tenants who have not yet shifted to the leasehold system? That is what we should like to inquire into. We should find Out the root causes. Why is it that, being given the freedom to choose, many tenants still continue with share tenancy and have not shifted to the lease-hold system? For me, that is the important question to answer. If I am not mistaken, the reason a tenant cannot easily shift now from share tenancy to leasehold is because he has no assurance — if he adopts the leasehold system — of financing and credit facilities. If he shifts to the leasehold system, I say that he will have difficulty in getting credit facilities and financing because it is not to be expected of him that he can get that financing and credit from the landowner, since he is already a lessee. He will have difficulties. Why? Because the ACCFA has proved to be a great disappointment. The funds of the ACCFA were exhausted, wasted, in transactions that we all know and which we all deplore. So the tenant who adopts the leasehold system cannot depend on the ACCFA for his financing or for his credit facilities. Neither can he turn to Chinese merchants now because we have prohibited the Chinese from engaging in the rice and corn industry. And neither can the tenants turn to our rural banks because our rural banks in actual practice do not give credit on the security of production or crop loans. Our rural banks require title to the land. They want the owners of the land to give security for whatever loans they will give to the lessees of these lands. That is the sad condition in which our tenants find themselves today and you cannot solve that by imposing on them this leasehold system. I dare say that even if you impose the leasehold system and our tenants cannot be assured the financing or credit facilities, you cannot solve the problem of our landless tenants. On the other hand, assure them of credit facilities. The millions that we are appropriating under this bill as pork barrel — let us not use them as pork barrel; let us use them for assuring our farmers, who want to be lessees, of credit facilities. Assure them of credit facilities and I will wager that without this bill, they will immediately leave share tenancy and adopt the leasehold system.

SENATOR MANGLAPUS: Let me proceed, if I may, to dare to answer some of the constitutional objections which have been raised, particularly by the distinguished gentleman from Quezon from whom I have learned practically all I know in Constitutional Law.

The distinguished gentleman from Quezon cited several points of unconstitutionality against this bill, the first one of which may be grouped under the provision of impairment of obligations and contract. I recall that early in the period of interpellation I had occasion to discuss this point with the distinguished gentleman from Manila, Senator Tolentino, who raised this question in interpellation. Well, I recall what I said that fundamentally the first answer to this challenge of unconstitutionality is that every contract written in this Republic contains in its provisions the unwritten reservation of police power of the State. But the distinguished gentleman from Quezon proceeded to criticize the bill also on other grounds, for-instance, the deprivation of property or liberty without due process because the leasehold relationship in this bill is imposed upon the tenant and the landlord.

Permit me to say first in answer to this criticism that this is not the first time that a relationship is being imposed on the landlord and the tenant by legislation in this Republic. Republic Act 1199 imposes the relationship of leasehold on the tenant and landlord, upon choice of the tenant; but it is an imposition none the less even if there is an intervention of the will of the tenant. If the tenant under Republic Act 1199 should choose to be a lessee, the landlord has no other choice but to permit him to be a lessee. This is an imposition on the landlord. He has no choice.

Under Republic Act 1199 there was introduced in legislation in this country the element of imposition over the relationship of landlord and tenant and that imposition was that if the tenant should choose, the landlord had no other choice but to make him a lessee. But you say that the tenant has a choice under Republic Act 1199. True.

Now, we go to, more fundamental questions on Constitutional

Law. I am wondering whether when this distinguished body passed the bill creating the Social Security System, it discussed the question of compulsion or the imposition of relationship. When this body passed the SSS Law under the Nacionalista Administration of President Magsaysay, did it consider that it was imposing the relationship of employer-beneficiary on the employer and the employee when it required that the employer should contribute to the insurance of his employees against its will? Was this not an imposition over the objections of such bodies as even religious bodies who complained that, perhaps, their system of private insurance was better than the SSS? And yet they have been required to enter into this relationship against their will.

But charges had been made that the means adopted hadbeen unreasonable because there is nothing in the share tenancy against "health, morals and public safety." Permit me to call the attention of this distinguished body that, while traditionally this phrase, "health, morals and public safety" had been used in Constitutional Law to circumscribe the scope of police power, jurisprudence shows that it is not just "health, morals and public safety" but other considerations like economic needs that may be taken into account by the courts of this land considering the scope of police power. I would refer to the case, for instance of Veix vs. Sixth Ward Building & Loan Association, 310 US 32 where the following words are found:

"The authority which a State has in the interest of the public over private contracts is not limited to matters of health, morals and safety, but extends to economic needs as well."

This, I think, is the very philosophy that has been used in many instances by our own Legislature when by legislative fiat it converted something that is not *malum per se* into a *malum prohibitum*.

I have said it before, and I will say it again, that at one point in our legislative history, overnight and all of a sudden, contracts of loans which provided that the loans then bearing interest at 15% on unsecured loans suddenly became illegal and punishable as a crime. May I ask, what power did the Legislature at that time have to declare all of a sudden that 15% was illegal and 14% was legal? What was the criterion that they used? There is nothing in the Ten Commandments that says, for instance, "Thou shalt not loan on 15%!" But the Legislature of this country, having in mind the public interest, overnight declared that relationship between borrower and lender paying 15% interest was illegal and the participants of this relationship should be punished for having committed a crime.

We have other instances: the child labor, company unions,

and Blue Sunday laws — *malum non per se* but made *malum prohibitum, malum per accidens.* What is wrong with driving on the left side of the street? And all of a sudden, the Philippine government under the American administration ordered us to drive on the right side of the street? There is nothing against "health, morals and safety" or even economics about driving on the left side of the street! But it was found within the power of the Legislature and the delegated power of the city councils to decide for the people that for its common good, everyone should drive on the right side instead of on the left side, principally because at that time the transport in this country came mainly from the American Army which used only left-hand drive vehicles.

It is true, as the gentleman from Rizal has said, that share tenancy as found in Act 1199 is allowed, and as the gentleman from Quezon has said, we have lifted its definition and, we have found no reason to change it, and have placed it in this bill. But I would like, to disagree with the gentleman from Rizal when he says that because share tenancy was defined in Republic Act 1199 it was the objective of Republic Act 1199 to keep it legal and to defend its legality or to perpetuate its legality. On the contrary, the provisions of Republic Act 1199 show that Republic Act 1199, intended to lead away our economy from share tenancy. That is why it gave the tenant the power of choice, that he could go to the landlord and say: "I would like to choose to be a lessee and you cannot stop me." This is the policy of Republic Act 1199. Yes, share tenancy is defined in Republic Act 1199, but it is defined precisely because the law wants to show What the lessee wanted to run away from and not what it wanted to perpetuate.

Mr. President, tenancy may not be a *malum per se.* I agree with the gentleman from Quezon and also with the distinguished gentleman from Pangasinan who obliquely supported that position. But if it is not *malum per se*, certainly it must be very close to it, otherwise there would have been no land reform movements abolishing tenancy in other countries. I am sure that it is not histrionics that moved the Indians to institute land reform in the vastness of the Indian continent, or Chen Cheng to institute it in Taiwan, or the United States to institute it in the Southern states, or Rizal to think about it as early as 1888.

I am not going to say that the figures that I am going to quote show unrest, but I am going to show figures to show the status of tenancy cases in the Agrarian Court. In 1955, 2306 filed, 2306 disposed: in 1956, 2592 filed, 2592 disposed; in 1957, 2603 filed, 2598 disposed, 5 pending; in 1958, 3870 filed, 3809 disposed, 61 pending; in 1959, 3863 filed, 3787 disposed, 76 pending; in 1960,

4392 filed, 4219 disposed, 173 pending; in 1961, 5187 filed, 4460 disposed, 727 pending; in 1962, 5019 filed, 3254 disposed, 1765 pending; .in 1963, 3837 filed, 1806 disposed, 2031 pending; or a total of 33,669 filed; 28,231 disposed and 4,838 pending.

I am not saying that this takes the proportion of the Huk uprising in Central Luzon. I am saying that this is an indication of the discontent, or the unrest, of the necessity for improvement of relationship, of the necessity for change; and even if there were not such an indication I would repeat what I said in the beginning that the aim of this bill is not merely settlement of unrest. Settlement of unrest is a by—product of this bill. The purpose of this bill is to place the tenant in a position of dignity so that he may be a contributor to the economy of this country.

I would conclude by recalling the argument that has least impressed me and that has been stated here and in the Lower House against this bill. The argument runs as follow: Land to the landless; why not car to the carless? Land to the tiller; why not jeep to the jeepney driver; why not pedicab to the pedicab driver?

With respect to those who used this argument, may I say that it is perhaps bordering on the malevolent. Factories and jeepneys are made by man. The lands are not made by man. Sun Yat Sen said, "Before Chinese were Chinese and there was China. The lands of China are made not by the hands of the Chinese but the hand of God." If I must be bolstered in our moral position that land is not to be taken or Viewed as a factory or a jeepney or a car, I 'will read What Pope Pius XII has said about. property and land:

"But if the productivity of the multitude can be stimulated by the hope of acquiring some property in land, it will gradually come to pass that, with the difference between extreme wealth and extreme penury removed, one class will become neighbor to the other. Moreover, there will surely be a greater abundance of the things which the earth produces. For when men know they are working on what belongs to them, they work with far greater eagerness and diligence. Nay, in a word, they learn to love the land cultivated by their own hands, whence they look not only for food but for some measure of abundance for themselves and their dependents."

And, may I add, some measure of dignity for themselves and their families.

The distinguished gentleman from Zamboanga and Basilan, in defense of his challenge of this bill that it is unconstitutional, has repeatedly said and made mention on this floor of the Negroes in the United States and of the fact that President Kennedy is willing to send a battalion in order to insure that one Negro entering the portals of a Mississippi university be unhurt, I would like to use that argument to show precisely that it is the kind of action that President Kennedy is doing that is contemplated in this bill. Why is the Negro being supported in Mississippi? Because he is in the minority? No, Mr. President. The Negro is being supported because he is the oppressed, because as President Magsaysay said, he has less in life and, therefore, he must have more in law. If we are asking the landlord to submit to this bill, we are not asking him to do so because he is in the minority; if we are helping the tenants, it is not because they are in the majority. We are following the philosophy of Republic Act 1199 then enacted under Magsaysay Who said that those who have less in life should have more in law.

I will not use the word revolution. Let it be called whatever you want—change, improvement, progress. I wonder if in invoking Ramon Magsaysay we remember that Ramon Magsaysay actually wanted to buy all the lands in the Philippines and distribute them to his beloved people. But he could not because he did not have the money; and he died without a Sixto Roxas to device the Land Bank. Ramon Magsaysay wanted to do a lot of things, but he could not do so because death cut him down too early .....

3 - Expropriation

(The following passages are from the Senate deliberations of July 2, 8, 17, 1963. They have been arranged not chronologically but topically.)

SENATOR ALMENDRAS: Mr. President, when we adjourned yesterday morning, the sponsor maintained that it is more expensive for the government to develop and give virgin lands to the tenants than to buy already cultivated lands for them. I also maintained, Mr. President, that it is more economical on the part of the government to give lands to the landless out of public lands. In most cases, by giving lands to the landless by opening public lands, the government will only build roads to these public lands, per my experience, Mr. Sponsor, when I was governor of the Province of Davao for almost eight years.

Now, I think the sponsor has agreed with me that there are so many alienable and disposable properties in our country. I do not agree with the figures submitted to the Chamber by the sponsor when he said that there are only around two million hectares of agricultural lands which are alienable and disposable. The records that I have, Mr. President, comes from the Bureau of Lands — Land Resources of the Philippines as of June 30, 1962. In this tabulation, Mr.

President, it shows here that possible alienable properties in our country reach a total of around 10 million hectares and there are only one million landless farmers in our country. With this 10 million, by giving the family-size farms of, say, three or four hectares each (this is even more than enough, Mr. President) I don't know why we have to expropriate properties. By giving out alienable and disposable properties, we will not be discriminating against people and I believe the increase in production will be more than by expropriating properties such as private agricultural lands.

I can show to you, Mr. President, and to the sponsor and to this august Chamber alienable and disposable areas. In Region 1, which comprises Abra, Ilocos Norte, Ilocos Sur, La Union, Mountain Province, Pangasinan, Tarlac and Zambales, there are 1,244,888 hectares. In Region No. 2, which comprises Batanes, Cagayan, Isabela and Nueva Vizcaya, there are 869,275 hectares. In Region No. 3, which comprises Bataan, Batangas, Bulacan, Cavite, Laguna, Marinduque, Manila, Mindoro Occidental, Mindoro Oriental, Nueva Ecija, Palawan,' Pampanga which is the home province of the President, Quezon and Rizal, there are alienable and disposable properties which are good for agriculture — 2,274,454 hectares. Even in Central Luzon alone, Mr. President, if these areas could be given out to the landless people, it is even more than enough for the one million landless people. In Region N O. 4, which comprises Albay, Camarines Norte, Camarines Sur, Catanduanes, Masbate and Sorsogon, there are alienable and disposable properties which are good for agriculture — 1,158,189 hectares. In Region No. 5 — Aklan, Western and Eastern Visayas, Antique, Capiz, Iloilo, Negros Occidental and Romblon — there are 1,266,002 hectares. In Region No. 6 — Bohol, Cebu, Leyta del Sur, Leyte del Norte, Negros Oriental and Samar —— there are 1,533,352 hectares. In Region N 0. 7 —— Agusan, Bukidnon, Lanao del Sur, Misamis Occidental and Oriental, and Sur-igao — there are 1,255,821. And in Region N0. 8—Davao, Sulu, Zamboanga del Norte, Zamboanga del Sur — there are 2,310,426 hectares.

Now, Mr. President, why do we have to expropriate properties inasmuch as there are still alienable and disposable properties in our country? We cannot compare our country to Thailand. We cannot compare our country to Japan or the United States where in those countries there are no more alienable and disposable properties. And, Mr. President, if here in our country we don't have any more alienable and disposable properties to be given to the landless people, there is no question of giving private property to the landless people. But, Mr. President, in as much as we have still alienable and disposable properties in our country which are millions, more than sufficient to accommodate this one million landless people, why do we have to expropriate private properties to give to the landless people? That is my question, Mr. Sponsor.

SENATOR MANGLAPUS: Thank you. Now, first with respect to the figures. The distinguished gentleman from Davao has given a figure of 10 million as the total alienable public agricultural lands. In answer, may I re-read into the records the list which I read last time in order to analyze the figure given by the distinguished gentleman. Out of the 29.1 million or roughly, 30,000,000 hectares of the Philippines, of the lands we have, 12 million and a half are permanent forests. We have seven million in cultivated lands. This indeed leaves 10,200,000 hectares, but they are not permanent forests or cultivated land. Now it would seem that from this figure the number presented by the gentleman is correct. However, I think we should break down the 10,000,000 into its necessary components.

Of the 10,000,000, in accordance with the figures of the Bureau of Lands and the Bureau of Forestry, 5,000,000 is non—agricultural land. This includes cities, urban lands, roads, creeks, etc. Three million is indeed agricultural land but land unsuitable for cultivation. The figure 2.2 was arrived at after deducting the non-agricultural land and land unsuitable for cultivation from the 10,000,00 the gentleman was referring to.

Now with regard to cost. The gentleman disputes my statement that it is much costlier to transplant present tenants from their own landholdings to the public agricultural lands. I don't know whether the gentleman has figures to support his contention, but I am going to read figures which I presented when I discussed this matter yesterday. I recall these figures I cited in my privilege speech. It cost the NARRA P43 million to transplant 30,000 tenant families to their resettlement areas. At this rate, 1,200,000 tenant families that we must resettle would cost us P18 billion to transplant. Aside from that we know the result of the resettlement of the NARRA and the LASEDECO is not very productive. Why? We go back to the original fears that were expressed on this floor by the gentleman from Quezon: What happens when you deprive the tenant of his traditional sources of credit? It has been alleged here, and I have not agreed with it fully—but I have gone with it preliminarily—that the landlord is one of the sources of credit of the tenant, although I have read into the record also that the tenant has other sources of credit and the landlord is only one of them. But if we remove the tenant from his present environ, what do we remove him from? We remove him from his sources of credit; we remove him from the social overhead capital; we remove him from good roads, from the nearness to the market; from his regular marketing connections which he needs for his produce, and we put him in a completely new environment, perhaps without the necessary government support like what happened in the case of the NARRA and the LASEDECO. All these arguments, I think, support our decision not to resettle these tenants but to keep them where they are but provide them with adequate government support so that the dispossessed landowner will be able to take over these large tracts of agricultural land and develop them. The record of Mindanao, the territory of the gentleman, will show that the most progressive and most successful farming operations in Mindanao are the large-scale operations because the large-scale operations can afford and conquer the vicissitudes and difficulties attendant in large farming in newly opened areas. These vicissitudes and obstacles are too difficult for the small farmers, as is now being demonstrated in certain sections of Mindanao.

SENATOR ALMENDRAS: Your Honor mentioned the NARRA. Does Your Honor have the figures to show how much was spent by the NARRA for traveling expenses of the officials, the per diems, because I was told that most of the money appropriated for the NARRA was spent for traveling expenses and per diems and not for survey Of lands and the building of roads?

SENATOR MANGLAPUS: Of course, that is a matter of proof. The gentleman is placing the burden Of proof on me to show where the money went. I think we are in a position to presume that P43 million was spent.

SENATOR ALMENDRAS: Is there any study made by Your Honor on this matter?

SENATOR MANGLAPUS: You made the statement here that the administrative portion that was taken from the P43 million certainly was not sufficient to vitiate the argument that to settle 30,000 families costs P42,900,000. Does Your Honor mean that P1 million or P2 million was spent for administration? If that is so, the P40 million will still make the resettlement of 1,200,000 tenants far beyond the capacity of the government today.

SENATOR ALMENDRAS: I would like to know, Your Honor, because I was told that most of the money appropriated for the NARRA was not used for the actual clearing of lands or in establishing irrigation system or in building roads but most of the money was spent for per diems and traveling expenses of the officials running the NARRA.

SENATOR MANGLAPUS: I think the gentleman has been in the Nacionalista Party administration longer than I and perhaps he would be in a pOsition to supply the figure.

SENATOR ALMENDRAS: I am not in a position because I am not a member of the Land Reform Committee that drafted this bill. I am beginning to doubt that not even a member of that Committee is a farmer.

SENATOR MANGLAPUS: Again I will say that we speculate here. The gentleman says that a large portion of the P43 million was spent for administration. I am willing to grant that P20 million out Of P43 million was spent on administration which is, of course, bordering on the ridiculous. Let us say that only P23 million was spent by the NARRA for the resettlement of 30,000 families and that P20 million was misspent. If that was misspent, I am surprised that no investigation was ever made. Let us presume that to resettle 1,200,000 families would entail P10 billion, which is still beyond the capacity of this government, and that is only to resettle in accordance with NARRA conditions and standards. We are trying to improve the conditions of the tenants, not to worsen it. Under NARRA conditions it was found not good to continue the resettlement, under traditional procedures it has not been found advantageous to resettle these tenants. These traditional procedures that we have been used to in resettlement have been found to be inadequate.

SENATOR ALMENDRAS: Do you think it is more expensive to open roads to undeveloped public agricultural lands rather than to expropriate properties occupied by private persons?

SENATOR MANGLAPUS: Well, Mr. President, following the Land Bank device that is found in this bill we cannot undertake the kind of resettlement that the gentleman would like us to make, because we have to undergo huge inflationary expenditures, the kind of thing we are trying to avoid. In the land reform undertaken in Japan and Taiwan they had to override terrific inflationary expenditures. If that is the question, the answer is—it would be costly and the matter cannot just be done.

SENATOR ALMENDRAS: I asked that question because if we will find that it would be economical for the government to open roads, I am quite sure from my experiences that the landless people, when they come to know that there are roads to be opened, would just follow and settle there and cultivate the lands.

SENATOR MANGLAPUS: That has been the experiment in the past. We have adopted in the past the policy of building and Opening roads, hoping that by so doing we would attract people. But the fact is that we have not succeeded and the people abandoned the idea because the government had not given them credit and the other necessary support they needed. It is also a fact that even in Central Luzon where the best roads are often found, we here in the Senate always hear complaints or get requests for pork barrel for improvement of roads. How much worse a situation would there be in virgin lands where we will still have to open new roads for the benefit of the farmers in order that they can transport their products to the market?

SENATOR ALMENDRAS: As far as pork barrel is concerned, the main purpose is political. Secondly, this pork barrel allocation is not used for opening of roads in the virgin lands. Pork barrel is usually employed for schoolhouses. I have not heard of any pork barrel being spent to open roads in underdeveloped areas, especially in Mindanao. I believe that if there are new roads to be opened in underdeveloped public agricultural lands, the landless people will just follow and cultivate those lands, especially if the government would appropriate money to survey those lands.

SENATOR MANGLAPUS: That policy has been pursued by past administrations. I am not partisan about this. Both the Liberal and the Nacionalista administrations in the past pursued that policy, but we have not succeeded in achieving the desired Objective. What we are trying to do is to settle these 1,200,000 tenants which we must do within the resources of the government. Of course, the argument would be that if we had enough money and we had enough resources, we could bring the tenants to the fastnesses of Mindanao so that the situation would be comparable to that Of the tenants in Central Luzon where they have good roads accessible to the market. If we had all of these things, I might agree with the gentleman from Davao. But it cannot be done. We cannot transplant the tenants in Central Luzon to Mindanao overnight. We cannot do it even if we spend R10 million for roads. We can develop Mindanao by opening up large-scale farming through those who can afford to overcome hardships and obstacles. This is the experience in Mindanao today, Mr. President.

SENATOR ALMENDRAS: I agree that it is more expensive for landless people, especially from Luzon, to resettle in Mindanao where there are plenty of alienable and disposable public agricultural lands open to the landless. Why do they have to go to Mindanao while there are lands in Central Luzon?

SENATOR MAN GLAPUS: It is more expensive for these 1,200,000 tenants to go to Mindanao. We are not against the policy of Opening up public agricultural lands. As a matter of fact there are definite sections in this bill which would attract those who are able to finance large-scale farming operations. The landowners Who would be deprived of their landholdings are to be given bonds which they can use as payment for public agricultural lands. How much does a hectare of land in Central Luzon cost now? Under Section 71 former landowners whose lands have been expropriated are entitled to» buy from the Land Authority public agricultural lands at a price not less than P250 per hectare and they are protected against expropriation as far as this bill is concerned and they will be given government support. There are already in Mindanao people engaged in large-scale farming operations who have been given government support and they are now succeeding.

SENATOR ALMENDRAS: May I know, Mr. Sponsor, whether it is more economical to open public agricultural lands than to expropriate private agricultural lands?

SENATOR MANGLAPUS: It is less expensive to open public agricultural lands. All we have to do is to declare that public agricultural lands are open, but I think the issue is not the opening. I think we are desirous of finding a solution as to how to settle the tenants into these public agricultural lands.

SENATOR ALMENDRAS: I think they will settle in those areas if roads will be opened in those regions.

SENATOR MANGLAPUS: Roads have been opened in Mindanao where there are lands intended for settlement, but the result of the performance has not been as expected.

SENATOR ALMENDRAS: I am talking from experience, that the moment the landless people know that there are roads opened in undeveloped lands, they just follow. What the government should do is to appropriate a certain. sum of money to survey the lands and give two, three, four or five hectares to every landless farmer, and when it comes to the necessary farm implements and work animals, then it is the duty of the government, maybe through the ACCFA or NARRA or any government entity concerned to extend loans. By doing that I think it would not be necessary for the government to expropriate private agricultural lands by compulsion, and there would be no discrimination against landowners. Production would be more because there will be more, public lands to be opened.

SENATOR MANGLAPUS: The policy outlined by the gentleman from Davao is the same policy followed in the past with respect to resettlement of tenants, and in all resettlement projects that have something to do with the opening of public agricultural lands. This has been the fundamental policy followed, and this is not the way that the tenants can be rehabilitated. It cannot be done within the resources of the government. We have to do this at minimum cost to the government and in a way by which the tenants will not be uprooted from their traditional sources of credit and sources of capital and nearness to the market. All those elements make the cultivation of their lands profitable. That is what I mean when I say that the idea of transplanting 1,200,000 to public agricultural lands is outside or beyond the resources of the government. If we were a rich country, perhaps after these people have been transplanted into the public agricultural lands we could open many beautiful roads and open many markets overnight and provide for all these things —— this would be possible. But we are trying to do this within the context of developing countries, like the Philippines. And this cannot be done in the way the gentleman would like us to do.

SENATOR ALMENDRAS: So the intention of the Committee as provided in the bill is to give these 1,200,000 tenants family-size farms of three or four hectares, and the landowner will be allowed to purchase 1,000 hectares each for him to develop, is that right, Your Honor?

SENATORMANGLAPUS: The landowners who have sold their lands, yes.

SENATOR ALMENDRAS: Whose property has been expropriated?

SENATOR MANGLAPUS: Yes, or has been sold by negotiation. May I add that it is not only the landowner that can buy, anyone who holds the bonds can.

SENATOR ALMENDRAS: Only a landowner whose property has been expropriated will be allowed to, own again say 1,000 hectares.

SENATOR MANGLAPUS: Or the holder of bonds.

SENATOR ALMENDRAS: My question is, how can you expect the landowners to develop another 1,000 hectares, in as much as they are not paid in cash except 10%?

SENATOR MANGLAPUS: In the first place, the bonds will pay for the land.

SENATOR ALMENDRAS: Does not Your Honor believe that it is more expensive to develop the land than the cultivated farm?

SENATOR MANGLAPUS: That is correct, but the policy of the government is to render the kind of credit assistance that large-scale farms need. As a matter of fact, several large-scale farms are operating on government assistance. The landowner who has the land, 1,000 hectares, can mortgage these and borrow the money. Imagine the amount of money that can be borrowed on 1,000 hectares?

SENATOR ALMENDRAS: So the intention of the bill, Your Honor, is, once the properties of the landowners have been expropriated; they could be given 1,000 hectares for them to develop.

SENATOR MANGLAPUS: They will not be given; they will be sold. Mr. President, may I say that 1,000 is the maximum. If the landowner does not care to have 1,000 —

SENATOR ALMENDRAS: So, if they do not have enough money inasmuch as they are only given 10% out of the property expropriated, then the Land Bank will extend loans to them?

SENATOR MANGLAPUS: Not only the Land Bank but the

land given to him will be mortgaged in any credit institution.

SENATOR ALMENDRAS: Instead of giving this to the landlord, why not give it to the tenants so that they can open public lands?

SENATOR MANGLAPUS: I do not quite follow that. The landowner will get, say, land that is purchaseable in exchange for the bonds paid to him in exchange for the land that he has disposed of. All right, he gets this piece of land, say, in Mindanao. Now, the question is: Where is he going to get the money to develop the land?

First of all, he does not lose anything in the transaction because there is an exchange of the land, perhaps, bigger. The bigger it is, the harder to develop. Where is he usually going to get the money to continue the cultivation of his present land?

Secondly, the land that he now possesses 'in Mindanao is mortgageable as collateral for loan, Mr. President.

Thirdly, as a landowner he is traditionally closely in touch with the credit institutions. We all know that some of these land-owners, as a matter Of fact, organize banks. They are closer to credit institutions and are more acceptable to the banks than the tenants.

SENATOR ALMENDRAS: Where do they get the cash inasmuch as only 10% is paid?

SENATOR MANGLAPUS: The question is where did they get the cash before to continue the development of their land? Second, the land is mortgageable. They can get cash from credit institutions. Any farmer can get money for his cultivation.

SENATOR ALMENDRAS: The landowners can bring money to this new area, they get their money from any banking institution?

SENATOR MANGLAPUS: Including government institutions.

SENATOR ALMENDRAS: Well and good. Now, if those facilities or privileges could be given to the landowners in order to develop the new area in exchange for the property that would be expropriated we might as well give them to the landless people to develop the new public land.

SENATOR MANGLAPUS: Because it costs so much to transplant these people to these new areas, and it will require far greater credit for the tenant to overcome the Obstacles individually, because a large-scale farming is in a far better position to overcome difficulties. This is the experience undergone by the farmers in Mindanao. It is far easier for large-scale farming to overcome the difficulties.

SENATOR ALMENDRAS: I will go to another question. Were there studies made where the tenants were asked whether they were willing to develop alienable and disposable lands if given to them by the government?

SENATOR MANGLAPUS: The studies that you ask for can be answered by the experience in the past, Mr. President. The government has made this offer in the past through the various agencies.

SENATOR ALMENDRAS: My question is whether the landless people were asked by the Committee if they were willing to go and develop the alienable and disposable lands of the government. We know they are willing to develop.

SENATOR MANGLAPUS: I have here behind me the president of the Federation of Free Farmers, and he has told me that the farmer far prefers that he be given the Opportunity to own the land which he is tilling. If that is the question of the gentleman —

SENATOR ALMENDRAS: If you let the farmer choose from which to work and develop between a cultivated farm and an undeveloped farm, there is no question that he prefers the developed farm.

SENATOR MANGLAPUS: He knows that the Obstacles of emergency land farming are unconquerable for a small farmer like him. That is why he prefers to stay where he is.

SENATOR ALMENDRAS: Your Honor, modesty aside, I do not know if there is any member of the Committee or of the Senate Committee who has more experience than I have. I am only a simple and practical man, and my solutions are practical. I have been a tenant and a farmer, and I am still a farmer. I maintain and believe, Your Honor, that if the one million farmers will be informed that the government will subdivide all alienable and disposable lands to them, we will have no problem. The question, however, is that we do not inform the public. If President Macapagal will announce that the seven million hectares of alienable and disposable lands will be given to the landless people, and there is no need to expropriate properties, rather than prejudice the owners of these cultivated properties, for sure if he is after reelection, he will be reelected. The question, Your Honor, is that the action. Here of the President is characterized by greed. Because if this bill is approved, he will go to the people and say: "The Nacionalistas are against giving land to the landless."

If he will inform the one million landless people or farmers that "there are still 10 million hectares of alienable and disposable lands which are good for you; I will Open roads; you go there with facilities; the government will organize engineering corps; I will spend for the survey of the land, give working animals," I am sure these landless people will go there. By so doing we will not prejudice the owners of the cultivated lands and their production will increase because there is more land to be cultivated. That is practical, and I think you will agree with me.

SENATOR MANGLAPUS: I would like to say in answer to the distinguished gentleman that the plan or the policy he has pointed out is again a practical one, conceding adequate resources on the part Of the government. If we had all the resources necessary to provide the tenant with the kind of credit that he needs after he has been uprooted from his traditional environs, if we had all the resources necessary to build the kind of roads and the markets for the tenant once he is already settled in these places, if we had P18 billion to transplant these families from Central Luzon to Mindanao, then I would say that I would move right now to withdraw this bill from discussion. But this is not possible, Mr. President.

SENATOR ALMENDRAS: It is not possible?

SENATOR MANGLAPUS: Our resources are far more limited than the requirements that would be imposed upon them by the plan of the distinguished gentleman.

SENATOR ALMENDRAS: Does Your Honor believe that there is not enough money to develop the alienable and disposable public agricultural lands?

SENATOR MANGLAPUS: There is not enough money if we want to develop them by transplanting tenants. But there is enough if we do it this way —— by opening public agricultural lands to big landholders who are the ones in the best position to make a success out of large-scale farming in virgin public agricultural lands.

SENATOR ALMENDRAS: There is not enough money if we are going to resettle landless people, say, from Luzon to Mindanao? But there will be enough money if we open lands right here in Luzon — there will be money?

SENATOR MANGLAPUS: No. Let us not speak of money here because the Land Bank is not going to pay out 100% cash; It is going to pay out 10% cash.

SENATOR ALMENDRAS: I agree with you, Your Honor, that to resettle these landless tillers to the already cultivated areas is more preferable on the part of the landless tillers. But don't you know, Your Honor, that by providing — my' own theory — or by just opening roads and clearing the lands for these landless tillers or rather landless people, the farmers will follow the roads?

SENATOR MANGLAPUS: With due respect-to the opinion of the distinguished gentleman —

SENATOR ALMENDRAS: Let me finish first...

SENATOR MANGLAPUS: Please.

SENATOR ALMENDRAS: And by this means, Your Honor, there will be no more tenancy because everybody will have lands. Whereas, in the present set-up there will be discrimination against the landowners. First: because after working hard, sacrificing so hard, only 10% will be paid to them. Imagine, only 10%. On all of the hard labor that they have made throughout the years only 10%. And for the remaining shares of stock and bonds, the landowners cannot be sure of that. Why?

First we cannot be sure that the Land Bank will not go bankrupt; second, I believe that production will be less. It will not increase production because you cannot expect to mechanize, say, one, two, three, four or 24 hectares. Mechanization of farms increases production, Your Honor, and there is no farmer who intends to mechanize one, 10 or even 24 hectares because machineries alone, tractors alone, will cost so many thousands of pesos. SO, I still maintain, Your Honor, that agricultural production will be less by doing this.

SENATOR MANGLAPUS: Mr. President, may I answer now? May I say, with due respect to the Opinion of the gentleman since he is a recognized farmer, that perhaps discussing this question purely in terms of roads may be oversimplifying the matter. Let me give the gentleman an example. Two days ago, we had a very interesting discussion here in which the gentleman from Quezon was involved when we discussed the income of the farmer. It was the position of the Committee to know that 45% of the income of the farmer comes from sale of crops and 55% from all other sources available to him in the area. One of the attendant results that comes from resettlement will be that of being uprooted from the environment with the usual sources of income available to him. This consists sometimes Of extra work in the community where he is already known; double crops because there is already irrigation; the condition of the soil already warranted; small businesses which are undertaken with the help of sources of credit that are available in the area. These are the sources of income that comprise 55% of the income of the farmer in the area. This cannot be solved by merely building roads and transplanting the tenants to these places where the roads are to: be developed. The roads will not give all the oher facilities and other sources of income. It may make him independent, but independent from what?

The NARRA has placed people in areas that are reached by roads. But it has been found, for instance in the case of Kidapawan, that while the tenants were settlers themselves, they found it necessary to become themselves tenants when their aspirations when they went to Mindanao were to be independent and to improve their living conditions. But when they got to Mindanao, 24% of them in the Kidapawan area had to turn. themselves again into tenants. No improvements at all, Mr. President. Why? Because the government — both the Nacionalista and Liberal administrations — in the past did not take into consideration other factors that are necessary in computing the productivity of the farms.

I am willing to concede the importance of roads. But roads, after all, are what we make them. In some places there are roads which are very vital. But there are roads constructed upon request of barrio lieutenants who come to Manila to seek the aid of the President, which both Your Honor and I decry.

We must place, Mr. President, if I may conclude this part of my remarks, the tenant in a better position than that which he is found today, and putting him in large places found in agricultural lands in Mindanao, even accessible by roads, does not put him in a better position than where he is today. It puts him, as was the experience of the NARRA, in a worse position and permits him to deteriorate rather than to improve.

SENATOR ALMENDRAS: Well, I cannot agree with Your Honor because to expropriate property is more beneficial, or rather good to the landless tenants if the lands that will be expropriated are along the national and provincial roads.

Well, are there studies made whether the NARRA settlers were contented or not?

SENATOR MANGLAPUS : The question is, were there studies made whether the NARRA settlers were contented or not.

SENATOR ALMENDRAS: Yes.

SENATOR MANGLAPUS: I don't know. Of course, the NARRA will always claim that everyone is contented. But I think we can deduce from the figures which we have already quoted, from the fact that they were only able to cultivate 54.8% of the total lands given to them, from the fact that in such areas as Kidapawan where there is now an incidence of tenancy of 24%, and from these figures given to me we find that the value of crops per hectare cultivated by NARRA is only P69. So that even if it could be shown that the NARRA settler is contented, maybe the production itself is low. All of this seems to indicate, whatever the tenant may say, the actual condition under which the tenant is living today following the policy of the government in resettlement.

SENATOR ALMENDRAS: Are there studies made why the production of NARRA settlers is less? The reason is because it may be that they do not have the irrigation facilities or they do not have the work animals.

SENATOR MANGLAPUS: This is precisely the point that I am making, that these settlers have been removed, first of all, from their accustomed environs where they have additional sources of income. They have been removed from their original sphere where they have sources of credit. The government may have attempted to give them credit, but this is not enough. They must be given credit as contemplated under the ACA.

SENATOR ALMENDRAS: Precisely, Your Honor, we must furnish what is needed by the NARRA settlers.

SENATOR MANGLAPUS: The government, of course, must do its share. There is doubt about that. That is why in this Land Reform Bill we are asking for sufficient appropriation in order that the government may do its share. But the program does not merely involve pure government assistance. We cannot deny that the tenants, even under present conditions, need government assistance. These are conditions that are not cured by massive government credit support, whether it is in Central Luzon or in Mindanao. And I repeat that in Mindanao, or wherever public agricultural lands may be found, you will not be able to duplicate the condition in which the tenants are found today. You will have to place the tenant in a far less advantageous situation than where he is now, unless we command the resources that other countries command, which we do not, for resettlement.

x x x x

SENATOR LIM: Mr. President.

THE PRESIDENT: The gentleman from Zaimboanga and Basilan is recognized.

SENATOR LIM: On the same page 24, line 28, including of course line 29, after the word "expropriated" delete all the words until "EXCESS" on line 29 and add the following after the word "expropriated" on line 28: "EXCEPT WHEN THERE IS EXCESS AGRICULTURAL LESSEES WHO CANNOT BE ACCOMMODATED IN SAID IDLE OR ABANDONED PRIVATE AGRICULTURAL LANDS." Then eliminate all the words on lines 30 and 31, so that the proviso will read from line 25 in capital letters as follows: "PROVIDED, THAT IF IDLE OR ABANDONED PRIVATE AGRICULTURAL LANDS ARE AVAILABLE IN A LAND REFORM DISTRICT, NO PRIVATE AGRICULTURAL LAND UNDER CULTIVATION WITHIN SUCH DISTRICT SHALL BE EXPROPRIATED EXCEPT WHEN THERE IS EXCESS AGRICULTURAL LESSEES WHO CANNOT BE ACCOMMODATED IN SAID IDLE OR ABANDONED PRIVATE AGRICULTURAL LANDS."

THE PRESIDENT: What does the Committee say?

SENATOR MANGLAPUS: Well, Mr. President, the Committee would like to explain its position on the matter as follows: Before we can know that there are excess agricultural lessees we have to expropriate the lands where these lessees are found. These lands are to be considered by the land project team and the area of the family-size farm that is proper under the circumstances that hold this particular estate. In other words, the amendment would be inoperative since we could not know what excess agricultural lessees there are until the estates themselves are studied and expropriated.

SENATOR LIM: No. Evidently Your Honor has not been following my amendment. As a matter of fact this is mostly,a correction in grammar, except that substantially there is one point, that if there are idle or abandoned lands available and there are no excess agricultural lessees and therefore there is no need for expropriating private agricultural lands under cultivation, we should not expropriate. The only trouble is that if we will not amend it in the way we are amending it, you can. simultaneously expropriate agricultural lands under cultivation together with idle or abandoned lands. That is too much. After all the Land Authority or the surveyors who will make surveys of the lands can easily find out whether there are excess agricultural lessees or not. I believe this amendment can very well be accepted.

I will reread it very carefully and slowly. I would like to read the proviso the way it should read if my amendment. were accepted:

"PROVIDED, THAT IF IDLE OR ABANDONED
PRIVATE AGRICULTURAL LANDS ARE AVAIL-
ABLE IN A LAND REFORM DISTRICT, NO
PRIVATE AGRICULTURAL LAND UNDER CUL-
TIVATION WITHIN SUCH DISTRICT SHALL BE
EXPROPRIATED EXCEPT WHEN THERE IS EX—
CESS AGRICULTURAL LESSEES WHO CANNOT
BE ACCOMMODATED IN SAID IDLE OR ABAN-
DONED PRIVATE AGRICULTURAL LANDS."

Your Honor will see that this is a good amendment.

SENATOR MANGLAPUS: May I be allowed to explain the position of the Committee. As already explained by the Committee some time ago during the period of amendments, the Committee has accepted the concept of priority as mentioned in this light: That we will expropriate idle or abandoned private agricultural lands and hold them for possible resettlement of tenants who may not be accommodated in the estates which are being expropriated. The wording as it is now would prevent the expropriation of tenanted lands before idle or abandoned lands are completely occupied.

SENATOR LIM: You cannot declare a land reform district unless the surveys, all the data and statistics have been gathered by the Land Reform Committee. As a matter of fact, I should like to say that I am trying to avoid simultaneous expropriation of lands under cultivation and idle land and/or abandoned lands. What is the use if there are only a few idle and abandoned lands? You will be encouraging inflation of money and burdening the Land Bank.

THE PRESIDENT: What does the Committee say?

SENATOR MANGLAPUS: The Committee would like to reiterate what was stated that the land that is to be expropriated from idle or abandoned private estates is to be held by the Land Authority for resettlement of tenants, even from other land reform districts. This was the concept in which the Committee accepted the amendment which pr0vides for order of priority.

It will be recalled that in the original bill there was no order of priority mentioned, but it was accepted only on condition that the idle. or abandoned private lands would be held by the Land Authority for possible resettlement, even from other land reform districts of excess tenants.

THE PRESIDENT: The body will vote on the amendment.

SENATOR LIM: Mr. President, I should like to speak in favor of my amendment.

THE PRESIDENT: The gentleman may do so.

SENATOR LIM: This bill has already very many defects. We are trying to tone down or minimize as much as possible, Your Honor, the defects of this bill. If that amendment is not going to be accepted, the objection, even among other senators, that I raised against this is that, even politicians can enter into the consideration of expropriation of private agricultural lands. It will remain in its full force and strength and depth and insidiousness because even if there are idle or abandoned lands in a certain land reform district and there is no need to expropriate private agricultural lands under cultivation, then because there is no excess agricultural lessees, the tentacles of the party in power, through the Land Bank and the Land Reform Committee and all the other agencies will have a Stronger grasp upon the portion of the population concerned.

So I believe that a careful scrutiny of this amendment will bear the conclusion that one objectionable feature of the bill can at least be thwarted. I do not want to make any explanation very lengthy.

SENATOR MANGLAPUS: I feel the gentleman deserves further explanation from the Committee, because I know the amendment has been submitted in all sincerity. Let me explain as follows: Let us take a land reform district. In this land reform district there are idle lands, and there are tenanted lands that are not idle. All right, if we follow the present procedure, which is the interpretation Of the Committee of Section 52, what would happen is that we expropriate both the idle and the tenanted lands. Why are we doing this? Because if we follow the procedure that is suggested by the gentleman, that is to say, expropriate only the idle lands and move all the tenants from the tenanted lands to the idle lands, what will happen is that we will reach a point, where, while we are holding the idle lands originally in reserve for excess tenants not only from the district but from other districts, there will be excess tenants who will no longer be accommodated in the idle lands or cannot be accommodated in the lands from which they are removed because the lands are no longer tenanted.

Even if Mr. A owns a 300—hectare farm in a land reform district, X, under your theory we would move the tenants if there are idle lands in the same district. We will move the tenants from the farm of A so that Mr. A's land ceases to be tenanted. Since it ceases to be tenanted, it goes beyond the pale of the power of expropriation that is granted to the Land Bank in this act. Since it is no longer expropriable, we reduce the possibility of resettlement by that much.

That is why I explained that if we accept this order of priority, we are thinking of holding this land not only for the excess tenants of the district, but also excess tenants outside of the district, and as near as possible to the many. But if we follow the procedure, we will be automatically excluding from the scope of expropriation those lands from which we have removed tenants to put them in idle lands, lands which originally could be expropriated.

SENATOR LIM: But as long as this land under cultivation is within the land district any time when the necessity comes, it can be expropriated. As long as there is no need for expropriating the private agricultural land under cultivation, we should not allow expropriation, but the moment there is need for expropriation, then it can be expropriated.

SENATOR MANGLAPUS: The effect is, as I explained, that we are in the process of evacuating, as it were, a tenanted land and putting the tenants in the idle land and automatically excluding that evacuated land from the powers of expropriation of the Land Authority, and we Shall reach a point where we have excess tenants in other land reform districts, and we will not be able to expropriate even these formerly tenanted lands that are under lease tenancy.

SENATOR LIM: If my amendment is accepted, you will remember that the land remains inside the land reform district. As long as there is no excess agricultural lessees, you cannot expropriate, if my amendment is approved, private agricultural lands under cultivation. That does not preclude the government from expropriating at any time when there are excess lessees from anywhere within the land district.

SENATOR MANGLAPUS: My reply, Mr. President, is that the effect of your suggested modus operandi would be that those lands from which we have removed the tenants, cannot be expropriated any more, even if we want to accommodate the tenants from other land districts.

SENATOR LIM: Give these tenants the chance to possess land. Now if there is enough land, idle or abandoned, why try to expropriate the other lands under cultivation when there is no more tenancy to abolish? Now, there is more tenancy in this private agricultural lands. Why are you going to abolish it? As long as there is space for all the landless on idle or abandoned lands inside the land district, we should not allow their expropriation.

SENATOR MANGLAPUS: If we were talking only of one district, this would be fine, Mr. President. But we are talking of the national scene, and we foresee situations where tenants may not be accommodated in one district alone and have to be moved to another district.

SENATOR LIM: But this whole proviso, Your Honor, refers only to a land reform district — to one reform district.

SENATOR MANGLAPUS: That's right.

SENATOR LIM: It does not talk about the whole nation.

SENATOR MANGLAPUS: Yes.

SENATOR LIM: It says here: "PROVIDED, THAT IF IDLE OR ABANDONED PRIVATE AGRICULTURAL LANDS ARE AVAILABLE IN A LAND REFORM DISTRICT." This is only a particular land reform district where there are more than enough idle or abandoned private agricultural lands. That is the only time that you should not allow expropriation. But the moment these idle or abandoned lands become lacking in area to accommodate all the landless people in that particular land reform district, then that is the time that you should expropriate. In other words, all I want, Your Honor, is to avoid simultaneous expropriation.

SENATOR MANGLAPUS: Well, you see, the trouble is, this is the way we accepted this concept — because we are viewing it from a national point of view. We foresee situations where tenants may not be accommodated in one district, either in the idle lands or in the expropriable tenanted lands, and, therefore, may have to be moved to another district. And if we follow the suggestion of the gentleman, we would be depriving ourselves or the government of the opportunity of expropriating those formerly tenanted lands which could have been expropriated. The moment we remove the tenants from a particular landed estate or piece of land, we exclude that piece of land from the power of expropriation. In the process, therefore, we are reducing the expropriable lands. Instead of inmcreasing the opportunities of other excess tenants, we are reducing their opportunities because we are excluding this particular portion of land from the power of expropriation.

SENATOR LIM: Probably, Your Honor, we do not really understand each other. There is nothing in my proposed amendment which would preclude that precisely. The amendment simply says that as long as there are still idle or abandoned lands sufficient in area to accommodate all the landless within a land reform district, we should not allow the expropriation of private agricultural land under cultivation. But the moment, any time, within that same land reform district, there are no longer idle or abandoned lands sufficient to accommodate tenants 'who have not yet been given lands, you can proceed to expropriate.

SENATOR MANGLAPUS: Under the provisions of the bill, we cannot, because the bill only allows expropriation in cases of cultivated lands or lands under tenancy or lease tenancy under the provisions of this bill. Once we have removed the lessees from the land, the land can no longer be expropriated. So, in the process, instead of increasing the available land for excess tenants, let us say, in other districts, we are reducing the possibilities; because by removing them, by transplanting them from the cultivated land to the idle land and making the cultivated land untenanted and, therefore, unexpropriable, we are depriving the government of the right to expropriate this land; and, therefore, we are reducing the actual hectarage that is available for expropriation.

SENATOR LIM: I believe otherwise. There is nothing in my proposed, amendment which would bring about that kind of a consequence or result.

If my amendment, however, is not accepted, the impression is that we are trying to really consider the landowners as enemies, as if they are not Filipinos also like the tenants, like the senators and congressmen, and all of us; as if we really want to squeeze the necks of the landowners here. Because it is very clear. Even if there is enough idle or abandoned land, still we want to expropriate as if we were trying to pit the poor, the landless, against the landowners; as if we want to finish some kind of an unfinished revolution against the landowners. Because as Senator Sumulong explained here and repeatedly by Senator Tafiada, Senator Primicias, Senator Tolentino and Senator Almendras, and all of those senators who spoke on this bill — Senator Puyat, Senator Ledesma and other senators —— we have precisely been saying that you cannot also squeeze the necks of the landowners just because they are in the minority. That is not social justice; that is not within the definition of the term "social justice." For example, it is because we want to pit the majority against the minority — the poor, the numerous poor, against the few landowners — that you could justify squeezing the necks of the minority.

In the United States, out of 200 million American citizens, just to protect the rights of one Negro, an American citizen, President

Kennedy spent, or the Government of the United States spent, $5 million and sent out 23,000 troops to the University of Mississippi — just to protect the rights of one American citizen out of 200 million Americans in the United States of America.

And here, just because we have only a few thousand landowners as against the countless landless — who by the way, I stated already, will be the most prejudiced by this bill, the tenants themselves, as I have already shown in my main speech against this bill several weeks ago —— now we want to make it appear that we really want to pit the poor against the rich, squeezing the necks of the landowners, because the landowners have been lording the tenants. You are telling the landowners:

"Now, you are going to be deprived of most of your property. 24 hectares is what we want to give you. And even in those land reform districts where there are enough abandoned and idle lands, just the same, if the government does not like your face, Mr. Landowner, we will simultaneously also expropriate your land." If that is so, Your Honor, there are not going to be tenants any more in these private agricultural lands under cultivation because they have already been transferred to these idle or abandoned lands; therefore, since there are no more tenants, what tenancy, therefore, are you trying to abolish unless the idea as I said — and I repeat it —— is to really try to squeeze the necks of the landowners, don't give them any chance at all? If that is the idea as this bill seems to contemplate in its over-all totality, in its attitude towards the landowners, then I believe we are being unjust and unfair. We legislators must legislate for the common good — not only for the rich or for the poor, or the middle class, but for the common good.

I said already here before, Your Honor, that I have no land whatsoever. The only piece of land awaiting me is the 6 feet by 4 feet there in the cemetery —— I do not know whether in Manila or in Zamboanga. It depends on my wife where she wants to bury me, although I told her: "You try to bury me in Zamboanga." But that is all. So, I am not against this bill because I am not against giving land to the landless. I have already explained that the tenants themselves will be the most adversely affected by this bill because they will never be able to own these lands — never! They will never be able to pay the monthly amortizations —— never! Not even in a hundred years. And now we even want to kill the goose that lays the golden eggs. We know that these landowners —— as Senator Sumulong just stated tonight — have sacrificed a lot also to develop these lands. And as Senator Ledesma said, with this bill, he does not agree with what you say that there will be more production; and I agree with him when he says that it will be less, that the production will even be decreased — the over-all production will even be decreased by an alarming proportion.

And so, I believe, Your Honor, that we should try to water down the bill. Let us try to tone down the bill; let us not try to make it appear that we have declared war against the landowners. Not all landowners are rich; only a small percentage of landowners are rich. As a matter of fact, those lands that are 200 hectares or over, there are only about 868 private agricultural lands all Over the Philippines ~ very few; and most of them, I think all of them, are mortgaged. So, we are trying to imagine that all the landowners are wealthy — are millionaires. No. Many of them I tell you are up to here — up to here (Senator Lim pointing to his neck) — in debt. Why should we make it very hard and very harsh, Your Honor. I consider this amendment, if properly understood, very important in the sense that we should attempt to tone down and water down this bill. And so, I would ask Your Honor that we might as well put it to a vote.

THE PRESIDENT: The Senate will now vote on the matter. All those in favor. of the amendment, please raise their right hands. (Some senators did so.) All those against the amendment, please do the same. (Some senators did so).

There are 8 votes in favor of the amendment, 11 votes against, and the amendment is lost.

SENATOR SUM ULONG: I have a pending amendment regarding the priority that should be followed in the expropriation of agricultural lands. 1 have already submitted this, I think two days ago, but we deferred consideration of it so that I may read the other provisions of the bill which was indicated by the sponsor.

SENATOR MANGLAPUS: The Committee recalls this amendment and recalls that it was suggested that the amendment might be acceptable if it were taken together with the criteria set down by the Land Authority and the Land Reform Team.

SENATOR SUMULONG: What I see in the bill is what is provided in Section 128, paragraph 3, page 57. This section 128, paragraph 3 gives to the National Land Reform Committee the following powers. I am reading sub-paragraph 3 of Section 128. I quote:

"(3) To formulate rules and regulations embody—
ing standards for (a) the selection of agricultural
lands to be acquired and distributed under this Act."

So, under this provision we are allowing the National Land Reform Committee to set the standards to be followed in the selection of private agricultural lands to be expropriated under this bill. And I submit that this is delegating legislative power to the National Land Reform Committee. And to avoid that objection I believe that we should, we in Congress ourselves, set the standards of the priority we believe should be followed in expropriating private agricultural lands.

SENATOR MANGLAPUS: Mr. President, the Committee recalls that it invited the attention of the distinguished gentleman from Rizal also to Section now 129 and Sections now 130 and 131 which provided not for the broad authority that is mentioned in the paragraph which has just been read by the distinguished gentleman but for much more specific standards laid down for the choosing of the areas of the farms, etc.

SENATOR SUM ULONG: I have read this provision also, Your Honor.

SENATOR MANGLAPUS: Now, the Committee stated that as long as this suggested amendment would not prevent the Land Reform Team from exercising the discretion that is provided for here and the judgment based on standards that are provided for in Section 131, the Committee would have no objection. It recalls that the amendment of the gentleman, if I remember correctly, provided for expropriation of lands according to priority based on the size. Am I correct?

SENATOR SUMULONG: The priority that I am —

THE PRESIDENT: Before we proceed any further. The Chair would like to inquire Whether the distinguished gentleman from Rizal insists on his amendment?

SENATOR SUMULONG: Yes.

THE PRESIDENT: Because the amendment has not as yet been submitted and nobody knows what the amendment is?

SENATOR SUM ULONG: I submitted it before.

THE PRESIDENT: Will the gentleman please restate his amendment so that the members of the Senate, including the Chair, may know what the amendment is?

SENATOR SUM ULONG: With pleasure. I will reiterate my proposed amendment, especially that we have now a revision of the bill.

THE PRESIDENT: Certainly. Please do so.

SUMULONG AMENDMENT

SENATOR SUM ULONG: My amendment is on page 24——

THE PRESIDENT: Page 24 of the revised version of the bill?

SENATOR SUMULONG: Yes. I am proposing that the words on lines 6 and 7: "IN THE FOLLOWING ORDER OF PRIORITY" be stricken out. And then between lines 31 and 32 insert the following as sub-paragraph "c," Which will read as follows:

"IN EXPROPRIATING PRIVATE AGRICULTURAL
LANDS UNDER THE TWO PRECEDING PARA-
GRAPHS THE FOLLOWING ORDER OF PRIORITY
SHALL BE OBSERVED: (1) THOSE WHERE JUSTI-
FIED AGRARIAN UNREST EXISTS."

That is the first order of priority. _

"(2) THOSE WHICH HAVE BEEN ABANDONED
OR LAYING IDLE."

That is No. 2 in priority.

"(3) THOSE WHOSE AREA EXCEEDS 1,024 HEC-
' TARES; (4) THOSE WHOSE AREA EXCEEDS 500
HECTARES BUT IS LESS THAN 1,024 HECTARES;
(5) THOSE WHOSE AREA EXCEEDS 144 HECTARES
BUT IS LESS THAN 500 HECTARES; AND (6) THOSE
WHOSE AREA IS MORE THAN 24 HECTARES BUT
IS LESS THAN 144 HECTARES."

I am proposing this priority, Mr. President, so that as between lands where there is no agrarian unrest and lands where there is agrarian unrest, why, certainly, the expropriation must first be made on lands where there is agrarian unrest.

THE PRESIDENT: May the_Chair also inquire what reaction the Committee has to this proposed amendment?

SENATOR MANGLAPUS: The Committee regrets that it cannot accept the amendment.

THE PRESIDENT: Is the gentleman from Rizal insisting on his amendment?

SENATOR SUMULONG: I would just like to briefly give the reasons behind my amendment.

THE PRESIDENT: The gentleman may proceed.

SENATOR SUMULONG: Mr. President, if we do not amend this bill and approve it in the form in. which it is now, I repeat, that this would result in Land Control and not Land Reform. I say that because we are leaving it to the so—called National Land Reform Committee to set the standards on what private agricultural lands to expropriate. That is a delegation of legislative power and there is nothing in the bill which clearly states what standards will be followed. It only says that whatever land the National Land Reform Committee may deem suitable for subdivision into family-size farms, then the land can be expropriated. That is the only thing said in this bill and that practically leaves in the hands of the National Land Reform Committee what lands to choose, to direct to be expropriated because the other agencies, that is the Project Teams and the Regional Councils, will just have to follow the policy to be laid down by the National Land

Reform Committee.

I object to giving this virtually blanket authority to the National Land Reform Committee because that will open the door to abuses and excesses on the part of the National Land Reform Committee. If land reform is really the objective of this bill, then we in Congress should set down the priority in the expropriation of private agricultural lands. And I submit that it stands to reason that we must first expropriate lands where there are agrarian troubles because that is the best justification for the government to step in to expropriate lands where there is agrarian unrest so that they may be subdivided and resold at cost to the landless tenants.

But unless we place this in the bill, it is possible that under this bill even if your land has no agrarian trouble at all, even if you have no tenants, still the National Land Reform Committee will just say: Your land is suitable for subdivision and, therefore we order the expropriation of your land. Under this bill even if your land is only 50 hectares. because it exceeds 24 hectares, even if there are big haciendas with an area of 10,000 hectares, they can begin with 50 hectares on the ground that the big hacienda is not suitable for subdivision, while the land with 24 hectares is suitable for subdivision.

We will give this National Land Reform Committee practically absolute power. We are making it a dictator in deciding what private agricultural lands to expropriate. And I fear— and I have grounds to fear — that unless we ourselves spell out the priority to be followed, then those who are not in the good graces of the administration will be the first ones to fall victims in the (expropriation of private agricultural lands; whereas, if you raise your right hand and affiliate with the party now in power, then even if there is agrarian unrest in your land, even if your land is a very big hacienda where there has been recurrent trouble, the National Land Reform Committee will just say, "Well, this big land is not suitable for subdivision and, therefore, it cannot be expropriated."

These are the reasons which impelled me, Mr. President, to submit this amendment and I, therefore, submit it respectfully to a vote by this Honorable Body.

SENATOR LIM: Mr. President, before we vote, would the gentleman kindly yield?

THE PRESIDENT: The gentleman may yield if he so desires.

SENATOR SUMULONG: Certainly.

SENATOR LIM: In View of the fact that Your Honor's amendment is lengthy, will Your Honor ask the stenographers to read it?

SENATOR SUM ULONG: I will gladly do it for them.

SENATOR LIM: Please do so.

SENATOR SUMULONG: The amendment I am proposing is as follows: "In expropriating private agricultural lands under the two preceding paragraphs, the following order of priority shall be Observed: 1) those where justified agrarian unrest exist. . ."

SENATOR LIM: That is in accordance with the present Land Tenure Law.

SENATOR SUMULONG: Yes, and I think that is in accordance with the mandate of our Constitution. It has always been the standing policy of our government that when a land is the seat Of agrarian unrest and continuous trouble between the landowner and the tenants, that is a very good ground that the land should be expropriated by the government so as to stop the agrarian unrest that has been besetting that land.

The second priority is abandoned or idle lands. So that if a land is abandoned by the owner, the government has every right to step in and expropriate that private agricultural land. The third priority will be the big landed estates, those Whose area exceeds 500 hectares. The fourth will be lands whose area exceeds 500 hectares but is less than 1024 hectares. The fifth will be those lands whose area exceeds 144 hectares but is less than 500 hectares. The sixth will be those lands whose area is more than 24 hectares but is less than 144 hectares. That is the order of priority that I am proposing.

SENATOR LIM: Well, Your Honor, I agree with those amendments which are very sound, although I don't believe they will be approved by this Body. I would like to make some kind of an appeal that if there are — I say if —— among us senators who are voting on this very vital amendment along partisan line, to please desist from continuing to do so because some of these amendments are really very vital and. we are all anxious to try to cure this bill, Your Honor;. and if Your Honor would submit this very vital amendment now to a vote, I am afraid the other amendments submitted by the Nacionalista senators will be defeated. So, I would like to ask Your Honor that on this very vital amendment, we postpone the voting because this is really a very vital amendment. I think the senators who listened'to that amendment will agree with me that it is really very vital. Will Your Honor agree to postpone voting on that amendment until tomorrow?

SENATOR SUM ULONG: I will accede to postponing the voting on this amendment because I believe that we should not leave everything in the hands of the National Land Reform Committee as to what land will be expropriated. If the standards I have proposed here are unsound and unreasonable, I am subject to correction and amendment. But I do not like. . .

SENATOR LIM: It will really be a Land Control Act unless this amendment of Your Honor is approved.

SENATOR SUMULONG: My idea is, we should not allow the National Land Reform Committee to begin with 50 hectares when there are big haciendas. We should allow the National Land Reform Committee to begin with big haciendas where there is agrarian unrest.

SENATOR LIM: Under the pretext that others are more suitable than the others?

SENATOR SUMULONG: That criterion of suitability for subdivision is not a limitation at all. Every land can be suitable for subdivision.

THE PRESIDENT: The motion to suspend consideration of the amendment is submitted. What does the sponsor say?

SENATOR MANGLAPUS: It is the position of the Committee, Mr. President, that there are specific standards. . .

THE PRESIDENT: No, on the motion to suspend consideration.

SENATOR MANGLAPUS: No, no. May I ask for a suspension for a few minutes because I feel there may be an area of agreement here. I voiced this when the motion was presented a few days ago.

(Suspension of the session)

SENATOR PRIMICIAS: Mr. President, I ask that we suspend the session for a few minutes.

SENATOR MANGLAPUS: Just a minute. I was addressing myself to the gentleman from Rizal, recalling that the Committee has always said that it has an Open mind on this question provided that certain conditions are met, and I feel that a suspension of the session for a few minutes might lead to an agreement.

THE PRESIDENT: Is there any objection?'(Silence.) The Chair hears none. The session is suspended.

(The following day)

THE PRESIDENT: The gentleman from Rizal is recognized to resubmit his amendment in order that the members of the Senate may know the subject of discussion.

SENATOR SUMULONG: Mr. President, I am restating and rewording the following amendment on page 24, lines 6 and 7. Delete the words "WITHIN A LAND REFORM DISTRICT IN THE FOLLOWING ORDER OF PRIORITY:" and insert in lieu thereof: "SUBJECT TO THE TERMS AND CONDITIONS AND PRIORITY

HEREIN BELOW SPECIFIED."

On the same page, between lines 30 and 31, insert the following:

"c. IN EXPROPRIATING PRIVATE AGRICULTURAL
LANDS DECLARED BY THE NATIONAL LAND
REFORM COMMITTEE OR BY THE LAND AU-
THORITY TO BE NECESSARY FOR THE IMPLE-
MENTATION OF THE PROVISION OF THIS ACT,
THE FOLLOWING ORDER OF PRIORITY SHALL
BE OBSERVED:
(1) ABANDONED OR IDLE LANDS;
(2) THOSE WHOSE AREA EXCEEDS 1,024 HEC-
    TARES;
(3) THOSE WHOSE AREA EXCEEDS 500 HEC—
    TARES BUT IS LESS THAN 1,024 HECTARES;
(4) THOSE WHOSE AREA EXCEEDS 144 HEC-
    TARES BUT IS LESS THAN 500 HECTARES;
(5) THOSE WHOSE AREA EXCEEDS 24 HEC-
    TARES BUT IS LESS THAN 144 HECTARES."

SENATOR TOLENTINO: Mr. President.

THE PRESIDENT: Before the Chair recognizes anybody, may I inquire first what does the Committee say to this amendment?

SENATOR MANGLAPUS : The Committee will ask for a two-minute suspension while we confer with the gentleman from Rizal on his amendment.

THE PRESIDENT: Is there any other matter that can be taken up while the amendment is redrafted, without suspending the session?

SENATOR MANGLAPUS: I think we are ready to continue with the discussion.

SENATOR SUMULONG: May I restate my amendment? This is a small modification. My amendment will be as follows: On page 24, on lines 6 and 7, delete the words "WITHIN A LAND REFORM DISTRICT IN THE FOLLOWING ORDER OF PRIORITY :" and insert in lieu thereof: "SUBJECT TO THE TERMS AND CONDITIONS AND ORDER OF PRIORITY HEREIN SPECIFIED," and on the same page, between lines 30 and 31, insert the following:

"c. IN EXPROPRIATING PRIVATE AGRICULTURAL
LANDS DECLARED BY THE NATIONAL LAND
REFORM COMMITTEE OR BY THE LAND AU-
THORITY WITHIN A LAND REFORM DISTRICT
TO BE NECESSARY FOR THE IMPLEMENTA-
TION OF THE PROVISION OF THIS ACT, THE

FOLLOWING ORDER OF PRIORITY SHALL BE OBSERVED:
(1) ABANDONED 'OR IDLE LANDS;
((2) THOSE WHOSE AREA EXCEEDS 1,024 HEC-
TARES;
(3) THOSE WHOSE AREA EXCEEDS 500 HEC-
TARES BUT IS LESS THAN 1,024 HEC-
TARES;
(4) THOSE WHOSE AREA EXCEEDS 144 HEC-
TARES BUT IS LESS THAN 500 HECTARES;
(5) THOSE WHOSE AREA EXCEEDS 24 HEC—
TARES BUT IS LESS THAN 144 HECTARES."

THE PRESIDENT: What does the Committee say?

SENATOR MANGLAPUS: The Committee, Mr. President, finds this new version of the Sumulong amendment acceptable.

THE PRESIDENT: The Committee accepts the amendment.

SENATOR TOLENTINO: Mr. President.

THE PRESIDENT: The gentleman from Manila.

SENATOR TOLENTINO: Yes, Mr. President, I was going to propose an amendment. On page 96, line 14, delete the entire line; on line 15, delete the word "by" after "resettlement" and, in lieu thereof, 1nsert "WHICH HAS BEEN FILED WITH"; and on lines 17 to 18 delete the words "have been issued AND PROPER NOTICES SERVED ON THE TENANTS."

THE PRESIDENT: What does the Committee say?

SENATOR MANGLAPUS: Mr. President, the Commit-
tee regrets, in View of the objectives of this bill, that it cannot accept the amendment of the distinguished gentleman.

SENATOR TOLENTINO: May I explain, Mr. President?

THE PRESIDENT: The gentleman from Manila may do so.

SENATOR TOLENTINO: Under existing law, Mr. President, the landowner can mechanize for the purpose of increasing production or for lowering cost of production, and the preper application for such purpose is to be filed with the Agricultural Tenancy Commission; and after certain inspections and requisites have been complied with, then the proper certificate should be issued and notices served upon tenants who may desire to contest the application. The point, Mr. President, is there are many applications pending with the government office concerned and have not been acted upon. The fact that these applications have not been given due course and have not been acted upon is the fault of the government. It is not the fault of the parties involved or interested. And the amendment is simply to cure the effects of this inaction on the part of the government agency concerned. Where the law authorizes a certain act to be done, as it is so authorized in Republic Act No. 1199, and then the government officials deliberately sit down on the applications, I think the Congress should see to it that we allow these applications to be taken into account and processed and due course be given to them—and not leave it within the power of government officials to frustrate the intention of Congress by simply sitting down on the applications once they have been filed. I think, in this case, there may even be cases of malfeasance on the part of government employees who have actually sat down on these applications. I understand that there are a number of these applications pending, and it is only fair that since these applications have been filed long before we took up the Land Reform Bill, they should be given due course. This bill has actually eliminated mechanization as a ground for taking over the lands from tenants by the landowners. In other words, in the future, there can be no more applications for mechanization, and I think that that is a retrogressive economic step because we all know that mechanization is resorted to for the purpose of increasing production or lowering cost of production. It seems that the purpose of this bill is just to provide social remedy irrespecive of the fact that it may be economically a retrogression and inimical to the general welfare because it might actually result, if it does not discourage, the increase of productivity.

That is why, Mr. President, I have presented this amendment and let the Committee reject it as it has rejected it. Let this Chamber reject it if it wants to reject it, but I want to make it of record that if there is reduction of productivity in the future because of failure in its mechanization, it will be the responsibility of those who want to eliminate mechanization in our agriculture.

THE PRESIDENT : Has the Committee an explanation to make?

SENATOR MANGLAPUS : Yes, I would just like to make it of record that the Committee is not against mechanization as the gentleman from Manila would imply. As a matter of fact, it was the Committee itself which inserted this Section 205 which does not exist in the original. But upon discovery of the fact during the hearings of the Committee it felt however that it could not agree to including in the exception every application that had been filed; it had to insist that proper notices be served on the tenants before the application be considered subject to the reservation of Section 205. For obvious reasons there is here protection for the tenant because he has been given notice by the proper government agency. I have no doubt at all that there may be occasion where the delay in giving proper notices may have been abetted by a government official, but we have provisions in our laws that provide remedies for government officials who delay action on applications in their respective offices. We felt that in arriving at a compromise position between our desire to facilitate mechanization and also in our desire to provide family-size farms to those who deserve them, this was the maximum position that we could accept.

SENATOR TOLENTINO: Mr. President, may I direct some questions to the sponsor on this point?

THE PRESIDENT: The sponsor may yield if he so desires.

SENATOR MANGLAPUS: With pleasure.

SENATOR TOLENTINO: I would like to know what is wrong in giving due course to applications already filed or pending? They will not be new applications and yet they are not going to be approved. I did not say that it will be approved. The bill also says that they will be given due course under the provisions of Republic Act 1199. So that if the application does not comply with the requirements of Republic Act 1199, they must be disapproved. But what is wrong with giving due course and acting upon them one way or another instead of just terminating them by fiat of law which we are putting up in this section? What is wrong with that? That is what I want to know.

SENATOR MANGLAPUS: Mr. President, we have already stated that the Committee feels that the maximum position that it can accept in this direction is the inclusion of applications where proper notices have already been served to the tenants. This we believe is for the protection of the interest of the tenant. We don't want of course to go into a lengthy discussion of the activities of the government agencies in this connection, but it is the experience of those who know about this matter that the government agencies concerned have not been too strict in dealing with these applications and a provision like that which the distinguished gentleman would like to insert here would open the way to all kinds of manipulation that would vitiate the objectives or the provisions of this bill.

SENATOR TOLENTINO: Mr. President, what I am talking about or asking for is the reason or What is the objection to acting on these applications. Can it be said that these applications have been filed in bad faith that is why we should not allow them to be acted upon? What we are asking only is action not approval. What is wrong? That is what I want to know. Is it the feeling of the Committee that these applications have been filed in bad faith? And why, if they were filed in good faith, why should these people who filed the applications be prejudiced by inaction or malfeasance possibly of the government officials?

SENATOR MANGLAPUS: Well, the Committee has already stated its position on that. But there are laws which provide for remedies for government officials who do not carry out their duties under the law.

SENATOR TOLENTINO: Mr. President, that is a very sorry excuse for inaction by government officials. Precisely, we wanted action to be done and here we will just allow them to commit malfeasance, anyway there is a remedy against them administratively or criminally. If we could do something in this bill to give due course to the pending applications, why don't we do it? Or is it simply because we don't want to give due course at all to them? Let us confess it if that is the fact that this bill is intended and the position of the Committee is not to give due course at all any more to the pending applications. That is what I want to know. Irrespective of the merits ——whether the Committee does not want to give due course to them any more.

SENATOR MANGLAPUS: Mr. President, the Committee would be very candid in his regard.

SENATOR TOLENTINO: Better.

SENATOR MANGLAPUS: The Committee feels that heretofore the certification of mechanization, with very good exceptions of course have been made the basis of Sec. 205, but the Committee feels that the filing of the applications for mechanization have been used by landlords to pressure tenants, a sword of Damocles over the heads of tenants. The effect of amending Section 205 so as to include all applications that have been filed even if no notices have been served would be to give due course to the threat that the landowner has been making over the heads of the tenants making use of the otherwise valid filing of applications for mechanization.

SENATOR TOLENTIN O: A threat of what, Your Honor?

SENATOR MANGLAPUS: There are many things that a landlord could threaten a tenant into, such as to go into a sharing that is not provided by law, like going into a 50—50 share tenancy.

SENATOR TOLENTINO: But after this bill has been approved, can he do that?

SENATOR MANGLAPUS: The gentleman assumes that all applications for mechanization were filed with the intention to mechanize. We feel that there must be a proper compromise since we cannot accept that all applications, Mr. President, were filed with the intention to mechanize; some were done actually to put pressure on the tenants. But notices that have already been served will be given due course. As a matter of fact, there is a representation made by those who appeared before the Committee. I can mention names here. One of them is Mr. Narciso of Pangasinan. Their request was that due course be given to certifications where notices have already been served.

SENATOR TOLENTINO: Maybe, that one individual had already a certificate and notice has already been served. What about the others? Just because that one individual falls under your construction, we amend that in order to suit that particular individual? Why not make it' uniform for anybody who filed applications in good faith? If it is true that applications were made in bad faith, that could be inquired into and the application rejected. What I am asking in my proposed amendment is that these applications be inquired into, processed and acted upon.

SENATOR TANADA: Mr. President, will the gentleman from Rizal and Manila yield to a few questions?

THE PRESIDENT: The gentleman may yield if he so desires.

SENATOR TOLENTINO: Gladly.

SENATOR TANADA: In order that we can solve this problem, can the gentleman from Rizal and Manila inform us how many applications are pending before the Court of Agrarian Relation which have not been acted upon? My reason for asking that question is if there is one, two or three, then perhaps the distinguished sponsor would agree. But if there are 100, then perhaps we will have to consider very seriously the effect of the amendment being introduced by the gentleman from Rizal and Manila. So I am asking this question. Everybody now wants to terminate this deliberation. Now, how many applications are pending that Your Honor's amendment would protect or cover? If there is only one, two, three, four or five, I am of the belief that the distinguished sponsor, the gentleman from Rizal and Ilocos Sur, would agree.

SENATOR TOLENTINO: Mr. President, I am not in a position to state the number of the applications. I understand there are many.

SENATOR TANADA: There are many. Can we not be given more or less a rough estimate of the number?

SENATOR TOLENTINO: We have some people in the technical staff assisting the distinguished sponsor, and perhaps they can furnish us the figure.

SENATOR TANADA: I wish to state for the record that I am in favor of the amendment introduced by the Committee to the original bill because this amendment introduced by the Committee to the original bill was due to the representation made during the hearings conducted by the Committee. Now, I would like to state also that I am in favor of the idea advanced here by the gentleman from Rizal and Manila to the effect that applications pending before the Court of Agrarian Relation before the filing of this bill and which therefore cannot be considered as applications filed in order to evade the provisions of this bill, Should be taken into consideration. I thought we could solve this problem by finding out whether the applications are numerous or just a few. I wish to thank the gentleman from Manila and Rizal for the answers that he has given and I will listen very carefully to the discussion between him and the distinguished sponsor.

THE PRESIDENT: If there are no other remarks on the matter, the Chair submits this to a vote. All those in favor of the amendment, raise their right hands. (Several senators did so.) Those who are against the amendment, raise your right hands. (Several senators did so.) The Secretary will include the Presiding Officer.

(The Secretary informed the Chair of the result of the voting.)

There are seven in favor of the amendment, and eleven against. The amendment is lost.

4 - Feasibility

(From the Senate deliberations of June 13, 14, 18, 1963.)

SENATOR TANADA: Mr. President, another objection to the measure is that it is impractical, that it will not work and it will not solve the problems it has set out to solve. Let us take as an example the case of the Land Bank which the bill will establish to finance the purchase of the estates.

What is the total farm area covered by tenancy which the government must purchase if our tenants are to be given land? (I am not including estates in excess of 24 hectares, without tenants, but which are also expropriable according to Section 52 (1) (b) which I have just discussed.)

Let us use the President's figures to determine the total tenant-hacienda area. In his message, the President states that there are 1 million tenants operating an average of 2.4 hectares each. This makes a total of 2,400,000 hectares under tenancy.

Based on an average price of P2,000 per hectare (which is very low, because some ricelands are now worth as much as P10,000), this would mean a total value of F'4,800,000,000 payable in stocks and bonds, of the Land Bank. These stocks and bonds are to draw a guaranteed income of 6% in interest or dividends as the case may be. Hence yearly there would have to be paid by the Land Bank, or in case of default of the latter, by the government, the sum of P288,000,000 in interest and dividends alone.

Originally, under the Macapagal Land Reform Bill as well as under the bill filed by the Liberal senators except Senators Cuenco and Padilla, and also under the bill reported by the Manglapus-Magsaysay Committee, the Land Bank is to be capitalized at P500 million of which P200 million is to be fully paid—up by the government. The other F300 million is to be issued to landowners as 40% payment on their expropriated lands. The provision IOf the bill regarding this matter is rather defective; but this is the intention of the bill according to Secretary Roxas when he testified in one of the Committee hearings. It would seem that the authors of the three bills apparently did not then realize that 40% of the value of all expropriable land amounts to much, much more than P300 million; the figure reaches P1 billion, 920 million (P1,920,000,000). Now, I ask: When the Bank runs out of its P300 million worth of stocks, how shall the other landowners be paid?

I ask this question because the bill specifically requires that 40% of the value of the land expropriated shall be paid in shares of stock of the Land Bank. If there are no more shares of stock of the Land Bank, because they have all been issued, how can the Land Reform Program of President Macapagal be continued or carried out? Of course, after the deluge of amendments that came three days ago, among other things, the 40% was reduced to 30% and what is more, to the surprise not to say dismay of those who know the state of our government finances, the capitalization of the Land Bank was increased not twice the original capital but three times, that is, from P500,000,000 to P1,500,000,000. Somebody must have discovered a gross error in computation — error in terms not of centavos, but in terms of millions of pesos. — so the bill had to be amended even before we had reached the period of amendments.

The distinguished sponsor, Senator Manglapus, was asked by the no less distinguished Senator from Rizal and Manila, Senator Tolentino, where we are going to get the money needed just to launch the Land Reform Program, which amounts to about P700,000,000, considering that our present revenues are not even sufficient to cover the sum of about P2,334,929,584 which is the total budgetary requirements of the government; and the distinguished sponsor Whose intellectual honesty has been demonstrated in the course of his sponsorship, answered that he did not know, he however hoped, fervently I am sure, that it will be forthcoming. Let us also hope that the money needed will come, otherwise we will have to pay dearly if we pass this knowing that we do not have the money necessary to finance the program.

Under the amendment increasing the capital of the Land Bank to P1,500,000,000, the government shall subscribe to P900,000,000 shares of stock, and the balance of P600,000,000 worth of shares shall be used in acquiring lands pursuant to the provisions of the Act. I regret to state that the amendment does not solve the problem. For 30% of the value of the expropriable land amounts to P1,440,000,000 which is very much more than P600,000,000 worth of shares of the Land Bank. We are now using 30% and not 40% because of the recent amendment introduced by the Committee.

Another amendment, of the more than 100 introduced by the Committee, is that 10% of the value of the land to be expropriated shall be paid in cash. Now, 10% of the P4,800,000,000 which is the value of the expropriable land under tenancy, is P480,000,000. The P400,000,000 to be paid in cash will not be enough, assuming that the government can get hold of this amount. And if the entire f400,000,000 will he used in buying lands, what will be the income of the Land Bank? When will it get the money to pay the interest and dividends on its bonds and stocks?

Assuming that it will invest P200,000,000 of the P400,000,000, and assuming a yearly return of 80% on the P200,000,000 invested by the government, which is the President's flown figure, that is if we can find enough enterprises which would give such a return, we have a yearly income for the Land Bank of P16,000,000. But the Bank has to pay interest and dividends on its bonds and stocks at the rate of P199,200,000. Where is the deficit of P183,200,000 yearly to come from?

From the former tenants? But these former tenants will be holding an average of, say, three or four hectares only. They cannot hold more because the bill requires that the lessees must personally cultivate the land. How much of the income from this can they set aside yearly to pay on the purchase price of their new lands? Certainly, not very much, and especially if we consider the interest he will have to pay on the principal which, according to the President, will be 8% per annum. Although Section 106 provides that interest on loans to farmers shall not be more than 12% and may be subjected to a 5% insurance fee payable at the time the loan is granted. And what will happen to the lessee's payment when crop is bad or is destroyed? One crop failure alone will destroy the estimates and paper computations of the experts who drafted this bill.

Incidentally, what will be the effect in the stock market if the Bank's F200,000,000 capital for investment is actually released? I will leave this for the economists to answer. However, I can say this, that with P200,000,000, it will not be hard for the government to acquire control of existing industrial enterprises. So that, in the end, by this bill, the government will control both industry and agriculture. And yet we say we want the government out of business — we are for free enterprise.

The bill apparently already anticipating such a deficit, provides that the government will cover the Land Bank's deficit. But where is the government to get a quarter-billion pesos yearly? And if the Land Bank is continuously in the red, its shares will be next to worthless.

What all this seems to mean is that with only P200,000,000 actual cash for purchase of lands, the Land Bank can buy in the immediate future only about P800 million worth of haciendas, out of the total that are worth aggregately some P4,800,000,000. This computation is based on the provisions of the Macapagal Land Reform Bill. The Land Authority will therefore enjoy a wide latitude of choice on which estates to expropriate. Does this not open avenues to abuses, graft and corruption? Could the power to expropriate moreover not be used to threaten or blackmail landlords or be used as political weapons to punish independent-minded landowners?

Now, shall we discuss the redemption of the bonds when they mature? Sixty per cent of the payment is to be made in bonds. If all the tenant-estates are expropriated, this would mean 60% of P4,800,000,000, or P2,880,000,000. Where does the President propose to get this fantastic sum of money at maturity of the bonds? Can the Land Bank possibly raise this amount when, as we have seen, it will most probably be operating at an equally fantastic deficit? It is doubtful that even the amortization payments of the former tenants could cover such a deficit and at the same time build enough of a surplus to pay the bonds upon maturity. This doubt is confirmed by reports the veracity of which cannot be denied, that tenants who acquired parcels of estates expropriated under existing laws have had to sell their parcels because they could not make both ends meet.

I have been furnished a computation of how much the former tenant would get as produce of a three-hectare riceland. This memorandum was prepared by one of the most progressive farmers in Central Luzon — Mr. Hector Moreno. In View of the importance of this particular point, I would like to speak lengthily on the same by referring to this memorandum. As I said, the computation is based on a three- hectare riceland producing 30 cavanes of palay per hectare, cultivated by a tenant or lessee family with a family of 6 persons, 2 adults owning 1 carabao, plow, harrow and cart. The gross harvest of this three-hectare riceland, according to this computation, will be 90 cavanes—3 x 30. Seeds at ¾ cavan per hectare will be 2.25 cavanes. Threshing at 4% will be 3.6. Harvesting at 8% will be 7.2 cavanes. Deducting these three items from 90 cavanes, you have the net harvest for the tenant, now owner of the land, in the amount of 77.95 cavanes. The family consumption of rice for one year at 1.5

gantas per day is 43.8 cavanes. The cavanes of palay disposable, therefore, would be 34.15 cavanes. This is the result of the operation which consists in deducting from the net harvest of 77.95 cavanes the 43.8 cavanes that the family will consume for one year. The sale of these 34.15 cavanes at P11.50 per cavan will bring P392.70. The sale of rice bran—we are already assuming that the rice bran will be sold, it is not always sold—will bring P4380. So the gross income will amount to P413650, but the tenant or the new owner of the land will have to borrow the minimum of P5000 necessary to prepare and cultivate the land per hectare. Now, the loan repayment of this P150.00 plus interest will be P175530. The interest that Mr. Moreno gives here is 17% because according to the bill the tenant shall not be charged more than 12% plus another 5% for insurance. So the net income will be P261.00 per year for those three hectares. Now the land valuation based on this rental, that is 25%, capitalized at 6%, will be P4,023.90. The amortization, therefore, based on 20 years payment at 8% interest on balances will be P371.05. Now, considering that the net income is, P261.00 and the amortization is P371.05, then the tenant will still be short, for purposes of amortization alone, of the amount of P110.05.

But, Mr. President, this computation does not include the expenses for supplementary food, for fish, for pork now and then, or carabao meat, for clothing for the family, for repair and maintenance of the house, for depreciation in farm implements, for depreciation of carabao because carabaos age, for school expenses of the children, for medical expenses due to illness in the family. These items are not included. Now, if we include these items, where will the tenant, the new landowner get the money for amortization? That is Why I consider this bill as impractical. . .

Now, the other computation is also based on a three—hectare riceland, but this time producing 50 cavanes. Because you know this rice industry will say that 50 cavanes is, for the present, almost untenable. Yes, there are farmers who produce 100 to 200 cavanes per hectare, but that is only in small quantities, exceptionally cared for like gardens cared for by housewives. They do not spend for fertilizer and they devote all their time to the cultivation of the gardens. But let us say this computation on the 3-hectare land producing 50 cavanes. Gross harvest will be 150 cavanes. Seeds at ¾ cavan per hectare will be 2.25 cavanes; threshing at 4 percent, 6 cavanes; harvesting at 8 per cent, 12 cavanes. Deduct these three items which amount to 20.25 cavanes from 150 cavanes, you have the net for the new owner of the land amounting to 129.75 cavanes. Rice for family consumption for one year, for a family of 6 persons at 1.5 gantas 1a day, 43.8 gantas. Deducting this rice consumed by the familyfrom the net of 129.75 cavanes, we have 95 cavanes which the new owner is free to dispose. At 1911.50 per cavan, he will get P538840. Sale of rice bran which will amount to 21.9 cavanes at P2 per cavan is P4380, and the gross income will be P1,032.20. Loan repayment of P150 plus interest Will be P175.50. Net income, P856.70. Amortization. based on 20-year payment at 8 per cent, P624.90. The owner of this 3-hectare riceland producing 50 cavanes will not lose but will net P231.80. But this again does not include the expenses for supplementary food, clothing, labor and maintenance, depreciation of farm implements, school expenses and medical expenses. I hope that the experts of the Presidential Committee on Land Reform will give us their answer to this computation. I did not have the chance to test the accuracy of this computation by asking the experts of the Presidential Committee on Land Reform because this computation was given to me only four days ago. SO, I will continue.

If this is to be the state of affairs of the Bank, I repeat, what value in turn can its stocks have? The authors of the bill in Section 77 have provided for a special guarantee fund to pay the Bank's "bonds, debentures, and other obligations, in the event that the Bank shall be unable to pay." This section provides that "for the purpose of such fund, there shall be appropriated formally the sum of P1 million out of any moneys in the National Treasury not otherwise appropriated, until the total amount of P20 million shall have been attained." But considering that the Land Bank is authorized to issue "five times its unimpaired capital and surplus" which could be five times P1,500,000,000, or P7,500,000,000, is the guarantee fund of P20 million adequate? Is it not now obvious that the bonds that the landowners will get as compensation for their lands are, to say the least, of very little value, and that, therefore, said bonds cannot at all be considered as a fair and full equivalent of the lands taken?

Admittedly, Mr. President, the Bank can space the issuance of bonds at say P1 billion a year, which will naturally reduce the obligation, but the burden will still be heavy for the Bank to bear. Besides, it would mean that the "deliverance" of the tenants from their economic difficulties will be delayed.

Consider now the reduction in government revenues that will result from the disappearance of income tax payments from present hacenderos. The haciendas will be divided into family—size farms, a size of necessity barely large enough to support the former tenant and his family. In all likelihood, the latter will not be paying any income tax because their income will not be large enough to be taxable. What then is to replace the taxes formerly paid by the big estate owners? The latter will now be deriving their income from the interest and the dividends on their Land Bank stocks and bonds, which under the bill are to be tax-free.

Yet, the government can ill-afford any loss of revenue. Government expenditures are mounting. They will mount further under the provisions of the Land Reform Program. For instance, P400 million will be appropriated for the Land Bank alone which must be paid by the government within one year from the enactment of this bill into law; P1 million yearly until the sum of P20 million is reached will be appropriated for the special guaranty fund; P5 million for the Land Authority; P10 million for its land survey and classification; P150 million for the newly created Agricultural Credit Administration; P5 million for the Agricultural Productivity Commission plus salaries for its 16,000, I repeat 16,000 "extension workers" (according to Secretary Abes); P100 million for the Special Cadastral Program Revolving Fund; P10 million for the Agricultural Land Administration: P5 million for the Court of Agrarian Relations which by the way will have one Executive Judge and 50 Associate Judges with the rank of Judges of the Courts of First Instance, 60 hearing officers with a salary of P9,000 per annum each, 51 clerks of court with a salary of P7,200 each and 51 deputy clerks of court with a salary of P5400 each; and P3 million for the Office of the Agrarian Counsel, whose head shall have the rank of first Assistant Solicitor General, with a Deputy and 80 Special Attorneys under him; all told, an appropriation of almost P700,000,000 upon passage of the proposed Act alone, not to speak of the recurring appropriations that will be necessary to pay salaries of the myriad officials and personnel created in the Act. I am beginning to wonder whether the measure is not just one mammoth spoils system being passed off as a Land Reform Program.

SENATOR MANGLAPUS: The distinguished gentleman from Quezon has cited figures which tend to show that if we go ahead with this program, the farmer would not be able anyway to pay the instalments on the land and, therefore, the land reform would fail because the Land Bank will collapse, because: it will not receive the proper support of payments from the tenants.

I would like to recall, Mr. President, at that time the distinguished gentleman from Quezon made the following computations:

First, he started with the assumption of three hectares as the average size of the family-size farm, and then he multiplied these three hectares by a maximum of 50 cavanes per hectare as produce and found a total produce of 150 cavanes of three hectares per year. Then he would deduct the seedlings, threshing and harvesting amounting to 20.25-cavanes, leaving a net of 129 cavanes. Then he would deduct the consumption of six persons at 1.5 ganta a day. Then he would have the figure of 85.95 cavanes, and he would multiply these by P11 per cavan. The total would vary a little, but I have a total of P945.45. If added then we should add half a peso or P40. This will be about P1,020.40. We would add also 29.9 cavanes of rice at P200 each, 43.80 or a total of 1,032. We add P40, that would be about 1,072, less laundry payment of P175.50. The difference would be P856570, less amortizations P624.90.

The gentleman from Quezon then found that there would be available for family living only P181,80. I wonder if that is exact. Add the P40 that is due or P271.80.

Now, he has used this example to show several things, in general to show that the land reform cannot succeed.

Second, that the Land Bank will not succeed because the family landholder would not be able to pay his instalments. Let me point out first that under our definition, page 92, paragraph 19 of a'family-size farm, this unit is an area of farm lands that will produce an income sufficient to produce a modest living, to provide for a yearly instalment on the land and reasonable reserve to absorb yearly fluctuation and income.

At this point, it is impossible to predict the exact average hectarage that would be found in each region by the Land Reform Committee to be the family-size farm unit and, therefore, I would submit with due respect to the gentleman from Quezon that the basis of the three hectares is probably somewhat arbitrary since it is not supported by actual research and findings. But with due respect to him, I will use this figure and his rate of production of 50 cavans to make another computation. He said that the total production would be 150 cavans — 50 times 3 hectares, 150 cavans. The net production after seeds, threshing and harvesting costs are deducted is about 129 cavans. I will also use this figure of 129 cavans, but I will not use his figures on family-size consumption because apparently they are not based on the actual statistics. The statistics apparently in the Philippines show that the average size of a family is not 6 but 5, to begin with, and this makes a lot of difference in the consumption and in the computation. The average consumption of rice is 4.4 cavans of palay per person per year, or a total family consumption of 22 cavans of palay — and not 48.8 cavans as would be one of the conclusions of his computation. Deducting 22 cavans from 129, you get an availability of 107 cavans to the family.

Now, let us also take the figure of the gentleman from Quezon of P11 per cavan instead of the supposed price of P1150. Now this is correct; it is P1150. The value of 107 cavanes at P11 per cavan is P1,177. Now, we have to increase this again by half a peso, which will make it about P1,227. Let us forget the income from rice bran, since rice bran is commonly used for the payment of the milling fee. The cash cost of producing one hectare of palay, according to a research study that we have here with us. is P67 per hectare. P67 times 3 hectares is P201. Now, P1,177, to this we add again the P50 residue ——make this P1227; less cost of production of P201, will equal P1,026. Now, let us also use P624.90 of amortization and interest he mentioned. P1,026 less P624.90 is about P401.10 available for family living, instead of the sum of P231 as arrived at by the distinguished gentleman from Quezon. He is correct if he says that P351 is still insufficient, or P401, as we have it here, would still be insufficient for family living. The average cash cost of living of our farmer is P750. Let us, however, not forget a very important fact about farming, and that is, that the means of livelihood of our farmers is not limited to the income that they get from their share in the crop. Let us) not forget that our farm families have other sources of income. A farm operator has non-farm sources of income. He can have industries, home industries, piggeries; he can go out and get a job elsewhere. The other members of the family also have other sources of income. As a matter of fact, income from the sale of land comprised only an average of 45 per cent of the total cash income of our farmers – not from the sale of land but sale of crops. A study that we have here of 5,195 farms shows that the operator's non-farm income average P176 and that other family non-farm income average P279, or a total of P455. Now, P401.10 plus P455 is P856.10 total income. This P856 may be just slightly over the cost of living of P750. It does not offer a large margin for fluctuation of income. This is true under the status quo — under the present system of tenancy. Under this system, the farmer works only 7.4 months out of 12 months; and the farm family works 7.7 months out of 16.3 months of available labor. This is what happens in a system of tenancy where the farmer does not get the entire benefit of harder work. The objective desired by this Land Reform Bill is precisely the incentive for the farmer to make the best use of the land and the maximum use of his and his family's labor. The incentive comes from the system where the benefits resulting from harder work and better management will accrue entirely to the farmer and his family.

Mr. President, this brings us, of course, to the fundamental objectives of this bill. I was going to leave this to the conclusion, but I would like to say this here: that it is not the objective of this bill merely to settle unrest. We may be able to prove that there is not a single dispute in land tenancy today (but I am sure that we cannot do this) and we would still insist on land reform because the settlement of unrest is only a by-product of land reform. Land reform seeks to increase productivity by making the tenant successively, first, a lessee, and then a landowner, by making him participate more in the increased production of his land, giving him the incentive to produce more by giving him the opportunity of get 'ting all that is coming to him after he has paid a fixed rental as lessee; and all that is coming to him after he has become the owner of the land.

The gentleman from Quezon has doubted the ability of the Land Bank to pay the 6 per cent dividend on the bonds or shares. He has assumed, of course, something which I have modestly tried to refute; and that is, the inability of the tenant to pay. However, I would like to call respectfully the attention of the members of the Senate to Chapter VII, Section 127, which provides that a Land Reform Project Team shall go about studying areas, agricultural areas in the country, and determine the suitability of any area for redistribution into family-size farms; the economic size of farm units; the feasibility of acquiring and distributing the area; and the financial and other requirements of the project. For this purpose, it may gather data, obtain opinions, conduct surveys and pursue investigations, and incorporate any information thus established in a development program for the area. In other words, the difficulty that is contemplated by the gentleman from Quezon isanticipated by Section 126 because no area will be recommended by the Land Reform Team unless the team is convinced that productivity in the area will ensure that all the provisions of this bill including the payment of instalments by the tenants Shall be made possible. The team has to take into consideration the conditions of the areas and that this is also taken into consideration with the members of the agencies that are to be established, such as the Agricultural Credit Administration and the other agencies of the government that are to assist in the productivity and the supply of credit of the tenant turned lessee and the lessee turned owner.

The gentleman from Quezon assumes that this is not possible. We assume that it is. He assumes 100% non-payment by the tenants who are to become landowners. We assume that under this bill there will be no areas that will be brought under the Land Authority, that will be brought under the purview and operation of this bill, unless the Land Reform Team has made sure that the difficulties: that have been anticipated by the gentleman from Quezon are also anticipated by them ahead Of time. If we assume 100% payment 'by the farmers, there will be no need for the P200 million, that is, the original P200 million provided for in the bill which is now P400 million because of the 10% cash payment. The collection by the Land Bank within 10 years can, be invested in long-term or short-term securities which will provide for further payments in the future.

I do not wish to tax the indulgence of this distinguished" body but I have here for examination of the members of the body an outline of how this may be carried out assuming a phase that will involve a portion of P100 million worth of' property every year, and I will have this at the disposal of the members of this body.

Mr. President, a lot has been made, about the money that is being appropriated for this bill. The gentleman from Rizal and the gentleman from Zamboanga and Basilan have delivered very eloquent words decrying the amount that is to be appropriated in this bill which in the first year would amount to P699 or P689 million. May I first remind this distinguished body that the yearly appropriation out of this total is only P28 million. Secondly, I am not going to use the word "revolution." I am just going to use the word new, novel, unusual, original. But I am going to recall that this Senate has year in and year out appropriated mil-lions of pesos for such things as public works. I recall that in 1960— 61, this body" passed a Public Works Act amounting to P500 million, and? I am wondering whether the record of this Senate will show that anyone complained that there was no such money available, that anyone ever wonders that this money would be available to the government to implement the Public Works Act.

We have before us this year P300 million worth of public works. I wonder how many Of us are going to ask Senator Antonino where he is going to get P300 million. We are here, Mr. President, involved in not just a yearly Public Works Act. We are involved in something that is fundamental to the economy and to the political life of this country.

I think, Mr. President, that our sense of values, with due respect to everyone concerned, should dictate that in considering an unusual situation like this that we should not equate it with the ordinary bills that we have so far been considering on this floor.

SENATOR ALMENDRAS: Your Honor, suppose a landlord has, say, 500 tenants. Like almost in all —— if not all—places, the tenants depend upon the landowner for loans all year round for the following purposes: for daily subsistence, expenses for the cultivation of the farm, repair of their houses, implements, etc.. and even for emergency needs like hospital fees, doctor's bills, baptism, funeral expenses, matriculation fees for their children come the opening of the school year.

SENATOR MANGLAPUS: Fiestas.

SENATOR ALMENDRAS: Yes, fiestas. After this bill becomes a law, who will replace the landowner as source of this credit?

SENATOR MANGLAPUS: Well, Mr. President, first, again the

hypothesis here is that the landowner is the exclusive source of credit of the tenant.

SENATOR ALMENDRAS: Yes.

SENATOR MANGLAPUS: Well, to begin with, we will assume that hypothesis, but I will show later on that this is not the general rule.

SENATOR ALMENDRAS: You maintain, Your Honor, that it is not the general rule, but it is happening now.

SENATOR MANGLAPUS: But "assuming that hypothesis, that is the reason we are appropriating P150 million for the Agricultural Credit Administration which will go into intensified credit operations on the barrio level. And even the extraordinary situations like that which Your Honor has mentioned, we feel, would be covered. And, I want to emphasize, that the facts are that the tenant has other sources of credit besides the landlord himself. As a matter of fact, from the figures that I read sometime ago, the sources of credit as of 1958 of the farmers were as follows: private individuals, 35 per cent; landlords, 18 per cent; relatives, 15 percent; merchants, 9 per cent; farmers, 6 per cent; registered institutions, 13 per cent; and others, 4 per cent.

SENATOR ALMENDRAS: So, it is the Agricultural Credit Administration, Your Honor, that will extend the credit. Now, does Your Honor think that the Agricultural Credit Administration which extends the loan can grant the loan at the precise time that the tenants need the money — say, in 1 or 2 days? Whereas, if it is the landlord, there is no need of any collateral, no need of processing the loan. The moment the poor tenant goes to the landlord, because the tenant is known personally to the landlord, the landlord just gives out the money. Now, how about the Agricultural Credit Administration? Does Your Honor think the Agricultural Credit Administration can facilitate the granting of the loan as fast as the landlord could give it to the tenant?

SENATOR MANGLAPUS: That is the reason we are providing for the expansion of the ACCFA and weeding out the cooperatives activity of the ACCFA and turning this over to the Agricultural Productivity Commission, so that the Agricultural Credit Administration will concentrate entirely on the facilitation of credit on the. barrio level with the massive support of P150 million provided by the government.

SENATOR ALMENDRAS: I think, Your Honor, that is only applicable on the part of this Agricultural Credit Administration as far as farm implements are concerned. But for, say, funeral expenses, accidental expenses, matriculation fees, fiestas, those that need immediate approval Of the loan — can the Agricultural Credit

Administration facilitate the granting of the loan in due time— say, in less than a day? Your Honor, I would like to make it clear. Supposing a member of the family of the tenant dies today and tomorrow will be the burial. The tenant needs the money very badly because it has been our practice, we Filipinos, that we have to prepare because of our visitors — buy pigs, chicken, etc. Can the Agricultural Credit Administration lend money immediately?

SENATOR MANGLAPUS: Mr. President, fundamentally, we are not trying to perpetuate the paternalistic atmosphere which has been the product of the present landlord-tenant relations today. What we are trying to do is to remove the tenant precisely from this ambiance and make him somewhat more independent than he has been. The increased productivity— which is to come after this bill is passed— out of his transformation to lessee and later on to landowner is supposed to take care of these other needs that the distinguished gentleman has enumerated. Furthermore, I would like to reiterate what I said: that the hypothesis of the gentleman is an exception rather than the rule— because I have already cited the figures that I have shown that the landlord provides 18 per cent and that there are other sources that are available. Some of them, of course, are not necessarily laudable sources. Perhaps they are usurious in their money-lending transactions. But we feel that we are putting them in a much better condition than that on which they are found by providing them with a businesslike way of obtaining credit, not depending on a paternalistic system, but one which, on the barrio level, will provide the credit directly.

SENATOR ALMENDRAS: That is granting, Your Honor, that the tenants have other sources of income — that the tenant can borrow the money at the important moment.

SENATOR MANGLAPUS: Again. Your Honor's hypothesis is, as I said, an exception. Rather than the general rule—-and it is very important and difficult to go by exceptions. The hypothesis is that without the landlord— under Your Honor's example—— the tenant is completely lost. This, Mr. President, we are not ready to accept. I think it is quite evident that in our society, our social structure is such that the tenant is able to depend on other sources of support for his living and even for these unnecessary expenses that Your Honor has listed —— or other sources besides the landlord. But assuming that in this particular hypothesis the landlord is not there anymore to provide for the baptism or for the fiestas, well, my only answer is, if the ACA cannot give the loan to him, let him postpone his fiesta. That, I think, will be very good for the economy.

SENATOR ALMENDRAS: Now, Your Honor, that idea of putting up agencies in all, the barrios, how many barrios are there throughout the Philippines?

SENATOR MANGLAPUS: 28,000 barrios roughly.

SENATOR ALMENDRAS: 28, 000 barrios Does not Your Honor think it is too expensive to put up agencies in each of the 28,000 barrios?

SENATOR MANGLAPUS: That is the objective of the ACA. One of the criticisms that has been levelled against the ACCFA is its inability to reach the people on the barrio level, and this is precisely one of the reasons the ACCFA has failed.

SENATOR ALMENDRAS: May I know from the sponsor if the Committee has made any studies as to how much is the figure to put up agencies in each of the 28,000 barrios in the Philippines?

SENATOR MAN GLAPUS: Mr. President, as I said at the beginning, there are two agencies concerned here. Where the ACCFA was alone before and it failed precisely because of this confusion of missions, we now have the Agricultural Productivity Commission and the Agricultural Credit Administration. Now, I want to call the attention of the distinguished gentleman to Section 118 which provides for a Division of Cooperatives in the .Agricultural Productivity Commission. This Division will take over the cooperatives function which the ACCFA so far has been unsuccessfully undertaking. Section 119 and Section 120 provide for the extension workers. It provides on page 51, line 12:

> "(6) To encourage the formation and growth of
> private associations, study clubs, committees and other
> organized groups of farmers, familiarize them with
> modern methods of farming and interest them to ac-
> tively participate, collaborate or take initiative in agri—
> cultural research, experimentation and implementation
> of projects in cooperation with the Agricultural Pro-
> ductivity Commission; and
> "(7) To promote, stimulate and assist in the organ-
> ization of farmer's cooperatives."

Once these cooperatives are established, the ACA can then use them as their outlets so that it Will not be a purely mechanical operation but the people on the barrio level will have actual participation in the organization of their cooperatives in coming in contact with a source of credit which is the AgriculturalCredit Administration.

SENATOR ALMENDRAS: Now, Your Honor, granting that Your Honor's idea will materialize by putting up Offices or agencies out of the 28,000 barrios...

SENATOR MANGLAPUS: No, that is not the correct

supposition. We are not proposing that elaborate agencies will be established in the 28,000 barrios. Obviously, that is not the objective. The objective is that every man in the barrio is supposed to be a member.

SENATOR ALMENDRAS: Now, in this 28,000 barrios, at least we need one man who will manage the office. Say, if only given P120 a month salary to one man...

SENATOR MANGLAPUS: No, Mr. President, let me interrupt.

SENATOR ALMENDRAS: Let me finish first, Your Honor Twenty-eight thousand barrios times P120 for every man to manage this office in every barrio, the amount that will be involved is P2,360,000.

SENATOR MANGLAPUS: Your Honor, you are assuming that that is the objective of the bill, that is, one man in every barrio.

SENATOR ALMENDRAS: Yes, you cannot expect an office or agency to function without any man to handle it.

SENATOR MANGLAPUS: I said we are not establishing an elaborate office in the barrio. We are establishing under the Agricultural Productivity Commission the cooperatives which will be run by the members themselves. There is no need for an ACA man in every barrio all the time. The need is for these cooperatives to be in contact with the ACA but for that we do not need one man in every barrio. It is unnecessary.

SENATOR ALMENDRAS: Now, how about the cooperatives? We still need men to manage them.

SENATOR MANGLAPUS: No, the cooperative by its own definition is run by the members themselves. What we need is a man to instruct them how to run them. But we don't need people to establish themselves there as permanent agencies in the barrios. If we had that, then we will not be needing the cooperatives. The cooperatives precisely take the place of the government agencies.

SENATOR ALMENDRAS: In that case, Your Honor, if the ACA cannot facilitate immediately the needs of the tenants, don't you think, Your Honor, that this bill will encourage usury?

SENATOR MANGLAPUS: Again, I deny the premise. I have never admitted that the ACA will not be able to assist, and secondly, that under the hypothesis of the gentleman a general rule may be drawn. I still would like to insist very respectfully that it is not the landlord who as a general rule is the exclusive source of credit. I have already read to the distinguished gentleman the sources of credit that have been found to be available, assistance that are available to the tenants. And the landlord as a source of credit is only 18% of the totality of the 100% source of credit of the tenants.

SENATOR ALMENDRAS: Eighteen per cent of the tenants?

SENATOR MANGLAPUS: No, no, assuming one farmer.

SENATOR ALMENDRAS: Yes.

SENATOR MANGLAPUS: It has been found that this farmer using 100% as the total sources of credit depends only on the landlord to the extent pf 18%. There are others, relatives, institutions, farmers, religious institutions and other private individuals.

SENATOR ALMENDRAS: Okay. Granting, Your Honor, that that is the only percentage — granting, although Your Honor always says that my questions are always hypothetical—- I admit that it is hypothetical ——- but it is happening, Your Honor.

SENATOR MANGLAPUS: As isolated exceptions. I am sure that we can have exceptions to the general rule, but as I said, as basis for legislation we cannot delay or allow exceptions to govern all things when we are legislating for the general rule.

SENATOR ALMENDRAS: That is why, Your Honor, I still maintain that the implementation of the bill must be gradual in order that tenants and landlords will be given time to adjust themselves.

SENATOR MANGLAPUS: That is precisely why We are happy to accept .....

SENATOR ALMENDRAS: When we passed the nationalization of rice and corn industry, we gave the aliens three years gradual adjustment, so there is no reason we could not give the tenants and the landlords time in order that they could adjust themselves. But the effectivity of this bill is immediate — upon approval of the President.

SENATOR MANGLAPUS: No, no. That is why I wanted to interrupt because I think the gentleman may be discussing the original provision of the bill. The consolidated version which we are now discussing happily incorporates into the present bill under discussion the provisions of the Lower House, the amendments of the Lower House which provide that the law will take effect only after the proclamation by the Land Reform Committee that all agencies that are necessary to assist in the proper implementation of the law are already operable in the areas. It is only then that the law will take effect. So that the situation that you contemplate comes to be, that is to say, the landlord ceases to be a landlord and now he is an agricultural lessor, only when all the agencies required to assist the lessee in that area are already operable. This is the ideal period of transition, because it insures that when the law takes effect the lessee will not be left hanging but will be within the reach of all necessary assistance that can be provided by the government.

SENATOR ALMENDRAS: But I believe, Your Honor, the amendment that was made in the Lower House is only as far as the abolition of share tenancy, but as far as expropriation proceedings is concerned, the Land Authority can immediately expropriate.

SENATOR MANGLAPUS: But, Mr. President, even under Act 1199, there is no such thing as gradual expropriation and in the other laws that govern the subject the government may expropriate at any time upon petition.

SENATOR ALMENDRAS: Your' Honor, I raised that question because we are talking about adjustment. How can the tenants and landlords make adjustment if the implementation of the law is immediate?

SENATOR MANGLAPUS: No, it is 'not immediate.

SENATOR ALMENDRAS: No, it is immediate as far as the expropriation proceedings is concerned. Now, as far as the tenants are concerned, as far as abolition of share tenancy, it is gradual.

SENATOR MANGLAPUS: You see, the first phase of this law is the one that is found in Section 4. The first phase, the initial operation of the government, will be to see to it that the tenant is transformed into a lessee.

Then the Land Authority and the 'Land Bank which, I think, Your Honor will agree to, will come in and make studies. The Land Project Team, for example, insures precisely that there is no automatic and haphazard implementation of the law insofar as the operation is concerned because according to the law there will be. no expropriation unless there is a land survey made by the Land Project Team. This is, as a matter of fact, Mr. President, better than the present situation. The government cannot operate without studies made by many regional teams such as those that are provided in this bill. So I want to disabuse the fears in the mind of the gentleman about the inadequacy of the bill. There are certain built-in guaranties. There will be no headstrong and ill-considered moves on the part of the government because of those provisions I have already mentioned.

5 -Compensation

(From the Senate deliberations of June 13, 14 and July 1, 3, 1963.)

SENATOR TANADA: Sections 34 and 35 of the bill provide for the rental to be paid by the lessee. These two sectimis, I consider as some of the most important sections in this bill. Section 34 states that the consideration for the lease of riceland shall not be more than the equivalent of 25 percentum of the average normal harvest during the three agricultural years preceding the date the leasehold was established after deducting the amount of palay used for seeds and the cost of harvesting or threshing. Section 35 on the other hand provides that "the consideration for the lease of lands on which are raised crops other than rice (coconut, mangoes, tobacco, abaca, sugar cane, citrus, etc.) shall not be more than the equivalent of 25 per centum of the average normal gross produce during the next three preceding agricultural years after deducting the expenses for the seedlings used, harvesting, loading,hauling and processing, whichever are applicable according tocustomary practice. . ."

The first thing that strikes fone's attention is the incredible fact that the rental for riceland is the same as the rental for coconut land, for sugar land, for fish ponds, etc., when basic differences admittedly exist among them in regard to methods of production, land conditions and their values. Just to cite one example, in riceland the lessee must prepare the field at least once a year by plowing and harrowing it and by cleaning and fixing the dikes, while in the case of the coconut land the lessee does not prepare the field in that manner. All that he does is to harvest every two months when the coconuts mature by picking the nuts from the trees or by just waiting for them to fall down. Another difference is, in the case of palay one has to wait only from four to five months from planting to harvest; while in the case of coconut one has to wait for eight years, generally speaking, to harvest. Now, if the conditions are unquestionably different why should the rentals be the same?

In Taiwan, recognizing these basic differences, orchards and tea plantations were excluded from the general operation of the Farm Land Rent Reduction and from "The Land-to-the—Tiller Act." (Reads quotations)

I raised these questions during the Committee hearings but the pride of authorship is strong and Sections 34 and 35 were only amended as to the rate of rentals. In the case of Riceland the rental was fixed at 25% for all kinds of riceland and in the case of other crops like coconut, sugar, mangoes, etc. the rental was raised from the ridiculously low rate of 20% to 25%. I am raising these questions again here hoping that Your Honors will see the absurdity of fixing the same rental for all kinds of lands and will act accordingly.

NOW, the next question is, are these rentals reasonable or confiscatory? Not enough data has been presented during the hearings conducted by the Senate Special Committee on Land Reform to enable us to give a categorical opinion. The time at our disposal was so short that we could not hear all those who wanted to testify. However, former Ambassador Manuel V. Gallego, in a memorandum that he sent me, claims that the rental of 25% for riceland is confiscatory. For according to Ambassador Gallego' s computation, in the case of land valued at P2,700 per hectare and the production is 30 cavanes of palay which is the average production and in the case where the land is valued at P3,700 per hectare and the production is 45 cavanes of palay, the percentage of gross income in relation to investment is very much less than 4%.

'What about the rental of coconut land? Here is what the Philippine Coconut Producers Federation, Inc., Candelaria, Quezon Chapter, has to say:

"Let us take up the example of a coconut farm of one hectare with 200 coconut fruitbearing trees. This will cost from P8,100 to P10,000 to acquire. The farm will produce an average of 1,200 nuts per harvest every 60 days; at the current price of P120 per 1,000 nuts, it gives a return of E44; deduct the expense of P750 (for harvesting and processing) and the return per harvest is P136.50. To give the landowner 20% of the same, he will get the paltry sum of P2730; multiply this by 6, representing the number of harvests a year, and the land, owner will get a total annual income of P163.80; deduct the realty tax of P1040 (1% of P1,040, assessed value) and he will have a net return of P153.40 on his investment of F10,000, or 1.53%. Is this a fair and just return? If the landowner borrowed the money used in acquiring the farm with interest at 6% per annum, he would not be able to pay even the interest on the loan."

The foregoing is a computation based on first-class coconut lands situated in the municipalities of Candelaria and Sariaya. Mr. Godofredo Reyes, Jr, executive director of the Philippine Coconut Producers, Inc., however, submitted the following computation based on the average production of coconut plantations all over the country:

1. Gross return per hectare   P750.00
2. Deduct: Harvesting, processing and
        selling expenses @ P15 per
        thousand. nuts or 6,000 x P15   90.00
3. Net basis for computing
        25% lease rental   660.00
4. Lease rental per year to
        landowner 25% of P660   165.00
5. Deduct land taxes at new rate   20.00
6. Net return to landowner per year   145.00

                        ----

7. Percent return to landowner P145
        divided by P6, 000.   0.024 plus %

It will appear, Mr. President, from the computation of both the Philippine Coconut Producers Federation, Inc., Candelaria, Quezon Chapter, and that of executive director Godofredo Reyes, Jr. of the

Philippine Coconut Producers Federation, Inc. that the percentage of the net return in relation to investment is less than 2-1/2%. And to the foregoing computation and observations may I add, that if the bill Which now fixes the rental at 25% — in the Malacañang bill it was 20% — becomes a law, the coconut landowner will receive less than What, under the current terms of tenancy in coconut land, the tenants are receiving. At present the tenants are actually receiving from 30 to 40 per cent of the produce after deducting expenses as their share. In other words if we approve this measure as it is, owners of coconut farms will be in a more precarious condition than the present condition of their tenants. And this is not all, for the worse is. yet to come; because if this measure is enacted into law and is implemented to its logical goal, the landowners of today will be the landless of tomorrow.

Allow me, Mr. President, to read some of the many telegrams I received from coconut planters. This telegram comes from Mr. Jose Allana of Cotabato, who is the vice-president of the Coconut Producers Federation:

Senator Tanada:

Twenty percent share for coconut landowner under land reform unfair stop do you think tenant will still strive to become owner cultivator under above provision when already gets eighty percent and does not have to pay taxes stop he is already practically the owner without the responsibility stop we are depending on you to correct the iniquity.

Another telegram is from Mr. Jose Ortiz of Cotabato, president of the Coconut Planters Association:

As agricultural pioneers Mindanao we feel present land reform bill cannot guarantee we will still own the coconut we are planting when they start to bear fruit stop urgent do something thanks.

Another is from Jose Garcia of the Coconut Planters Association:

If present practice coconut farms giving tenants forty to fifty percent unfair to them why is it fair under land reform bill to give landowner only twenty percent when he invests for the land and coconut plantation and pays taxes stop please help thanks.

There are many others, Mr. President, but I believe that I have read representative views from coconut landowners, and it is for you, gentlemen, to decide.

What about the rentals for other crops? Are they reasonable or confiscatory? Not having received any data on them, and I doubt whether our own Committee has, I am not in a position to give an opinion. I venture to say, however, that we cannot fix the rental for said crops unless we have the necessary data and information.

Before going to another point I wish to state that if the computations made by Ambassador Gallego and the Philippine Coconut Producers Federation Inc., Candelaria, Quezon Chapter are substantially correct, then the rental fixed by this bill for riceland and coconut land is arbitrary and therefore, unconstitutional.

Another constitutional defect of the bill is its failure to provide just compensation for the lands to be expropriated. According to Section 79 0f the bill, payment is to be made thus: 10% in cash, 60% in bonds of the Land Bank, and 30% in stocks of the same Bank. This 'plan of payment is to all intents and purposes the same as payment, unless of course the owner agrees thereto, has been declared unconstitutional, as it does not constitute just compensation. (Cites Court decisions)

The State Supreme Courts have invariably held that while only few Constitutions prescribe the means of payment by which compensation shall be paid in expropriation cases, "there is an implied requirement that the compensation be in money: and that statutes providing that the lands taken shall be paid other lands, stock and/or bonds in satisfaction are, therefore, unconstitutional. (Vanhorne v. Dorrance (a.c.) 2 Dell. 304, 1 L. Ed. 391, Fed. P. 1040, 70 P. 1083). (Italics supplied).

Let me quote from another decision.

Just compensation for property taken by condemnation means a. fair equivalent in money, which must be paid at least 'within a reasonable time after the taking, and it is not within the power of the legislature to substitute for such present payment future obligations, bonds or other value advantage. '(City of Waterbury v. Plat Bros & (30., 56 A.586, 858, 76 Conn. 435, citing Butler v. Ravine Road Sewer Com'rs. 39 N.J.L. 665; Bloodgood v. Mohawak & H,R.R. Co., N.Y., 18 'Wend. 9, 35, 31 Am. Dec. 313, Sanborn v. Belden, 51 Cal. 266; Burlington & C.R. Co. v. Schweitkart, 14. P. 329). (Italics supplied).

The Federal Supreme Court repeatedly sustained the interpretation given by the State Supreme Courts as to the meaning of "just compensation." Thus:

In the constitutional provision that the property of no person shall be taken for public use without just compensation, "just compensation" means pecuniary recompense to the person whose property is taken, equivalent in value to the property." (Chicago, B. & Q.R. Co. v. County of Otoe, 83 U.S. (16 Wall.) 667, 674, 21 L. Ed. 375; US. v. Miller, 317 US. 369, 87 L. Ed. 336; Brooks-Scanlon Corp. v. United States, 265 US. 106, 68 L. Ed. 934).

The term "pecuniary" has acquired a settled legal meaning

and has been defined as, "monetary, relating to money, consisting of money." (Black Law Dictionary).

Contrary to certain claims, our Supreme Court has already ruled that the compensation to be paid the owner Of the property expropriated is the money equivalent of the property taken.

In the case of City of Manila v. Estrada. 25 Phil. 208 our Supreme Court quoted with approval the following:

For the determination of the market value of land, which is that sum of money which a person, desirous but not compelled to buy and a price to be given and received therefore, is beyond doubt difficult. The test is logically and legally correct, but it cannot be applied to stocks, bonds and personal property generally. Still, it is this test which admittedly must be applied, even when the value of the land and the damages are found in separate sums.

And in the cases of M.R.R. v. Velasquez, 32 Phil. 286, and Province of Tayabas v. Perez, 66 Phil. 467, our Supreme Court said:

The fundamental rule in expropriation matters is that the owner of the property expropriated is entitled to just compensation, no more no less, when possible to make the assessment, than the money equivalent of the property, just compensation having always been understood to mean the just complete equivalent of the loss suffered.

But assuming for the sake of argument that in expropriation proceedings the owner of the property taken may be paid in bonds or in shares of stock, still the stocks and bonds in this case that the owners shall receive as compensation for their lands cannot be considered a fair and full equivalent of the property taken.

The shares of stock which the landowners will receive, which shall be 30% of the value of the land have very limited rights. For Section 82 of the bill expressly provides that the holders of said shares of stock shall not have the right to participate in the direction and administration of the Bank or to bring derivative suits against the Bank. It is true that they are negotiable but who will take such shares considering their little value because of their limited rights?

The bonds that the landowners will receive, which shall be 60% of the value of the land taken, will be worse than the shares of stocks of the'Bank. The bonds shall be payable in pesos and they generally mature in 10 years. The value of the bonds on the date the owner receives them may be equivalent to the fair value of 60% of the land expropriated; but this does not mean anything, for he cannot cash them on that date. It is the value of the bonds upon their maturity that will count. But 10 years hence the value of the bonds will not be much because, according to the statistics gathered by the Central Bank, the trend of the purchasing power of the peso has been fluctuating downward since 1949, and as of the month of April 1963, it dropped by about 22% from the 1955 level. And there is no reason to believe that the downward trend of the value of the peso will be arrested. On the contrary the signs are that it will continue to drop and even at a faster rate. Consequently the purchasing power of say, a P10 thousand bond delivered today, will be only about P5,600.00 10 years hence which is the date of the bond's maturity. This certainly cannot be considered just compensation.

Another unconstitutional provision of the bill is Section 57. Not much attention has been paid to this section. And I would like to invite the attention of the members of this body, especially of the sponsors whose intellectual honesty has been demonstrated during the days we have been discussing this bill, to this section because this is the first time that we provide in our statutes a section like Section 57. This section enjoins the court to use as basis "the annual lease rental income authorized by law capitalized at the rate of 6 per centum per annum," in determining what is "just compensation." In other words, the government, the present administration, fixes the basis of the computation of what is to the landowner — the buyer in effect practically telling him: "The price of this land shall be this or that." This section, I, submit, is unconstitutional because it constitutes an unlawful encroachment upon the judicial function. Let me quote the ruling in a case which I cited in the text of a speech on this point.

> *The right of the legislature of the State, by law,*
> *to apply the property of the citizens to the public use,*
> *and then to constitute itself the judge in its own case*
> *to determine what is the 'just compensation' it ought*
> *to pay therefor, or how much benefit it has confer-*
> *red upon the citizen by thus taking his property with-*
> *out his consent or to extinguish any part of such com-*
> *pensation by prospective conjectural advantage, or in*
> *any manner to interfere with the just powers and*
> *province of courts and juries in administering right*
> *and justice, cannot for a moment be admitted or*
> *tolerated under our Constitution. (Isom v. Mississippi*
> *Cont. R. Co., 36 Miss. 300, quoted with approval in*
> *Monongahela Navigation CO. v. United States) (Italics*
> *supplied).*

But it may be asked, what does our SupremeCourt say on this matter? Could rental be considered as a proper basis for determining just compensation? Allow me to quote What our Supreme Court said in the case of City of Manila v. 'Corrales, 32 Phil. 85:

> *In expropriation proceedings, the question of the*
> *value of the property is always a difficult one to de-*

cide. Men vary so much concerning their opinion of the real value of property. The best the courts can do is to hear all the witnesses which the respective parties desire to present, and then, by carefully weighing such testimony, arrive at a conclusion which is just and equitable. The value of property cannot always be fixed by its actual rental value. There is a difference between the actual value of the property and the price for which it is rented at any particular time. What property will rent for is a variable quantity. The amount paid by the use of property is not always a constant quantity. The amount which tenants will pay depends upon their particular necessities at the time. The value of property cannot always be capitalized on its rental value. Neither can the value of property for expropriation purposes be based upon its actual cost of construction. In determining the value of land appropriated for public purposes, the same considerations are to be regarded as in the sale of property between private parties. The inquiry must always be — that is the property worth on the market, viewed, not merely as to the use to which it is at the time applied, but with reference to the use of which it is plainly adapted; that is to say, what is it worth, from its availability for a valuable purpose?

Speaking of rental value as basis for determining the value of the property for purposes of expropriation, I wish to point out the malevolent ingenuity of the Malacanang Land Reform Bill. To be sure that the government will not pay such for the lands it will expropriate, the bill reduces the rent of the lands; then it directs the courts to compute the value of the lands on the basis of the reduced rental. But when it comes to taxation, the tax is based not on the rentals it has fixed but on the rent potential of the property. A more Machiavellian scheme will be hard to find.

SENATOR MANGLAPUS: I should like to proceed with that initial statement that I made about open-mindedness. Take the instance of coconut lands. As co-chairman of the Committee, I have —— together with Senator Magsaysay ——made it very clear from the hearings of the Committee up to the time this was brought to the floor, that we are open-minded as to any suggestions that would improve this bill insofar as permanent crops are concerned, because we see that there is a distinction to be made. The distinguished gentleman from Quezon said that there is in this bill —— and he said this with tongue in cheek —— a malevolent ingenuity because it reduces rent and then makes it the basis for rent. First, may I say that the rent here is basically the same as the rent in Republic Act 1199. Second, he said that the rent that is outlined and provided for in this bill is unfair. This would require an explanation, of course. But third, it also presumes that rent should never be the basis for the valuation of land, which again does not seem to be supported by jurisprudence. It is true that in the case of the City of Manila versus Corrales — I think cited by the distinguished gentleman from Quezon — it was decided that the rental which was fixed by one of the parties should not be the proper basis for the valuation of the land. But permit me, if I may, to read from the decision. It is found in the Philippine Reports, Vol. 32, page 96, City of Manila vs. Corrales. The Supreme Court here opens the possibility that rents could be the basis for valuation of property. It says:

"There may be cases where the value of the property can be fixed upon its actual rental value. For example, Where 'the property has been rented for a number of years at a fixed rate, then such rate ought to be used as the basis of the actual value of the property."

Of course, it could be seen from this decision that the contention of the defendants would seem to be untenable, but it submits the possibility that rent could be the basis of valuation of property.

SENATOR TANADA: I would like to state that when I made reference to the malevolent ingenuity of the bill, and I would like to repeat here that it is really malevolent, I was not referring to rentals. I was referring to the fixing of just compensation, not to the rentals. Of course, I would like to respect the wishes of the distinguished sponsor that he be allowed to finish, that that has been our practice here. But perhaps it would be more interesting if, after every point that he has raised, we are allowed to answer right away. At any rate, I will have no objection to the distinguished gentleman from Rizal and Ilocos Sur to continue his speech. I only wanted to correct that point.

SENATOR MANGLAPUS: Well, on that point as I recall, the distinguished gentleman from Quezon said that the malevolence stems from the fact that while the value of the property was based on the rental, the rental was first reduced and then was made the basis. Of course, I stand corrected, but the gentleman said it is malevolent.

SENATOR TANADA: On the fixing of just compensation.

SENATOR MANGLAPUS: Because just compensation is based on the rent, something like that. The rent was arbitrarily reduced. That was his statement.

THE PRESIDENT: The gentleman from Rizal and Ilocos Sur has manifested his desire to continue with his speech, but those who seek to interpellate him may place on record their reservations to interpellate.

SENATOR TOLENTINO: I was about to ask the permission of the gentleman if I could just ask one question to verify if he is reading from the decision. It is not to argue with the distinguished gentleman but only to clarify.

THE PRESIDENT: What is the desire of the gentleman from Rizal and Ilocos Sur?

SENATOR TOLENTINO: I do not intend to argue.

SENATOR MANGLAPUS: This is, of course, urban land. This is one point that I am going to raise. This case refers to urban land.

SENATOR TOLENTINO: What I was going to ask was whether the rent was fixed by the parties or the rent was imposed by law. That was what I wanted to ask.

SENATOR MANGLAPUS: Mr. President, may I answer that? The rent here is one that is contended by the defendants as having been fixed by the parties, but the principle is that rental, according to the Supreme Court, could be a valid basis for valuation. Whether this rental is fixed by law or by the parties, as far as our bill is concerned, is not material.

SENATOR TOLENTINO: I was referring to the decision. If the Supreme Court said that the rental could be made the basis of valuation, that means the rental that the owner fixed considering the value of his property. In the present bill it is the government that fixes the rental and the value of the property is not considered. So it would be possible that the value of the property could actually be deduced from the rental fixed by the owner. That is why I asked whether that rental in the Corrales case is fixed by the owner.

SENATOR MANGLAPUS: The rental has been agreed upon, but I used that as an example that the Supreme Court has an open mind. Whether the rental is fixed by law is not quite material. It is not market value that is being considered here as against the contention that the market value should be the exclusive basis of just compensation.

SENATOR TOLENTINO: The implication here, Your Honor, is that the value of the property could be deduced from the amount of the rental that the owner charges. It is the owner that charges the rental on the basis of what he believes is the value of his property. But under our bill now it is the government that imposes the rental not on the value of the property but on the products. These are two different criteria.

SENATOR MANGLAPUS: That is why I called attention to this citation because it refers to urban land, while we are referring here to agricultural land.

Mr. President, the argument on just compensation. by those

who oppose this bill so far would continue to say that, in all cases lands or real properties should be valued at its market value and in cash for purposes of just compensation in the exercise of the right of expropriation by the government. I say, to begin with, that in all these cases cited by the opponents of the bill, there was no law at all which provided otherwise. In other words, these cases were interpretations of the bare letter of the Constitution. Secondly, that in all cases the issue of cash was never an issue. In all these cases the market value was expressed in cash simply as a descriptive element.

Now, Mr. President, may I refer to the Encyclopedia of American Law and Procedure to show that this jurisprudence is rather open-minded on this point. According to this bill we would be paying the landowner 10 per cent cash, 60 per cent bonds and 30 per cent shares in the Land Bank. These bonds and shares are to be liquidated at a certain time and cash delivered to the landowner. The Encyclopedia of American Law and Procedure, Volume 12, pages 214-215, says: "In case where a tract of land or other property is taken, compensation must be made in money at the fair market value of the property. The money need not be paid at the time possession is taken of the property, if a certain method of obtaining it within a reasonable time thereafter is provided."

Of course, it may be said till Kingdom comes. What is the reasonable time? The fact is that this jurisprudence is open-minded regarding the time when the cash shall be delivered, assuming that cash must ultimately be just compensation at the time the cash is to fall into the hands of the seller or the landowner. Let us briefly investigate the nature of the compensation that we are actually giving to the landowner which is 10 per cent cash. We have no quarrel about that. There is the 60 per cent bonds, but there is much more. May I recall, Mr. President, that these bonds when compared to the properties for which they are being exchanged compare favorably to some of the criteria which have been used in judging the justness of compensation. The land of the owner is certainly not more liquid than the bonds which are to have the properties outlined in the bill upon acceptance of constructive amendments such as those emanating from the distinguished gentleman from Manila and Pampanga. The returns are guaranteed to the landowner, returns that are tax-free based on 6 percent which, if we follow the computation that has been presented before our Committee, would seem to guarantee to the landowner returns higher than that they are receiving under present conditions, land that has been considered on the floor during the whole debate as appreciated, but it seems to me that this matter begs the question and this is not taking into consideration that this is precisely one salutary effect of a bill like this, that land is not appreciated beyond the land value, that if this land reform bill is passed, the land will assume a more reasonable trend of appreciation and that therefore the appreciation of the land, which is the proper appreciation of the title that it should not far exceed the appreciation that the bonds and shares have. It is purely speculation to say that at the time the bonds are written and valued much less at that time, because again I would say that we are forgetting that it would be one of the salutary effects of the bill, we are arresting the necessary rise of value of real estate in this country, particularly in agricultural real estate.

Now, let us investigate the bonds a little. What is the landowner going to be able to do with these bonds? He is going to be able to buy public lands .as many as 1,000 hectares for him to develop in a scientific manner, provided that he does not restore therein the same share-tenancy system that he left behind in his old homestead.

I want to repeat that the landholder who holds the bonds may sell these bonds to others, if he does not wish to take advantage of the privilege to buy this land from the Land Bank. He may sell this land to others who are interested in exploiting the public agricultural land that has come under the title of the Land Bank.

I am addressing the landlords who are in this hall to take note that this is added liquidity to the bonds because once the Land Bank has acquired the land, that land is at the disposal of the Bank. The Committee foresees that there will be cases when you will be approached by prospective buyers of land, so that you may be tempted to sell the land before it is expropriated or negotiated by the government. You may be able to liquefy and sell the bonds at some premium to those who are eager to exploit public agricultural lands. There is a constructive amendment in the Lower House which has been included here in the list submitted by Senator Puyat which we are ready to accept and which would add further to the liquidity of the bonds, that is to accept it as payment of reparations. This has passed the experts' scrutiny and in fact has been recommended by the distinguished gentleman from Manila and Pampanga. We are ready to accept another Puyat amendment which would make these bonds mortgageable to government banking institutions because under the present bill there is no specific provision that would allow it.

THE PRESIDENT: The gentleman from Manila is now recognized.

SENATOR TOLENTINO: Mr. President, in this Section 80, my proposed amendment is to delete the entire text of Section 80 and in lieu thereof insert the following as the text that should be Section 80.

"SEC. 80. MAKING PAYMENT TO OWNERS OF LANDED ESTATE.— THE LAND BANK SHALL MAKE PAYMENT IN THE FORM PROVIDED BY THE COMPETENT COURT TO' THE OWNERS OF THE LAND EXPROPRIATED BY THE LAND AUTHORITY FOR DIVISION AND RESALE TO FARMERS. IN CASES OF LANDS ACQUIRED BY NEGOTIATED SALE WHOSE PRICE SHALL HAVE BEEN APPROVED BY THE COURT THE TERM OF PAYMENT SHALL BE AS AGREED UPON BY THE LANDOWNER AND THE LAND AUTHORITY INCLUDING THE USE OF BONDS AND SHARES OF STOCK ISSUED BY THE LAND BANK. THE COMPENSATION SHALL BE EXEMPTED FROM THE PAYMENT OF THE TAX ON CAPITAL GAINS."

That is the entire section as I would like to have it proposed.

THE PRESIDENT: What does the Committee say?

SENATOR MANGLAPUS: The Committee thanks 'the gentleman for making that suggestion. However, it regrets with heavy heart —— it must also say that the same suggestion in substance came from the gentleman from Quezon ——and it is indeed with heavy heart that we must decline to accept this amendment because in effect this would reduce compensation exclusively to cash. We feel that that is the end result of this amendment and, as explained in the period of discussion, we are not in a position to accept anything less than the formula that we have already given in View of the fact that a total cash payment would result in several undesirable disadvantages to the economy of this country. First of all, we haven't got the cash; the government hasn't got the cash. And second, the cash compensation would result in inflation which would be beyond the control of the government. That has been seen in such example as that which happened in Japan where there was inflation, one which they were able to control only because of the healthy position of the Japanese economy.

SENATOR TOLENTINO: Mr. President.

THE PRESIDENT: Gentleman from Manila.

SENATOR TOLENTINO: May I be allowed to explain my proposed amendment?

THE PRESIDENT: The gentleman may proceed.

SENATOR TOLENTINO: Referring to the payment of the price in the case of negotiated sale there should be no controversy because then in that case that would be subject to agreement and, therefore, it will depend upon the landowner to accept a certain percentage of the compensation in cash and certain percentages in bonds or in shares of stock of the Land Bank. I don't know also if there would be any disagreement with respect to the last sentence of my proposal that the compensation, whether in expropriation or in negotiated sale, shall be exempt from the tax on capital gain. ....I feel that the real controversy lies in the first sentence of my proposal to the effect that the Land Bank shall make payment in the form provided by the competent courts to the owner of the land expropriated by the Land Authority for division and resale to farmers.

Mr. President, I am proposing this amendment in an honest endeavor and effort to try as much as possible to eliminate what we consider the constitutionally objectionable features of this bill. . . .

Now, I am going to show why these provisions of the present bill are unconstitutional. In the first place, this provision imposes upon the landowner, in cases of expropriation, the receipt of at least 60% in bonds of the Land Bank, and the balance, around 30% or less, in shares of stock of the Land Bank, and only 10%} to be paid in cash. Can we validly make an imposition by law that a person whose land is taken by expropriation should accept bonds?

Mr. President, what is the implication when we compel a person who gives up his land in expropriation to accept a bond of the Land Bank? What is a bond? A bond, I understand, Mr. President, is simply an evidence of indebtedness. It means that the holder of the bond, the landowner, becomes a creditor of the government or the Land Bank who issues the bond. It means that this bill now forces the landowner not only to give up his land in expropriation but also to agree to become a creditor of the Land Bank. In other words, the landowner is forced to become a creditor.

Mr. President, I do not know by what stretch of legal reasoning we can compel a person to become a creditor. To compel a person to become a creditor means that you are compelling him to lend his money to some other person; and when you lend your money to some other person, you must be free to choose the person to Whom you are lending your money because you must have assurance of his capacity and willingness to pay. You cannot compel a man to become a creditor; but the worse part of it is that this bill, by forcing the landowner to accept bonds, actually compels him to lend his money to the government. And on top of this, the creditor, the landowner, who is being forced to lend his money, has no choice in fixing the terms and conditions of the loan. Where can you find such terms of credit? When you extend a loan, it is the creditor that imposes the terms and conditions of the loan. But in this case, the creditor will be the one to swallow the terms and conditions of the bond that will be issued by the Land Bank. This is an imposition that can find no justification under our Constitution when we are living in a Constitution that guarantees freedom and right to property.

Let us go to the shares of stock. What is a share of stock? A share of stock is an undivided interest in the ownership of a corporation. A certificate is issued. We sometimes call the certificate the share of stock and the certificate is merely the documentary evidence of the extent of the investment of the individual in the corporation. Therefore, when you compel the landowner to accept certificates or shares of stock in the Land Bank, What do you ask him to do? You ask him to accept, to become a shareholder or a part owner of the Land Bank. A share of stock is an investment in the enterprise or corporation. The stockholder is an investor in the corporation. I thought all the while, Mr. President, that we are in a democratic society and under this administration there is free enterprise and under free enterprise a person must be free to choose where he will invest his money; and yet here under this bill the landowner has no freedom to choose where he will invest his money because this bill says, "No, 30% must be given as your investment in the Land Bank."

Mr. President, any person who invests must know whether the enterprise in which he will invest is acceptable to him or not. He must know whether there is reasonable chance for profit or success of that enterprise. But in this case, even if the landowner believes that this Land Bank will be surely heading for bankruptcy, the bill says, "No, you get 30 per cent in shares of the Land Bank." Where is the freedom there? All of this is an imposition. It is totalitarian in nature, and yet we want to put up a phraseology in a bill under an administration that boasts of its commitment to free enterprise.

Mr. President, this is enough to show that imposition of bonds and shares of stock would be unconstitutional because it compels a person to become a creditor, and there is nothing in the law or in the Constitution that can force us or compel anyone to become a creditor of the government, and it imposes upon a person an investment which he does not want at all and thus depriving a person of the freedom to invest.

But aside from this very clear and very fundamental objection, let us go to judicial authorities. I would like to quote, Mr. President, certain decisions of courts, and I would like the distinguished Committee that would like to insist on the phraseology of this section to please take particular note of these decisions.

I have a quotation here from Volume 18, American Jurisprudence, Section 128, pages 752 to 753, and I will read the paragraph of the section. It says:

> "Few Constitutions prescribe the means by which
> compensation shall be paid, but it is invariably held
> that there is an implied requirement that the com-
> pensation be in money. Hence, it is that statutes have
> been held to be unconstitutional where they provide
> that the Owner of lands taken shall be awarded other
> lands in satisfaction, or that he shall take his payment
> in warrants or in stocks or bonds of the corporation ao-
> qm'ring the lands in condemnation proceedings. x x x."

That is very clear, that statutes have been held to be unconstitutional where the owner of the land is compelled to accept as payment stocks or bonds of the corporation acquiring the lands. These are shares of stocks and bonds. of the Land Bank which will acquire the land because the title of the land will be transferred to the Land Bank.

Now, let me quote Corpus Juris, Volume 20, Section 278, page 842:

> "The great weight of authority is to the effect
> that payment for property taken under the power of
> eminent domain must be made in money in the absence
> of an agreement to the contrary. (That means the
> agreement by the landowner.) The landowner cannot
> be compelled to accept in payment other lands, or a .
> grant of a right of way over adjoining land. (This is
> important.) Nor can he be required to accept the bonds
> of the condemning corporation x x x."

These are bonds of the Land Bank. The owner cannot be compelled to accept them.

Now, let us go to specific cases under the Corpus Juris and under the American Jurisprudence the different cases are cited. In the case of Vanhorne versus Dorrance, 2 Dall. (Pa.) 304, page 315 appearing in 1 Law Edition :391, 28 Federal Case 16, 857, we have this decision of the court:

> "No just compensation can be made except in
> money. Money is a common standard, by comparison
> with which the value of anything may be ascertained.
> x x X. True it is, that land or anything else may be
> a compensation, but then it must be at the election of
> the party: it cannot be forced upon him."

And this bill would force upon the landowner the bonds of the Land Bank.

Another case, the case of Waterbury versus Flatt, 76 Conn. 435, Volume 56, Atl. 856. I quote:

> " 'Just compensation' means a fair equivalent in

money, which must be paid within a reasonable time after the taking, and (please note) *it is not within the power of the legislature to substitute future obligations, bonds or other valuable advantage for money."*

Mr. President, I do not suppose anything can be clearer than the understanding of what is a bond and share of stock, and considering these judicial authorities, if we want to really provide in this bill a method of payment that can be sustained under the Constitution, I believe that I have discharged my duty in calling the attention of this chamber to the unconstitutional features of this Section 80. I believe that I have complied with my duty to try to insert in this provision of Section 80 words or phrases that will conform with the requirements of our Constitution so that We can uphold this bill in court and so that the objective of the land reform can be really achieved. The failure of this Section 80 may undermine the entire system of land reform contemplated in this bill. I should like, therefore, to make particular appeal to the Committee and to those who want to maintain the wording now of this section as it is to these authorities and to consider that we cannot compel anyone to become creditor nor compel anyone to be an investor in any enterprise that is not of his own free choice.

With regard to the objection that there will not be enough cash to expropriate all the landed estates in this country, well, if we do not have enough cash Why do we want to get the landed estates? Does this mean that if we need, let us say, for our family one sack of rice a month and we do not have enough cash to pay for that sack of rice, we will be justified in simply resorting to illegal method to get this sack of rice because we need it? The objective is good, and nobody will disagree with the objective. But however good the objective may be we have the Constitution that tells us along what path we must travel in going towards that objective. And assuming that we will have the money, the Central Bank, let us say, will print the money and will provide somehow for the payment of these landed estates, then there is the objection that there will be inflation. That is true there will be inflation when the Central Bank prints all the money needed for the acquisition of the landed estates. But, Mr. President, a wise administration should know how to program the expropriation so that there will be no sudden release of funds at one time. The administration should know when and to what extent, expropriation should be undertaken in a particular year so that the release of these millions of pesos will not take place at one single time and the effects of runaway inflation may be avoided; that is, not to be safe-guarded by unconstitutional provisions in this bill.

So, Mr. President, with these words I feel that I have enough support both in reason and in law and under the Constitution and jurisprudence for the proposal that I am making. I leave the rest to this Chamber, to the Committee to decide whether we shall continue with an unconstitutional provision in this bill or we shall abide by the Constitution in trying to attain our objective. Thank you.

THE PRESIDENT: Is the Chamber ready to vote on the matter?

SENATOR MANGLAPUS: Mr. President, before the Chamber votes may I just take up a few minutes to answer the gentleman.

SENATOR SUMULONG: Mr. President.

THE PRESIDENT: What is the pleasure of the gentleman from Rizal?

SENATOR SUMULONG: Mr. President, I would like to speak in favor of the amendment introduced by the gentleman from Manila.

I shall not repeat the argument... I just want to call the attention of the Senate to certain provisions of the bill which will show that this manner of payment to the landowner is a system of high financing which can by no stretch of the imagination be regarded not only from the legal standpoint but from the standpoint of common sense, from the standpoint of any businessman to be considered as just compensation.

I maintain, Mr. President, that under the provisions of this bill, that with every P2.00 paid-in capital of the Land Bank, this bank can get P10.00 worth of land. Under this bill — please take note — the Land Bank is given a borrowing capacity of five times its capital and surplus, so that for every P2.00 paid-in capital of the Land Bank it can borrow P10.00 simply by issuing bonds with a face value of P10.00. So for every P2.00 paid-in capital, it will have P2.00 cash and P10.00, in bonds. And so if you are a landowner and you have a land worth P10.00, the Land Bank can go to you and say: "I am expropriating your land and, in payment, I will give you P1.00 because that is 10% in cash." Ten per cent of P10.00 is P1.00. So the Land Bank can use 10% in cash and give it to the landowner and say: "This is your payment in cash. So I will borrow from you the P6.00. As evidence of y indebtedness to you, here is a bond with a face value of P6.00," and that is just compensation under the bill because the Land Bank, as I said, can borrow five times of its paid-in capital. . .

Mr. President, this reminds me of what happened in Cuba, because in Cuba when Fidel Castro came into power, and he decided to expropriate American properties, he said: "I am expropriating the properties of the Americans and I am going to pay them in bonds"— bonds with long terms of 25 years or more. They wanted the

American government to accept bonds. And what did the US. government and people do? They said: "That cannot be. You must be thinking that we are fools and that we would allow ourselves to be paid in bond." And so the answer of the American government was: "You are not expropriating, you are confiscating." And because of that the US. government put an embargo on all imports from Cuba.

This is Fidel Castro's style of paying for lands, by means of bonds for a long term of: years.

SENATOR MANGLAPUS : I wish to thank the gentleman from Manila and the gentleman from Rizal, and of course, also the gentleman from Quezon for the speeches that they have made here which are very enlightening on the point of censtitutionality of Section 80 as it is now drafted in the bill.

First, I would like to reply to the remarks made by the gentleman from Manila and then to the remarks made by the gentleman from Rizal. Mr. President, the burden of the arguments of the gentleman from Manila seems to be that we cannot force anyone to become the creditor of the government.

Mr. President, before 1948, this might have been a valid argument. But I am afraid that since the passage of the Central Bank Act Which removed our monetary system from the gold standard and placed it on the fiduciary system, we have all become creditors of the government. May I call the attention of the distinguished gentleman not to the provisions of the law but to the P1.00 bill that all of us are carrying around these days. And may I read into the record the words that are found on the PLOO bill. It says: "This note is a liability of the Central Bank and is fully guaranteed by the government of the Republic of the Philippines." Before 1948, Mr. President, our money was not in this form. It was backed by reserves in gold or in dollars. But after 1948, bills issued by the Central Bank constituted or established a creditor—debtor relationship between the owner of the bill and the government. This is evident from the provisions of the Central Bank Act and from the words that are found in the bills themselves. As a matter of fact, Mr. President, part of the Central Bank assets today, the assets that back these bills are in the form of obligations of the government. Before 1948, no such thing existed, but since 1948 a man can go to the Central Bank and he will be told that of the assets that back the bills that are found in his possession; among these assets are found obligations and debts of the government, Mr. President.

Now, the distinguished gentleman has cited US. Authorities to show that bonds have been outlawed or overruled as a means of payment for properties that are being expropriated. It would be interesting to know, Mr. President, what kind of stocks and bonds were those that were overruled by the Supreme Court of the United States in those cases cited by the distinguished gentleman from Manila. It is my suspicion that these are stocks and bonds issued not by the government or by a government institution but by such institutions as railroad companies which, as we all know in American and Philippine jurisprudence, have power of eminent domain. I think an investigation into those cases will Show that these were not bonds of the same quality and liquidity as the bonds that we are providing for in Section 80, but bonds issued by private railroad companies or other companies that have been given the right of eminent domain by delegation of the United States Congress.

Mr. President, the distinguished gentleman has said that if there is no cash there should be no purchase. This is just like saying that when we are faced with the situation, let us not use ingenuity, let us not use the genius of an economist,rlet us not use our brains, let us not use legislative power in order to remedy social problems such as those found in tenancy cases.

Mr. President, I would like now to answer the statement of the gentleman from Rizal that bonds...

SENATOR TOLENTINO: Mr. President.

SENATOR MANGLAPUS: May I finish. . .

SENATOR TOLENTINO: Mr. President, before the gentleman goes to the argument or statement of the gentleman from Rizal, I would like to ask some questions.

THE PRESIDENT: The gentleman may proceed.

SENATOR TOLENTINO: Mr. President, I would go along with the statement of the distinguished sponsor that our money now constitutes a promise by the government or by the Central Bank to pay. It is an Obligation. But will the distinguished gentleman not also tell us that this is by law made legal tender?

SENATOR MANGLAPUS: That is correct.

SENATOR TOLENTINO: Will the gentleman agree to provide in this bill that these bonds of the Land Bank be legal tender?

SENATOR MANGLAPUS: Mr. President, the gentleman has changed the nature of the argument. We are discussing whether the government cannot force anyone to be a creditor of the government. That was the point raised. There was no question raised as to whether these bonds of the Land Bank will be as liquid as legal tender—as money. That was not the point I was answering.

SENATOR TOLENTINO: That is why we have to progress in our argument. Is the gentleman willing to put in this bill a provision that bonds and shares of stock of the Land Bank shall be legal tender acceptable in the payment of all private and public obligation?

SENATOR MANGLAPUS: No, because this runs counter to

the objective of the law, which is non-inflationary. We do not want to provide in the law anything that will provide for inflationary pressures in the currency of the government. I am going to answer one of those remarks, including the remarks of the distinguished Floor Leader who mentioned about inflation on the floor this evening. And so, if the gentleman will allow me to continue...

SENATOR TOLENTINO: I was only after that point. I admit that our currency is a, managed currency. _ But if the P1.00 bill is being compared with the bonds and shares of the Land Bank, all I want to know is whether we can make them legal tender.

SENATOR MANGLAPUS: While the gentleman has made the Observation—and made it the burden Of his speech—that no one may be forced by law to be _a creditor of the government, I showed that by the wording of the text of the Central Bank bill and by the wording of the Central Bank Act, we are all creditors of the government.

SENATOR TOLENTINO: Mr. President, there is no comparison between money, which is under the absolute control of the government, and the bond of the Land Bank which is. . .

SENATOR MANGLAPUS: We are not comparing in our argument. There is no comparison between money and bond. The argument of the gentleman is whether we can force a private person to become a creditor of the government. There is no comparison between money and bond. As a matter of fact, the argument avoided the question of comparison. There was no mention of money, and, as I said, this will be answered in my remarks.

SENATOR TOLENTINO: Mr. President, the issuance of money by our government is not just a statutory authority. That is inherent in government, not just the case of compensation. You will find that in the law itself, and that is why we are making the differentiation. If the distinguished sponsor claims that we can be forced to be creditors because we are, holding P1.00 bills, my only point is, if we want to make a parity, why not make the bonds Of the Land Bank legal tender. So that I will withdraw my amendment—dust put that in the bill.

SENATOR MANGLAPUS: I will agree that no law can be made to allow the issuance of money in general. But a law was made to allow the issuance of the Central Bank notes under the Central Bank Act, and these constitute an obligation of the government to the people and, therefore, we are all, by law, creditors of the government.

SENATOR TOLENTINO: Yes, because the control of currency is one Of the inherent powers of sovereignty, not the expropriation of land. You find that only in an express grant of the government.

SENATOR MANGLAPUS: The gentleman has modified his argument and I will be ready to answer that question in that light after I have finished my argument.

SENATOR TOLENTINO: If that is the pleasure of the distinguished sponsor, thank you,

SENATOR MANGLAPUS: (Continuing:) Mr. President, the gentleman from Rizal has very eloquently cited thecase of Fidel Castro in Cuba as argument, that bonds cannot be acceptable because when he said Fidel Castro expropriated the properties of Americans, he offered bonds maturing in 20 years and the Americans said that was not just compensation.

I am not a Castroist, I am not a communist, but I would be the first to disagree when he says that the act of expropriation or the act Of Offering bonds is a demonstration of communist ideology. I have here the American Journal of June 1963, the latest issue, which has in its pages the article of Robert Alexander, professor Of Economics, Rutgers University, who speaks here of agrarian reform in Latin America. Mr. Alexander says:

"The form of payment for appropriated land has
also been of great importance. It is generally impossible for the government to pay in cash for all the
land it wants to expropriate. As a result, virtually
all the reform laws have provided for payment in in-
terest-bearing government bonds. In Mexico, Guatemala, Bolivia and Cuba the legislation has called for
complete payment in bonds, although in the Cuban
case these bonds have never been issued. In Venezuela
the government pays 10 per cent of the expropriation
price in cash, and the rest in bonds of from 10 to
20 years' duration, paying not more than 5 per
cent interest per year. The new Columbian law
provides that when unused land is expropriated, payment shall be made in 25-year bonds, paying 2 per
cent interest." ' .

Mr. President, certainly, Mexico is noncommunist. It may not be strongly anti-communist, but it is certainly anti-communist. Guatemala is now anti-communist; Bolivia is also non-communist. So, Mr. President, I think it is idle to quote Fidel Castro here because Latin America, I would say, is an example where bonds have been used properly and successfully.

SENATOR SUMULONG: Mr. President, just on this point if the gentleman will yield.

THE PRESIDENT. The gentleman may yield if he so desires.

SENATOR MANGLAPUS: With pleasure.

SENATOR SUM ULONG: When I talked of Fidel Castro, I did not mention anything about communism.

SENATOR MANGLAPUS: If I remember correctly theword Your Honor used was "communist." I may not have heard right, but the record will show that the gentleman used the word communist or communistic. If the gentleman denies it, I stand corrected.

SENATOR SUMULONG: Do I understand from Your Honor that Your Honor considers it a mistake for the American owners not to have accepted the bonds being offered by Fidel Castro for the lands expropriated by him?

SENATOR MANGLAPUS: I am not saying that. This is a matter where the United States government is in an ideological conflict with the Cuban government. It has broken relations and the general situation is completely obscured by he foreign relation situation. I say that that is not applicable in our case because there is no question of foreign relation.

SENATOR SUMULONG: The American Congress and the American government, to retaliate, declared an embargo on imports from Cuba because of the action of Fidel Castro. And simply because Cuba was unfriendly towards the United States, even when the Cuban government had no cash it expropriated anything and told the owner, "Well, we have no cash. We will pay you out of bonds."

SENATOR MANGLAPUS: With due respect to the gentleman from Rizal, because I know he is the chairman of the Committee on Foreign Relations and I have limited experience in foreign policy, may I say that this is a matter of judgment for those students of American-Cuban relation. I find that, in the refusal of the Americans to accept Cuban bonds, there is the element of obstructionism because of the relation between the United States and Cuba. This is an element not found in the present situation. I thought that the gentleman used that as an example of why we should not use bonds. It is incontrovertible that in many Latin American countries, noncommunist and anti-communist, bonds have been used.

SENATOR SUMULONG: Do I understand that if the relation between the United States and Cuba were not strained as it is now, if Your Honor were standing in the shoes of the Americans, you would believe that you should accept the bonds offered by Fidel Castro as payment for these properties?

SENATOR MANGLAPUS: I am not defending the Cuban situation. I am only making it a starting point for revealing here that in Latin America bonds have been used in payment of expropriated lands. Asa matter of fact, the example of Cuba is not squarely on point because the properties of the Americans in Cuba were not all real estate. They consisted of shares in oil companies, etc., which is not squarely the issue here. The issue here is bonds in exchange for lands.

SENATOR SUMULONG: It is a question of choice of policy. In the United States, according to the decisions cited here by the gentleman from Manila, Senator Tolentino, they do not consider as just compensation any other payment except payment in money, in legal tender, whereas in Latin America, like Cuba, they pay in bonds.

SENATOR MANGLAPUS: On that I would not quarrel with the gentleman from Rizal as far as ideology is concerned, but I would not favor his line of argument. He is trying to show that expropriation is purely an anti-democratic act. Expropriation is not an anti-democratic act because, as a matter of fact, it is provided in our Constitution.

SENATOR SUMULONG: So Your Honor believes that when the time comes that the government should want to own lands, it can say, "We have no cash. Whenever we expropriate the land Of anybody, instead of paying in cash, we just pay in bonds and preferred shares of stock," and that would be constitutional.

SENATOR MANGLAPUS: It will all depend, if there is serious national policy involved such as the social condition Of the masses. But if serious points are not involved, then I myself would doubt the wisdom and even the legality of issuing bonds at the caprice of the government. Thus, if the Latin American countries use bonds, it is a matter of policy based on the desire to remedy social conditions.

SENATOR SUMULONG: I am sorry I interrupted Your Honor. I wanted to raise these points Which occurred to me at the moment.

SENATOR RODRIGO: Mr. President.

THE PRESIDENT: What is the pleasure of the gentleman from Bulacan?

SENATOR RODRIGO: Mr. President, with the permission of the sponsor, may I make a statement.

It seems that it can be implied from the authorities read by the gentleman from Manila from American Jurisprudence and Corpus Juris that in the United States the 100 per cent doctrine is that in matters of expropriation, cash must always be paid. I listened very carefully as the gentleman from Manila read the quotations from American Jurisprudence and Corpus Juris, and I heard from the quotations that the weight of authorities holds that only cash can be used, and I noticed also that the Corpus Juris and the American Jurisprudence refer to state-decided cases, not cases decided by the United States Federal Supreme Court. When the Corpus Juris and the American Jurisprudence say, "On the basis of state-decided cases the weight of authorities is that cash should be paid," this means that in some states, the minority, yes. But in some states of the United States there are decisions to the effect that compensation can be paid not necessarily in cash but by other means.

SENATOR MANGLAPUS: Mr. President, I have a few more words to say before I end my speech. I merely wish to comment on the point raised on the ability of the tenant to pay. I believe we have taken that up in our discussion with the gentleman from Quezon, and I also believe that the present is not to be used as a basis to project to the future the ability to pay. These are present conditions which we are convinced would be improved upon the passage of this bill, upon increasing the productivity of the tenant. Also, with the comment that this bill provides for high financing in the matter Of Land Bank operations, because for every P1 the Land Bank issues P10 or for every P10 only P1 remains, I would like to say that, as a matter Of practice in our commercial banking operations, for instance the Philippine Bank of Commerce, for every P1 only P070 remains in the bank, the rest are invested or loaned out. In the matter of the Land Bank the mere fact that for every P10 only P1 remains in cash does not show high financing. Secondly, the P1 is dissipated in the form of land, so that the assets of the bank remain intact and, as we all know, land is a much more stable asset than cash itself.

With regard to the Floor Leader's statement of doubts regarding the value of bonds at the end of its maturity period, may I say that the reason we are for bonds instead of for cash, is that we would like to try to avoid inflation till the end of the transition period. But if we insist on inflation here, finally may I say that one of the reasons the bill provides, for bonds and shares of stock is that precisely shares provide for a hitch against inflation for the landowners because shares, as we all know, appreciate also with inflation and when we give the landowners 30 per cent in shares of stock and 60 per cent in bonds, we are providing, partially of course, with a hitch against any possible inflation, which inflation is precisely What we are going to avoid if we provide for bond payment instead Of cash payment.

SENATOR TOLENTINO: Mr. President.

THE PRESIDENT: Gentleman from Manila.

SENATOR TOLENTINO: May I just make a very brief statement.

THE PRESIDENT: The gentleman may proceed.

SENATOR TOLENTINO: As I said, all my intention was to help in eliminating what we believe might prejudice the validity of this measure after we have approved the same. We stated our reasons. We have cited decisions of court which could be of persuasive effect in this jurisdiction. Now, it has been observed and stated by the distinguished sponsor that: possibly—and I will go along with him in regard to decisions, which I have cited from American courts to the effect that it is unconstitutional for the Legislature to require the landowner in expropriation proceedings to accept bonds or shares of stock—it may refer to public service corporations like railroads but not to the government.

Mr. President, in these decisions it is not the identity of the expropriating agency or authority that is involved. What is involved is the meaning of the phrase "*just compensation*." That phrase "just compensation" is, in our Constitution, in the same manner that it must be in the Constitutions of the other states of the American Union in which these decisions were rendered and so, the context of these decisions must be viewed" in the light of the definition of "just compensation," and in the definition of "just compensation" this court holds that "just compensation" can be made only in money. When it goes further and says that the landowner cannot be required to accept bonds or shares of stock, that is simply explanatory and a logical consequence and natural effect that follows from the statement that "just compensation" must be in money. So it is immaterial what is the expropriating agency. In this particular case given that we are considering, it is not the Republic of the Philippines that is expropriating. We are creating a corporation that will live for 50 years; and being a creation of the Legislature, this corporation might even be shortened by the Legislature. Under the Constitution the Congress can terminate the existence of any corporation created by this body. It is not the Republic of the Philippines that is going to expropriate. It is the Land Bank, and that is a corporation like any other corporation, only that it shall be controlled by the government, not even wholly owned by the government because we allowed in this Bank that shares of stock be issued to landowners.

As far as that is concerned, our attention Should be centered on what is just compensation, and that should be in money.

Now, Mr. President, the observation of the distinguished gentleman from Bulacan that Corpus Juris states, "that the great weight of authority is to the effect that just compensation must be made in money and that the owner cannot be required to accept bonds." Yes, the phrase "the great weight of authority" is used, but every lawyer knows what is meant by that phrase. 'When you say "great weight of authority" you ordinarily follow the interpretation of the majority of authority. You do not follow the minority. That is the meaning of "great weight of authority."

In the case of American Jurisprudence it says: "But it is invariably held that the compensation must be in money."

So, Mr. President, it is up to us whether we want to follow

these judicial precedents or not... It is our individual duty as senators to follow our conscience. For my part it is simply a duty to call the attention of this chamber to this existing jurisprudence and that having been done, I believe that I have performed what to me is a very important duty because this provision affects the interpretation of the Constitution. I believe sincerely that if this provision is allowed to remain as it is, it is unconstitutional. With due respect to contrary opinion, I believe that this is unconstitutional. My proposal is intended to give a leeway to the court in determining whether it should permit as partial compensation bonds or shares of stock but would not control or bind the court to require the owner to accept said shares of stock.

SENATOR PUYAT: I would like to propound a question to the distinguished sponsor because upon his reply my vote will be cast accordingly.

THE PRESIDENT: The sponsor may yield if he so wishes.

SENATOR MANGLAPUS: With pleasure.

SENATOR PUYAT: Mr. President, when we talk of values, it is very important that we take into consideration the time element, and when we talk of stocks and bonds the time element becomes a very important consideration.

I was impressed 'by the statement made by Senator Padilla that in some cases holders of bonds and stocks may prefer to hold on to the bonds and stocks if by monetizing these bonds and stocks we create such inflationary impact, so that the purchasing value of the currency will fall to a level that it will not be to the better interest of the bondholders and holders of certificates to monetize these papers. On the other hand, however, we must recognize the fact that in our country we have a very limited bond-and-stock market, so that while it is true that bonds and stocks may both appreciate or depreciate in value, our experience in our country is that the more normal tendency is for these papers to depreciate in value.

Now, the distinguished chairman of the Committee on Banks, Corporations and Franchises referred to the land reform program in Venezuela, and I am reading a very pertinent provision, Article 178. And I will read this portion because, perhaps, we can amend this provision by adopting part7 of this article. This is Article 178:

This article ties up the value of the land expropriated with the cash that will be given to the owner of the land. So that in a way, by adopting a graduated scale such as this you mitigate the bad effects of inflation. My question is, would the sponsor entertain an amendment adopting a similar pattern, or would he adopt or accept an amendment that would make these bonds convertible so that if it is to the better interest of the bondholder, he does not convert these bonds into cash, but if he finds it to his better interest, he may have to convert these bonds into cash?

SENATOR MANGLAPUS: That amendment has already been suggested by Senator Manahan.

SENATOR PUYAT: I was convinced with that, but I wanted to make that clear on the floor. We want vital arguments that can be adduced to.

SENATOR MANGLAPUS: One .of the immediate reactions of the Committee has been for the maximum retention. The gentleman Will recall that in our discussion in the executive session and in caucus, the Committee emphasized that the large majority of the land available for expropriation will be less than 144 hectares, and according to the schedule prepared in that amendment and formally submitted, most of the lands that will fall under expropriation would be covered by the full cash or top priority in cash payment, and for this purpose we would need perhaps more than P400 million more to carry out the expropriation program. This matter has been thoroughly studied and this is one of the most serious objections— the inflationary consideration.

SENATOR PUYAT: Mr. Sponsor, in reading this article I was not suggesting that we adopt exactly similar percentages or the same values. We could modify the formula so that if the cash involved would not be so big, we could adopt this totally. A provision such as this would be better than the provision we have now in the bill.

SENATOR MANGLAPUS: Mr. President, may I state, depending on the maximum retention possible in the bill, that the Committee might consider this, but We cannot decide this until after the maximum retention is known.

SENATOR PUYAT: So the sponsor would prefer that the discussion on this provision be made later.

SENATOR MANGLAPUS: I was suggesting that we finish the discussion of this provision, and if the gentleman feels, after the retention provision is already considered and finished, like asking for reconsideration the Committee will not have any objection if it feels that there is a new basis for reconsidering this section based along the line of the Venezuelan law.

SENATOR PUYAT: Would the sponsor accept an amendment to make the bonds that would be issued convertible?

SENATOR MANGLAPUS: Convertible into what?

SENATOR PUYAT: Into cash.

SENATOR MANGLAPUS: Who Will pay the cash? L

SENATOR PUYAT: Whoever issues the bonds.

SENATOR MANGLAPUS: Then the effect would be thesame.

SENATOR PUYAT : No, because as I said, when you

consider values, the time element is important. As has been stated these papers may either appreciate or depreciate in value. If these bonds appreciate in value very few people will convert them into cash, but if the condition is so that it would be to the better interest of the bondholders to convert his bonds into cash let us give him that privilege.

SENATOR MANGLAPUS: I think that would lead to the pitfall which we are trying to avoid. We feel that there are in the bill certain provisions for conversion of bonds into other things besides actual cash, like shares of government reparations payment, etc., which might be sufficient to meet the demands of the landowners for transformation of their bonds into cash.

SENATOR PUYAT: I appreciate that by accepting that amendment you might produce inflationary pressure, but as I said suppose the trend for these papers appreciate in value. Does not Your Honor think the bondholders would prefer to hold on to their bonds? Rather, let us not assume that all the bondholders would want to metalize their bonds. Many of the bondholders would hold on to their bonds instead of metalizing them and, as Senator Padilla very well said, when you metalize you create inflationary pressure. So, it is to their better interest to hold on to their bonds.

SENATOR MANGLAPUS: This might be conceivable if the bonds were concentrated to a few individuals. But I think we should remember that these bonds will be distributed among a, large number of landowners and we feel that the trend will be in the immediate transformation into cash of all these bonds. I am sorry that the Committee cannot consider the suggestion of the gentleman from Manila and Pampanga.

SENATOR PUYAT: May I just make this comment, that precisely the bonds will be spread over thousands and thousands of bondholders, and the fear that there might be simultaneous attempts on the part of bondholders to metalize does not seem logical. If the bonds will be held by few individuals, there would be that danger feared by the gentleman, but since these bonds will be held by thousands of people, then that danger is less likely to happen because these bonds will not be metalized at a certain brief time. I just want to call attention to that, and with the answer given by the sponsor, I am now in a position to vote on the amendment.

THE PRESIDENT: The chamber will now dispose of the amendment.

SENATOR TOLENTINO: Mr. President, I was going to propose an alternative amendment which might be acceptable to the Committee. Instead of deleting the whole provision of Section 80, we will retain atleast the first paragraph. So the first paragraph which reads as follows will remain: "The Land Bank shall make payments in the form herein prescribed to the owners of lands acquired by the Land Authority for division and resale to small landholders. Such payment shall be made in the following manner: ten per centum in cash, at least sixty per centum in six per cent, tax—free, redeemable bonds issued by the Bank in accordance with Section 76, and the remaining balance in shares of stocks issued by the Bank in accordance with Section 77." That will be retained.

Then I propose that we eliminate the second paragraph which is anyway unnecessary, and instead of the second paragraph we insert the following: "THE FOREGOING SHALL NOT BE WITHOUT PREJUDICE TO WHAT THE COURT MAY DEEM JUST COMPENSATION IN EXPROPRIATION CASES." This may be a suitable amendment because at least the mention of bonds and shares of stock will not be removed.

THE PRESIDENT: What does the Committee say? Does the Chair understand that this amendment is being submitted formally in lieu of the original amendment?

SENATOR TOLENTINO: I am only sounding out the sponsor regarding this alternative amendment.

THE PRESIDENT: The sponsor may answer.

SENATOR MANGLAPUS: Mr. President, the sponsor would like to state that the Committee has great admiration for the tenacity and resourcefulness of the distinguished gentleman from Manila, but for reasons, I have already stated, with due respect to the gentleman, I regret to say that the Committee cannot accept his first amendment as well as his second amendment. . . .

SENATOR TOLENTINO: Then I am not going to insist on this as an alternative. I will leave the first amendment as it was proposed.

THE PRESIDENT: The Senate will now dispose of the amendment of the gentleman from Manila. All those in favor of the amendment Will please raise their right hands. (Some senators did so). All those against the amendment will please raise their right hands. (others did so).

The Secretary will include the vote of the Chair on the negative side. There are 9 votes in favor of the amendment and 12 against. The amendment is lost.

SENATOR LEDESMA: Mr. President.

THE PRESIDENT: The gentleman from Iloilo and Negros Occidental is recognized.

LEDESMA AMENDMENT

SENATOR LEDESMA: On page 40, line 27, after the word

"GOVERNMENT," add the following: "PAYMENT FOR ALL TAX OBLIGATIONS OF THE HOLDER THEREOF OR ANY DEBT 0R MONETARY OBLIGATION OF THE HOLDER TO THE GOVERNMENT OR ANY OF THIS IN STRUMENTALITIES INCLUDING THE DEVELOPMENT BANK OF THE PHILIPPINES AND THE PHILIPPINE NATIONAL BANK."

THE PRESIDENT: What does the Committee say?

SENATOR MANGLAPUS: Mr. President, this amendment has already been suggested formally to the Committee in writing and has been carefully studied and regretfully, the Committee has found the amendment unacceptable in view of the fact that it militates against the objective of the Committee on non-monetization of the land bonds and it figures that the idea of tax payment or obligation payment to the owners of the bonds would have the effect of monetizing.

THE PRESIDENT: Is the chamber ready to vote?

SENATOR LEDESMA: May I be given the chance to explain my amendment.

THE PRESIDENT: "The gentleman may do so.

SENATOR LEDESMA: Mr. President, I do realize the point raised by the sponsor, but on the other hand, we have seen also that the way the measure has been presented we cannot avoid the Central Bank printing paper money in some cases; and in this specific case, Mr. President, here is a landowner Whose land has been subjected to expropriation. This land is mortgaged to one of these government .instrumentalities. He has no other income, he has no other source of income but this land which has been the subject of expropriation. I was just wondering, Mr. President, how could this landowner pay his indebtedness to these government instrumentalities? Suppose he is in arrears in the payment of his taxes or some obligations to the government and this property subject to expropriation is his only source of income. I wonder how we could solve the problem of this landowner.

SENATOR MANGLAPUS: I wish to make a brief comment if I may be allowed by the gentleman from Iloilo.

SENATOR LEDESMA: Yes.

SENATOR MANGLAPUS: At present with the landowner holding the land, they are not paying their obligations with the land itself. They are paying their obligations with the income from the land.

SENATOR LEDESMA : Correct.

SENATOR MANGLAPUS: Now, we are providing that the land will be acquired with interest bearing bonds tax free. We feel that this will provide the landowner with the same kind of income, even more in many cases, which will provide them with the resources for the payment of their obligations.

SENATOR LEDESMA: Yes, perhaps the distinguished sponsor is correct if we accept the statement here that the payment will provide more income to the landowner than the actual income he is getting from the land. But I think that is going a little bit too far. If I may be allowed to say so, that is assuming that the valuation which is being embodied in this measure really would provide the landowner with an income much greater or at least equal to the income that the landowner is presently deriving or receiving from the piece of land. That is speaking with all frankness and sincerity.

SENATOR MANGLAPUS: Speaking of valuation, I think the gentleman will recall that the provision on just compensation has already been amended so that the court has much greater leeway in evaluating the land. We have provided with the compromise arrangement of the gentleman from Manila for a provision which will not limit the court to even what we feel are well studied choices provided in the bill or will limit the court to use other evaluations so that the fear that the evaluation of the expropriation might not be realistic, I think, should subside in the case of this new amendment.

SENATOR LEDESMA: Yes, with due respect to the statement of the distinguished sponsor, may I categorize on this assertion as purely hypothetical for the time being. I would like to repeat my example again, following the explanation of the distinguished sponsor.

Here is a landowner. He has this property. This property is being subjected to expropriation. The property has been mortgaged to a government financial institution. During all these years, he has been fulfilling religiously his commitment to this financial institution. Here comes the government. The land is the subject of expropriation and he is being told that what he will receive from the government will be more than enough to meet his obligation. Now, I ask. Suppose this is not enough, then What is going to happen, granting and I will accept at its face value the statement of the distinguished sponsor? May I say also that supposing that is not the case.

SENATOR MANGLAPUS: Perhaps, we should analyze the proposition. We are supposing a mortgaged land. Now, when the land is mortgaged, I think the following routine is followed: The land is appraised by the lending institution. Usually the appraisal is not really the market value, but it is usually, less. And with that appraisal, a maximum of 60% is given by the bank.

SENATOR LEDESMA: Depending on the influence of the borrower.

SENATOR MANGLAPUS: Correct and since the appraisal is lower than the actual value or sometimes the appraisal is equivalent only to 40% of the real market value of the land. Now, in other words, the obligation of the landowner is to repay a maximum of 40% of the value of the land. On the other hand, the bonds that we are paying would be given to them on the basis of the value as found by the court and would be paying 6% interest. And perhaps, even assuming that the 6% would be less than the actual receipts or earnings that the landowner gets from the land, since the loan is not on the basis of 100% but Only 40, then the 6% of the bonds would be sufficient to cover amortization and interests on the loan.

SENATOR LEDESMA: I do not wish to dispute the figure of the distinguished sponsor here. I am prepared to accept his figure, but I am submitting this just in case the figure does not tally with the statement of the distinguished sponsor here. What are we going to do? There is one little detail here, that the landowner is just paid 10% in cash and the rest is in bond. Now, as has been stated here by the distinguished sponsor, let us assume that he gets 60%— the loan value of the land is 60%. Let us presume that 60% is a little bit higher than the 10% in cash.

SENATOR MANGLAPUS: May I correct that — 60% of the appraised value.

SENATOR LEDESMA: Assuming that that is the appraised value, could we presume that the 60% should be much higher than the appraised value of the land?

SENATOR MANGLAPUS: _ The landowner does not sell his land in order to pay for the amortization. It is held as security for the mortgage and the landowner does not sell his land in order to pay the mortgage. He earns from the land to pay the mortgage, and we feel that the compensation that he is going to get out of the bonds plus the added outlets that have been built into Section 85, such as the creation of a bond market by virtue Of a provision here regarding the sale. Of public agricultural lands and also the insertion of their acceptability as collateral in government financing institutions, plus their availability as payment for reparations goods and their acceptability as surety or performance bonds, and with all these added features of liquidity, will be sufficient to make up for whatever possible deficiency the landowner may find in the income that he gets from the land.

SENATOR LEDESMA: I am submitting what to my mind is a practical problem. I do realize the practicability of the assertion made by the distinguished sponsor, but I am submitting a practical problem. Yes, we are giving him all these privileges, but common sense tells us that before he can enjoy these privileges he would like to pay his indebtedness. . .

SENATOR MANGLAPUS: His indebtedness?

SENATOR LEDESMA: ....on the property that is subject to expropriation. Now, if there is a lien on that property, this property passes to the government. He is paid in bond. My question is, how is he going to clear his indebtedness, his obligati'On, when he is getting 10%? Yes, he was able to borrow only 60% of the appraised value, but the 60% is bigger than the 10% that is made in cash payment.

SENATOR MANGLAPUS: If the loan is from a government financing institution, and I think most of them would be from government financing institutions, the government will be compelled to accept the bonds as collateral.

SENATOR LEDESMA: Could we clarify that?

SENATOR MANGLAPUS: That is the amendment of the gentleman from Manila and Pampanga.

SENATOR LEDESMA: That is the only point I am trying to raise, Mr. President.

THE PRESIDENT: Is the chamber ready to vote on the matter?

SENATOR MANGLAPUS: If the gentleman is not satisfied with the explanation here, may I refer him to page 36, line 14, which reads:

"THESE INSTRUMENTS OF INDEBTEDNESS
MAY BE MORTGAGEABLE IN ACCORDANCE
WITH ESTABLISHED BANKING PROCEDURES
AND PRACTICES TO GOVERNMENT INSTITU-
TIONS NOT TO EXCEED SIXTY PER CENTUM
OF THEIR FACE VALUE TO ENABLE THE
HOLDERS OF SUCH BONDS TO MAKE USE OF
THEM IN INVESTMENTS IN PRODUCTIVE EN:
TERPRISES."

SENATOR LEDESMA: Page 36, Your Honor?

SENATOR MANGLAPUS: Page 36, line 14.

SENATOR LEDESMA: Page 36, line 14. It says:

"THESE INSTRUMENTS OF INDEBTEDNESS
MAY BE MORTGAGEABLE IN ACCORDANCE
WITH ESTABLISHED BANKING PROCEDURES
AND PRACTICES T0 GOVERNMENT INSTITU-
TIONS NOT TO EXCEED SIXTY PER CENTUM
OF THEIR FACE VALUE TO ENABLE THE
HOLDERS OF SUCH BONDS TO MAKE USE OF
THEM IN INVESTMENTS IN PRODUCTIVE EN—
TERPRISES. THEY SHALL ALSO BE ACCEPT-
ED AS PAYMENTS FOR REPARATION EQUIP-

MENT AND MATERIALS."

It seems to me, Mr. President, that this does not meet the point that I have raised. Yes, we could use them as collateral to borrow, but supposing that the landowner uses this as collateral but the amount that we could borrow is only 60%. That would not be enough to pay his indebtedness.

SENATOR MANGLAPUS: The bonds would be in the amount of 60% of the value of the land. Now, the mortgage principal would not be more than 40%. So, he has 60%, which is more than 40%.

SENATOR LEDESMA: Your Honor has stated here the mortgage is usually around 60%.

SENATOR MANGLAPUS: No, I said that the mortgage would be 60% of the appraised value of the land, and the appraised value is less than the real and actual value, and the mortgageable value is 40%. Now, the bond constitutes 60% of the value of the land.

SENATOR LEDESMA: But he cannot borrow 60% of the 100%. He can borrow only 60% of the 60%.

SENATOR MANGLAPUS: Mr. President, this is a good point raised and I think a perfecting amendment would be introduced here so that the bonds would respond. I think the gentleman from Manila and Pampanga who introduced this amendment himself 'might be able to suggest a perfecting amendment here.

6 - LAND AND IDEOLOGY

IN OUR debates on land reform on the floor of the Senate, I had occasion to stress repeatedly that the paramount objective of the Code was social, not economic. Productivity was certainly an important, an extremely important objective but not so important that its consideration could be allowed to prevail over that of social change.

During those thirty days of discussion, the issue of social change vs. economics must have been raised more than a dozen times. At every challenge, our response was two fold: First, that there was no conflict between the two objectives in the context Of the bill; second, that assuming the conflict, the immediate problems of social deterioration in tenanted lands, particularly (but not exclusively) in Central Luzon must first be tackled even to the postponement of benefits in production.

Early in the debates, we had to stop a drive to involve the government in another attempt at massive resettlement of tenants in public lands, leaving the tenanted lands in the hands of the landlords.

"There are many public lands still available in Mindanao," said its proponents. "Why not settle the tenants there and leavethe landlords to cultivate their land on a mass, scientific production basis?"

The answer had to be patiently spelled out.

This alternative had been tried before and found to be a failure. In the early 1950s, tenants were suddenly uprooted from their traditional ambiance from their sources of secondary employment, secondary credit, the warm closeness of extended family assistance, the ready, albeit imperfect, network of roads, markets and communications, and planted in the open vastness of Mindanao. Large numbers of those would-be independent settlers, unable to weather the abrupt convulsion in their lives, quickly deteriorated back to tenancy, share-cropping for established landowners in their area.

Furthermore, on the basis of actual cost of settlement of a few thousand families under the old program, it would now require an appropriation of 19 \billion pesos to resettle in this fashion the 1,200,000 tenant families that await their redemption all over the country.

The Code, in fact, provides for a "pluralistic" approach to modern farming. The tenants are to become owner—cultivators of their own land and organize cooperatives for production and marketing. The landlords will have the choice, with their cash bonds, to invest in industry or in large scale farming. The Code directs that public lands shall be made available to the bondholding landlords at P100 per titled hectare. At a. probable average selling rate of 192,000 a hectare of his land, each landlord should be able to acquire twenty hectares of public land for every hectare of his own that he sells to the Land Bank.

It is the landlord —— and not the tenant — who is better prepared to conquer the challenges of newly opened public land and engage in unitary (as distinguished from cooperative) largescale, scientific cultivation. The Code gives him this opportunity while at the same time doing away for good with the age old evil of tenancy.

Why is tenancy an evil? Because it is paternalism in its most deceptive and insidious form. A kind, benevolent landlord (and we have many of these) can at best treat his tenant as a child, making his decisions for him, not only those decisions that have to do with planting but even those that have to do with the tenant's own being and life — including who the tenant's daughter might marry.

This is the way share-cropping tenancy has worked all over the world. The tenant's mind persists in child-like innocence, uncreative, unproductive, crushed by the over-powering paternalism of the system.

After a few generations of it the tenant community learns to accept notions, beliefs and practices that debase human dignity.

As late as 1914 in Catholic Austria, tenants observed the rule of its ins primes noctis, or "right of the first night" under which the tenant bridegroom was expected to yield his bride to his landlord on the wedding night. In their minds this practice had come to be regarded as a way by which "noble blood" might be introduced into .their monotonously peasant strain. When a parish priest in a town near Vienna decided to condemn the practice publicly he was called down by his bishop. Honest history will reveal what monstrous variations of this rule may be found in Philippine and Asian tenancy.

Our land reform movement is faced with strong resistance on the part of landlords (except, we are told, in some parts of Pampanga.) But its most formidable enemy is our party system itself. Neither of our two major parties is ideologically committed to agrarian change. .(We might add that, being artificially protected by law, they find no need to commit themselves to anything fundamental and ideological.)

We passed our Land Reform Code in a purely pragmatic mood. There was no ideological frame of reference, no overall party article of faith with which it could be identified, no national plan of priorities in which it could be located.

The result is what we see today. The land reform program must go begging for funds, must complete with lesser needs for appropriations, must get involved in petty personal politics. On the very Senate floor during the debates on the Code, this formidable enemy reared its head. In the face of determined opposition from both parties, we had to give up the chapter on the revision of the agricultural land tax, which would have speeded the implementation of the Code immeasurably by providing the disincentive to holding large tenanted tracts and the gloved but determined push so that the landlord might move to industry or modern, untenanted farming. '

We need not wonder about aimlessly in search for a Christian Social ideology that will give us the vision of our future.

A bold transcendental encyclical has just come out of Rome which promised to achieve immortality. Paul VI, in "Populorum Progressio" (On the Development of People) raises the burning theme: "Development is the new name for peace."

He calls for a recognition of the social limitations on private property: "Private Property does not constitute for 'anyone an absolute and unconditional right. No one is justified in keeping for his exclusive use what he does not need, when others lack necessities." (Sec. 23)

He calls for land reform: "If, certain landed estates impede the general prosperity because they are extensive, unused or poorly used or because they bring hardship to peoples or are detrimental to the interests of the country, the common good sometimes demands their expropriation" (Sec. 24).

He calls for planning: "Individual initiative alone and the mere free play of competition could never assure successful development. One must avoid the risk of increasing still more the wealth of the rich and the dominion of the strong, whilst leaving the poor in their misery and adding to the servitude of the oppressed." (Sec. 33)

He calls for central and intermediate planning and decentralized implementation: "Hence programmes are necessary in order 'to encourage, stimulate, coordinate, supplement and integrate the activity of individuals and of intermediary bodies. It pertains to the public authorities to choose, even to lay down the objectives to be pursued, the end to be achieved, and the means for attaining these, and it is for them to stimulate all the forces engaged in this common activity. But let them take care to associate private initiative and intermediary bodies with this work. They will thus avoid the danger of complete collectivization or of arbitrary planning, which, by denying liberty, would prevent the exercise of the fundamental rights of the human person." (Sec. 33)

He blames "free trade" for the poor economies of former colonies: "In other words, the rule of free trade, taken by itself, is no longer able to govern international relations. Its advantages are certainly evident when the. parties involved are not affected by any excessive inequalities of economic power: it is an incentive to progress and a reward for effort. That is why industrially developed countries see in it a law of justice. But the situation is no longer the same when economic conditions differ too widely from country to country: prices which are 'freely' set in the market can produce unfair results. One must recognize that it is the fundamental p1 inciple of liberalism, as the rule for commercial exchange, which is questioned here " (Sec. 58).

He calls for contractual justice between nations. "The teaching of Leo XIII in Remm Novarmn is always valid: if the position of the contracting parties are too unequal, the consent of the parties does not suffice to guarantee the justice of their contract, and the rule of free agreement remains subservient to the demands of the natural law. What was true of the just wage for the individual is also true of international contracts: an economy of exchange can no longer be based solely on the law of free competition, a law which, in its turn, too often creates an economic dictatorship. Freedom of trade is fair only if it is subject to the demands of social justice." (Sec. 59)

This new ideology rooted in the old Christian ethic bears a devastating relevance to the social and economic problems of the

Philippines —— from tenancy to our "special relations" with the U.S.

If the land reform and the tensions of our development are to be overcome, it will require a citizenry moving in organized response to this ideology.

Pope Paul VI's appeal to youth (Sec. 74) is a fitting conclusion: "May all those who wish to belong to Christ hear His appeal: 'I was hungry and you gave me to eat, thirsty and you gave me to drink, a stranger and you took me in, a naked and you clothed me, sick and you visited me, a prisoner and you came to see me.' No one can remain indifferent to the lot of his brothers who are still buried in wretchedness, and victims of insecurity, slaves of ignorance. Like the heart of Christ, the heart of the Christian must sympathize with this misery: 'I have pity on this multitude.' "

DECENTRALIZATION

INTRODUCTICN

This section consists of several passages extracted from the records of the Senate deliberations on the Barrio Charter Revision Bill ,(1963) and the Decentralization Bill (1965).

The first group of extracts, entitled "The Movement: Advances and Setbacks," is intended to acquaint the reader with a brief history of the movement for local autonomy and some of the names associated with it in the past and in the present. The second group, entitled, "The Decentralization Bill: the Heart of the Matter," is meant to shed light on the essential elements of the bill and some of the basic issues they generated.

1 - The Movement: Advances and Setbacks

(The following is the sponsorship speech delivered extemporaneously by Senator Manglapus on February 3, 1963, in support of the bill to revise the Barrio Charter.)

Mr. President, I rise this morning to sponsor Senate Bill No. 82, which amends the Barrio Charter already passed by this august body in the year 1960.

Mr. President, I feel that in sponsoring this measure, my task is not complicated —rather, it is simple —for I feel that there is no need to persuade the members of this august body of the philosophy of barrio autonomy. The voting record on the Barrio Charter bill in 1959 demonstrates that all of the senators voted in favor of that bill. I am also proud to state that the grant of further barrio autonomy is part of the platform of the party to which I belong.

The credit for the Barrio Charter belongs to you, gentlemen of the Senate. It is because of you that today there is new life in the barrios, there is a new sense of participation among the people in the rural areas, there is a new self—reliance revived by the Barrio Charter. We have built a pyramid on a solid base, and that solid base is the growing political maturity of our people who live not in the centers of population but in the distant rural areas.

I am reminded, .as I sponsor this bill, of a great man who now lives in India, who in that part of the world may be considered as one of the leaders in the movement for village autonomy in Asia. This man is Jayaprarsan Narayan who said recently in India that in the building of our society it does not matter who is at the apex of the pyramid. What matters is how strong the base of that pyramid is; whether it is a barrio in the Philippines or a panchayat in India, it is imperative that the base be strong and acquire .a sense of participation in government. Our people are beginning to have that sense.

But I think we are all agreed that a law must be alive, must be living, must be responsive, and as the sponsor of the bill in the Lower House said, it must be subject to change.

Congressman Antonio Y. de Pio, writing a letter recently to Senator Manahan, said he admits that certain defects and deficiencies in the law have become evident. As co-author of the law with Vice President Emmanuel Pelaez, Mr. Pio admits that the law is far from perfect. There is need for some changes to make it. responsive totthe growing needs of the barrio people.

There were needs unforeseen in 1959 that have now become obvious by experience, and your Committee and the authors of this bill took pains to invite to a public hearing responsible members of the government and of private organizations who are by their profession and occupation engaged in research on barrio autonomy.

I want to mention in this connection a group based in the University of the Philippines in Los Bafios, headed by Prof. Buenaventura Villanueva, which is engaged in research on barrio autonomy.

I want to mention the cooperation of the joint Executive-

Legislative Tax Commission, the General Auditing Office and the Presidential Action for Community Development,

Certain unforeseen requirements have come up since 1959. For instance, it was not foreseen in 1959:

1) that there could be serious disputes on whether or not the "poblacion," which is the center of population in a town, may be considered a barrio;

2) that the lack of barrio boundaries could be a serious deterrent to the full implementation of the Charter;

3) that many barrios would fail to receive their 10 percent share of real estate taxes because of the extremely difficult administrative requirements imposed by the Secretary of Finance and the General Auditing Office;

4) that the barrio assembly as constituted under R.A. 2370 could have difficulty in convening a quorum so that as a result its performance as a policy—making body would be far from efficient;

5) that municipal, city or provincial officials would be reluctant in fully implementing the provisions of this Act for fear that it would diminish their powers or revenues;

6) that electoral and financial procedures as well as the organization of the barrio council, as provided for in RA. 2370, could be conducive to or would even aggravate inefficiency in barrio governments; and

7) that the lack of authority of barrio officials to enact their own budget could be a serious drawback to genuine barrio autonomy.

Mr. President, these are some of the many important problems that necessitate a thorough revision of the Barrio Charter.

As indicated in the Explanatory Note of Senate Bill 82, there are 10 major changes envisioned in the bill:

First, the explicit provision that the "poblacion" shall be considered a barrio. This would clarify the existing uncertainty on the legal status of the "poblacion." We have about 1,400 poblaciones. If we follow the interpretation of a former Executive Secretary that a "poblacion" is not a barrio, we would be denying the residents therein — about 1.5 million — the same political rights given to those residing in other sections of municipalities.

Second, the determination of barrio boundaries by municipal councils Within 60 days after the approval of this Act. This would solve the serious problem of undetermined barrio boundaries and would facilitate the allocation of the 10 per cent share of the real estate tax to the barrios.

Third, the expansion of the barrio assembly and the modification of its structure, organization, procedures and powers. This would solve the inherent weakness of the barrio assembly as a deliberative body, would make it a more efficient organization in asserting the sovereign rights of barrio residents, 18-year-olds and illiterates.

Fourth, the holding of barrio plebiscites to decide on ordinances, resolutions or decisions passed by the barrio council or the recall of any member of the barrio council. Through the plebiscite, members of the assembly will have final judgment on policies promulgated by the barrio council or on the behavior of any of its members. It would also facilitate tax consciousness, since no revenue measure could be effective without its approval through a plebiscite.

Fifth, the modification of the membership, electoral procedures and the rights of succession in the barrio council. I believe, Mr. President, this is necessary to make the barrio council more efficient in the formulation of policies and to make barrio elections systematic, clean and peaceful.

Of course, I do not imply that the past barrio elections are unclean, unreliable or disorderly. Far from it, Mr. President. But since we are legislating not only for the present but for the future, we want to be sure that coming barrio elections will be without fraud or disorder.

Sixth, the definition of the duties and responsibilities of all members of the barrio council. I believe that a more detailed listing of the duties and responsibilities of the members of the barrio council will prevent unnecessary disputes and, instead help create a more efficient working team in the council.

Seventh, the extension of the privileges given to barrio lieutenants under RA. 2370 to all members of the barrio council. This is only fair, Mr. President, considering that the barrio council works as a team and privileges given to one should be given to all.

Eighth, greater autonomy in the enactment of barrio ordinances by the barrio council. This bill provides that failure to act on barrio ordinances 90 days after submission to it by the barrio council would mean an implied approval of said ordinance. This, Mr. President, would prevent delay in barrio council operations.

Ninth, the authority of the barrio council to enact budgetary appropriations. This, Mr. President, would facilitate careful expenditures of barrio funds, would enable barrio residents to know where their money is going, would result in greater stability of barrio finances, and ultimately would result in more barrio improvements.

Lastly, the authority of the municipal treasurer to employ necessary personnel to take care of the accounting of barrio funds. Since these funds are deposited with the municipal treasurer and considering that there are many barrios in every municipality, the additional workload of the municipal treasurer could be tremendous. Hence, the authority to allow him to hire additional personnel is justified.

Mr. President, I want to reiterate that we should give credit where credit is due. 'We should give credit to the members of this body who voted affirmatively on the Barrio Charter. I believe it is only proper to give credit to men in our history, current and distant past, who contributed to the movement for local autonomy in this country.

Mr. President, local autonomy is as old as the pre—Spanish barangay. When the Spaniards came the barangay became a unit of administration, direct supervision and control of the Spaniards. In 1881, in Barcelona, Graciano Lopez-Jaena began his crusade for local autonomy when he said:

El dia que el triunfo corone nuestros ideales, el dia en que la republica brille en los horizontes espanio-les, tendremos ocasion de implantar una reforma am-plia, una ley municipal y provincial altamente radical, democratica con vida propia, independiente y auto-noma, cual cumple y honra a nuestras convicciones republicanas.

The day that triumph shall crown our ideals, the day that our republic shall shine in Hispanic horizons, we shall have occasion to implant ample reforms — a truly radical law for the provinces and municipalities, which shall have their own democratic existence, in-dependent and autonomous, in keeping with our repub-lican convictions.

Mr. President, we have our own democratic independent existence, in keeping with our own convictions. But this crusade of Graciano Lopez-Jaena found better expression in Article 82 of the Malolos Constitution which was daring in granting local autonomy to our local government, more daring than was our Constitution of 1934.

Before ending, Mr. President, I should like to give credit to a member of this body who fought for local autonomy, especially for the barrios, for initiating a specific movement for barrio autonomy in this country. I feel that I should at this point remind our people that in 1958, before anyone thought of bringing local autonomy down to the barrio level, it was the now Senator 'Manuel Manahan who said in August 1958 during the birthday anniversary of the late President Quezon the following words:

"I offer, as a solution to our most pressing national problem, that we give our rural folk barrio home-rule.

Barrio home-rule decentralizes pOwer and makes the barrio the cornerstone and key participant in the processes of our government. The barrio citizen knows what is best for him and should be rescued from the strait-jacket of democracy, but having been denied too long the active exercise of it, they have become cynical about its values and processes. Quezon dreamed of making every man a force in the community, and this dream took shape in the hands of Ramon Magsaysay. It is for us now through the barrio home-rule to bring it to reality.

Mr. President, the municipalities and provinces must also be given their share of autonomy. I am glad to note that there are many bi-partisan bills that are being filed in both Houses of Congress to grant more autonomy to municipalities and provinces. In the meantime, in the consideration of this bill, let us remember that it is the base of the pyramid that must be strengthened.

Mr. President, I will close by quoting Thomas Aquinas who said, "Freedom is the spontaneous obedience to the Law." (And Senator Osias caused this to be translated into Ilocano and Tagalog on the floor of the Senate.) Thomas Aduinas said that spontaneous obedience to the law is the most effective form of freedom and obedience. Spontaneity means the voluntary participation, the sense of taking part, in the activities of the community and of the nation. This is the meaning of the Barrlio Charter and this is the reason we seek to amend the Barrio Charter in order to strengthen the spontaneous obedience to law, the freedom of our people. Thank you, Mr. President.

2 - Decentralization and the Constitution

(This is an excerpt from the Senate deliberations on the Decentralization Bill on February 4, 1965.)

SENATOR ZIGA: I would like first of all to congratulate the distinguished sponsor for the zeal and dedication with which he has embarked on this decentralization project. I would like to state here for the record that I am whole-heartedly in support of the idea of decentralization. But I would like to qualify my statement by asking a few questions.

I notice in Sec. 2 of the draft of the bill under consideration that as a declaration of policy it is the intention of the sponsor to transform our local governments gradually into effective instruments to which the people can, in a most genuine fashion, govern themselves and work out their own destinies. Is it the policy of the Decentralization Bill that decentralization be gradual?

SENATOR MANGLAPUS : That is correct, Mr. President. We are only decentralizing, as the lady will note, three functions.

SENATOR ZIGA: Yes. Is it the opinion of the distinguished sponsor that we can decentralize our overcentralized government in one sweeping piece of legislation?

SENATOR MANGLAPUS: Those who are for decentralization, if they wish to achieve in full their desires, would ultimately want to amend the Constitution. But what we are doing now is seeking to decentralize within the framework of our Constitution.

SENATOR ZIGA: Yes. 5 What I am trying to say is that decentralization really need not be just effected in one bill but it could really be a long process.

SENATOR MANGLAPUS: Well, perhaps the word "long" may be difficult to accept at this time. At least it will be a process which will involve more than one step, and this is only the first step.

SENATOR ZIGA: Well, I would like to call the attention of the distinguished sponsor to the statement in the explanatory note to the effect that "after 18 years of independence we have not freed ourselves from the shackles of an overcentralized system of. government, a system imposed by the colonial powers." In this connection, is the distinguished sponsor aware of a provision in the Constitution, particularly Section 10 (1), Article VII, which reads as follows:

The President shall have control of all the executive departments, bureaus, or offices, exercise general supervision over 211 local governments as may be provided by law, and take care that the laws be faithfully executed.

Now, a perusal of this provision will readily give the impression that some form of autonomy is really intended to be exercised by the local governments. In fact the provision merely speaks of "supervision" which has been interpreted by our courts as overseeing, or the power or authority of an officer to see to it that the laws are complied with and that the subordinate officers perform their duties. Thus, Article VII of the Constitution, Your Honor, expresses a desire for general autonomy, so that from the very beginning, from the date of the final drafting of our Constitution that desire to increase autonomy for local governments is there, and it must not be forgotten that this present system was conceived and organized to meet the needs and the limited experience of our people in self—government when the Americans cr me into power at the turn of the century. Thus, in the Constitution we have a general desire expressed for increased autonomy for local governments. Does not the sponsor agree with me in this interpretation of Article VII of the Constitution?

SENATOR MANGLAPUS : Mr. President, the Committee, of course, respects the views of~the lady from Albay regarding Article VII of our Constitution. 1 merely would like to point out the very fact that this article referred to by the lady from Albay has been the subject of conflicting Supreme Court decisions. As the lady will recall the original decisions interpreting this provision favored "control" and not just "supervision." It is only in later Supreme Court decisions that some concession was made to the principle of local government, and the original decision penned during the Commonwealth period which would interpret this so as to include control was modified. To us this represents a situation which requires correction and clarification. We cannot do it without amending the Constitution. We cannot make a final correction without amending the Constitution, but we can implement the latest interpretation of it. We can do this .by approving this bill. The lady correctly states that perhaps at the time the Constitution was formulated a certain caution was exercised by the framers of the Constitution because of what she refers toas "limited experience." This was of course 30 years ago, in 1934. It is now 1965, and it is perhaps with all the added experience that we have had since the year the Constitution was framed that we are now in a position to be a little bolder in the interpretation of this article by giving added powers to our local governments. I would like also to point out that it would seem that the framers of the Malolos Constitution were somewhat more confident of the capacity of the local governments, even more confident than the framers of our Constitution in 1934 perhaps because they had not yet had the experience themselves. But Article 82 of the Malolos Constitution specifically mentions local powers, not only obliquely as does the present Constitution. Article 82 specifically lays down the limitation to which national power can go in supervising or dictating to local governments, whereas in our case we have done it the other way. We have given the positive power to the national government and we have left the task to the Supreme Court to interpret this. I merely want to point this out to show that in the past even our revolutionary leaders seemed to have had confidence in our local governments' ability to take care of their own affairs if given the chance. I hope this will answer the doubts of the lady from Albay arising from this phrase which we used in the explanatory note which, of course, is not part of the bill. If the lady feels that this is rather general and we should include a phrase which would do more justice to the framers of our Constitution we would have absolutely no objection.

SENATOR ZIGA: Well, in connection with the interpretation of the word "supervision" as used in the Constitution there are already several cases on that which interpret the Presidential power over local governments to mere general supervision and not control.

SENATOR MANGLAPUS: That is correct.

SENATOR ZIGA: I would cite the cases of Mindanao versus Salvosa and Ebron versus Reyes, so that supervision under that provision merely means supervision, or overseeing that the laws are fully executed by the subordinate officers. After the constitutional provision I would like to refer the distinguished sponsor to Republic Act. No. 2264, the Local Autonomy Act, and the Barrio Charter Act known as Republic Act No. 2370 which were passed in 1959, so that within this period of time from the drafting of the Constitution up to now there have been definite steps taken by our government for the purpose of giving increased autonomy to the local governments, so that it would. not be quite correct to say in the explanatory note that "18 years after the grant of independence we are still shackled by an overcentralized system of government."

SENATOR MANGLAPUS: I take it the lady is for a correction of the sentence in order to render justice where justice is due. As a matter of fact, that would be more flattering to the author of this bill, because we also have something to do with the revising of the Barrio Charter. As a matter of fact, Senator Manahan was originally the innovator in the matter of barrio home-rule. I would have no objection to amending this in order that it may not appear unjust to those who have taken steps to decentralize even before this bill.

The Decentralization Bill: the Heart of the Matter

1 - Decentralization and Efficient Government.
(From the Senate records, January 29, 1965.)

SENATOR PUYAT: In the new decentralization bill, three functions now undertaken by the national government are sought to be transferred to the provincial and local governments. What were the considerations that motivated the authors of the bill in pinpointing these three functions: agricultural extension, rural health and education? Of the many functions now exercised by the national government, why these three? And why is it felt that to achieve the purpose of this bill, these three functions should be under the management and supervision of provincial and local governments?

SENATOR MANGLAPUS: Mr. President, may I state, in answering the distinguished gentleman from Pampanga and Manila, first, that it is of course the ambition of the Committee to decentralize ultimately as many functions as possible. Now why did we begin with the modest step of decentralizing only these three services, and why specifically these three services? We thought that we should begin, not with all services but only with selected services, because I think this would satisfy those who might express the fear that we are taking too bold a step without measuring the consequences. We chose these three services because studies have shown that agricultural extension, rural health and education are better administered by the governmental units closer to the people. In most cities today, as a matter of fact, these services are already decentralized to a great degree. In the case of field extension of agricultural work, this is financed out of local funds although local officials have no voice on the amounts that should be used.

I think the gentleman should note that we had a bill some years ago restoring to the disposition of provincial governments the funds for agricultural extension. And as a matter of fact, Mr. President, at some time or other-in the past these three services were decentralized. But for lack of resources they were subsequently nationalized.

May I just recall, for example, that there was a time that intermediate schools all over the Philippines were conducted on the local level. It was only when developments showed that the national government was absorbing most of the resources and there was no accompanying increase of provincial resources that Congress found it expedient progressively to nationalize always these functions. But now, in taking this step we feel that we can go back to what after all was the original foundation of these services by ceding to the provincial government those resourcesit would need to carry out those functions.

SENATOR PUYAT: In other words, it is the feeling of the author of the bill that by transferring the funds necessary the local government would have the personnel, the machinery and such other factors as would effectively and efficiently administer these functions.

SENATOR MANGLAPUS: Yes, Mr. President, that is the feeling of the Committee. The provinces will after all merely absorb the machinery already in existence today and would now have the resources with which to maintain that machinery and keep it going.

SENATOR PUYAT: Now, considering that these activities are of a national scale, is there no danger that when you start decentralizing these activities, these activities may finally end up as fragmented programs depending on the administration of the different provinces and that there might be no central coordinated thinking but that the program would be carried out in accordance with the views and the thinking of the provinces and local governments?

SENATOR MANGLAPUS: The Committee looks on that statement of the gentleman with utmost sympathy and this is the reason We insisted in including in the bill lines 24 to 30, page 2, providing for the unity and integration of programs and activities and uniformity in general standards under the aegis of the national offices. And for this purpose, we will find that the bill provides for the periodic consultation between the national offices and the provincial offices in order that the guidelines set down by the national offices may be followed.

SENATOR PUYAT: Yes, I am aware of that provision. But I call attention to the fact that where a provision like this exists, where all that the national body or office can do is provide for the broad policies and set up guideposts but not the control of the funds and the actual implementation is in the hands of another governmental agency, our experience in the government shows that it is the governmental agency that controls the funds and has the final say, and that the recommendations of the policy-making body are often overlooked or totally disregarded. That is what I am afraid of.

All right, you have this national office establishing the policies. This office should be the coordinating agency but your funds will be in the hands of the provincial and local governments. Now, suppose the people handling these funds think otherwise; they see fit to overlook and to totally disregard the recommendation of the national office. What happens to this activity that must be carried out by necessity on a coordinated national level? You cannot have an educational system fragmented into what the different provinces feel. We cannot afford to have a rural health program fragmented into what the different provinces feel.

SENATOR MAN GLAPUS : I couldn't agree more with the gentleman from Pampanga and in answering him, I would like to refer him to Section 21 of the bill found on page 16, which reads briefly as follows:

> Within 60 days before the start of any fiscal
> year, the national offices concerned shall formulate,
> jointly with the Provincial and City Agriculturists,
> Provincial and City Health Offices, and Division and

City Superintendents of Schools, the general program
of activities for the coming fiscal year for field agricultural extension work, rural health work. and public
intermediate school education, respectively. It shall
be the responsibility of the Provincial Governor and
the City Mayor to carry out such program of activities
in their respective jurisdictions.

May I also refer the gentleman to Section 23, which provides
penalties for any violation of the provisions of this section by the
officials concerned.

Now, may I explain that the philosophy of this bill is to pin
point responsibility. Aside from the safeguards which are found in the,
penalty clause of this bill, which would provide for punishment of
officials who do not follow the provisions — and this would include
those who do not follow the program as formulated under the
provisions of this bill — I should like to make it clear to this body that
the philosophy of this bill in decentralizing functions on the provincial
level is to pin point responsibility. And I would like to refer particularly
to lines 23 to 25 on page 16, which read as follows:

It shall be the responsibility of the Provincial
Governor and the City Mayor to carry out such program of activities in their respective jurisdictions.

Aside from the penalty clause involved, the feeling of the Committee
is to establish the responsibility of the provincial governor and the city
mayor.

Today, when there is a breakdown, when there is inefficiency
in the rural health services, in the extension work or in education, it
is difficult to pin point responsibility. The provincial governor stands
up during election time and he normally disclaims any responsibility
for what goes on in his province on the ground that he has nothing to
say in the conduct of the services.

On the other hand, it is the people of the provinces who are
left without resort, without remedy since, obviously, the mere fact that
one province 'is discontented with the health services or educational
services may not be reason enough for the national leadership to
concentrate their efforts at improving the service because one or two
discontented provinces may not be sufficient to topple the party in
power. Therefore, we seek to pin point responsibility in the provincial
governor so that if he or his party should seek again the mandate of
the people, first, he can say when something good has been done
that he is responsible for it; and if nothing good has been done, then
the people can say that it is the provincial governor who is
responsible for it. And having pin pointed that responsibility the

people can take advantage of the desire of incumbent officials to continue in office. Thus, there will be reason to improve the services and to maintain services in coordination with the national government.

SENATOR PUYAT: Now, precisely, Mr. Sponsor, at this point I ask this question because these two sections are very specific. "It shall be the responsibility of the provincial governor and the city mayor to carry out such program of activities in their respective jurisdictions." What I was referring to was in the formulation of the program. There is the governor and local officials sitting with national officials and the governor says, "I know better the conditions in my province and I cannot agree with your program. It is this program that I want." Who will settle the difference? It is there, because once the program is agreed upon this provision would govern. But in the preparation of the program, in the setting of that program, suppose there will be a conflict of views and opinion, who will be the referee and whose opinion should prevail?

SENATOR MANGLAPUS: The answer to that will come under several remedies. First, the legal remedy, the normal legal remedy against officials lower than the President who do not carry out their functions properly under the law. They will be compelled judicially to perform their functions in accordance with law.

SENATOR PUYAT: This is not yet a responsibility of the provincial government. They are still in the process of setting up the program. This is a matter of divergences of opinion.

SENATOR MANGLAPUS: The gentleman is referring to the agreement in the program itself and not in the implementation.

SENATOR PUYAT: I think that your sections 21 and 22 will answer my question if there has been an agreement on the program. But supposing in the preparation of the program there is already disagreement, and I am anticipating that you will have that problem.

SENATOR MANGLAPUS: Well, it is the expectation of the Committee that in all of these meetings between the national officials and local officials some sort of a consensus will be developed. The final arbiter of this, of course, as indicated in the words of lines 23 to 25, will be the people themselves. If there is no program arrived at because of lack of agreement and the provincial government pushes on to implement its own program using its own resources, it will seem to me that the ultimate and final arbiter will be the people of that province. If they feel that what their government has done is in keeping with the best interests of the people of the province, then we see no reason the governor should not be allowed to carry out a program as he sees fit. However, if the gentleman would like to see this portion improved so that some safeguards are included in order to make sure that agreement is reached, then the Committee will be very pleased to entertain it.

SENATOR PUYAT: In a democracy it is understood that all divergences of opinion are finally left to the people for decision in the polls but that may take some time and the people may not be fully conscious of the issues involved and in the meantime a lot of injury may be inflicted on the public service. That is why I feel that there is a need for a more expeditious formula that will settle such differences.

SENATOR GANZON: Mr. President.

THE PRESIDENT PROTEMPORE. Gentleman from Iloilo.

SENATOR GANZON: With the permission of the two gentlemen, in order that this matter can be threshed out by them and for the enlightenment of the members, may I interpose one point here?

THE PRESIDENT PROTEMPORE: The gentleman may proceed if there is no objection on the part of the gentlemen on the floor (There was none.)

SENATOR GANZON: Mr. President, the gentleman from Pampanga mentioned here a possible disagreement in the program of activities of local government in agriculture, for example, between the mayor or governor and the Manila office, say, the Department of Agriculture. And then there is another point which I wish to be included in the discussion. The local government like the national government has a law-making body. The municipal council, for example, is the policy-determining body and it makes programs and policies which the mayor and governor execute. Now, since it is the municipal council or board which appropriates the funds, it also feels under obligation and authority to provide the program of activities of, let us say, agriculture Which is the topic now. Now, supposing the municipal board or city board or the provincial board files a resolution: "January 2 —— This shall be the program of activities in the field of agriculture of the municipal government for the year 1965." I ask the sponsor, Mr. President, where does the municipal board or the law-making body come in, in the event that there is not only a conflict of views between the local executives and the Manila office but a conflict of views between the municipal board and the mayor as against the national government?

SENATOR MANGLAPUS: Well, the answer to the difficulty posed by the distinguished gentleman from Iloilo goes to the fundamental philosophy of this bill. This bill fundamentally decentralizes to the provincial, not to the municipal level although there are certain additional releases on control that we are conceding to the municipal officials. Basically, however, decentralization is to the provincial level.

Now, going to the specific example cited by the gentleman from Iloilo where the municipal council or government would seem to disagree with the provincial government, the answer in the bill is very clear: that it is the will of the provincial government that should prevail because we are decentralizing the responsibility to the provincial level. The question raised by the gentleman from Pampanga is different because we are decentralizing to the provincial government and he wants to know just how much coordination is there between the national and provincial governments.

SENATOR GANZON: I am not yet through, Mr. Senator, with the permission of the gentleman. On that point I was referring to the conflict of views not only on the local level, the municipal level, but the provincial board as against the governor or the provincial board and the governor as against the national government.

SENATOR PUYAT: That question of the senator from Iloilo becomes very important especially when the governor of one province belongs to one party and the provincial board is in the control of officials belonging to another party. We are liable to have these disagreements.

SENATOR MANGLAPUS: May I then refer to the provision of the bill which says :.

It shall be the responsibility of the Provincial
Governor and the City Mayor to carry out such program of activities in their respective jurisdictions.

The coordination is going to be conducted on the level of the national offices with the provincial and city heads or office concerned, namely, the Provincial and City Agriculturists, Provincial and City Health Officers, and Division and City Superintendents of Schools. As soon as that program is formulated then it becomes the responsibility of the chief executive of the province or city to carry out the program. Therefore, it would seem to me that it is under these circumstances where there is no doubt at all that the provincial chief executive or city executive would have a final say in determining just what the position of the provincial government should be, vis-à-vis the national government on this matter.

SENATOR PU YAT: Well, I think that point is clear. If there is an agreement on the program there are provisions. The question I raised is on disagreements in the formulation of the program. Perhaps. we should clarify this point on formulation.

SENATOR MANGLAPUS: Yes, I agree that between the provincial and national positions there might be room for improvement on this paragraph in order to make sure that some agreement is reached.

SENATOR PUYAT: And so as not to delay the implementation of the program.

SENATOR MANGLAPUS: Correct.

SENATOR PUYAT: Now, Mr. Sponsor, one of the activities that you intend to transfer is that of intermediate education. It is commonly known that the financing of our public school system, and part of that is the intermediate grades, is still an unsolved problem. This is our big headache. Everytime we discuss the budget we find that 1n spite of the increased appropriation there are always in a number of schools, between 10,000 to 15,000 schoolrooms, every year to be covered by special or supplementary appropriation. Do you feel that while we have a national problem of this magnitude, it would be timely to transfer these activities to the provincial governments at this time?

SENATOR MANGLAPUS: Yes, Mr. President, because the main reason for this annual uncertainty on appropriations for schools is the fact that there are no specified revenues that are segregated and set aside for these expenditures. They are specified items in budgets, but the revenues are not specified. Now, the virtue of the change we are making in this bill is that we are segregating the revenues, namely, the three taxes mentioned in this bill, into a fund which would respond exclusively to the needs of the intermediate schools and the other two functions we are decentralizing. That is why we feel that all this annual uncertainty will be avoided.

SENATOR PUYAT: ...which you are calling a decentralization fund.

SENATOR MANGLAPUS: A special fund.

SENATOR PUYAT: Well, my position on this matter is quite clear. All these years I have been advocating against the creation of additional special funds. It has been our experience that once a special fund is created, the control or the supervision of the national government over that special fund practically disappears. National revenues become a proliferation of special funds. And what do we discover now? In a review of the extant laws we find there are special appropriations the purpose of which no longergexist and the funds for which still are there, and because of the presence of these laws we cannot even integrate the funds under these special laws into the general fund, thereby immobilizing several hundred million pesos, money that our national government can very well make use of. But that is not the danger here. I know that you are separating certain sources of income to cover this and that. Judging by your figures, I find that if your proposal is carried out without any amendment, now that the share of the local governments in these taxes amounts to only 16 per cent, the share of the local governments will increase to

31 per cent. On the other hand where the share of the national government now is 84 per cent, that share will drop to 69 per cent. Now, do you not feel that, by taking away such a big portion of funds from the national government, you may weaken the national government so as to render it ineffective in performing other essential services, since all of these funds are under the discretion, supervision and control of the national government? The national government has to shift funds for one purpose to another. Once you create a special fund for this particular purpose the national government, in spite of more urgent needs, will never be able to touch these funds again unless we amend this section of the bill that may become a law. Do you not think that danger exists and that such a policy may be dangerous?

SENATOR MANGLAPUS: Mr. President, the gentleman poses two questions here. One is a doubt cast on the basic wisdom of creating special funds and the other on the dangers that would arise from the fact that we are, as a matter of fact, segregating certain definite amounts from the disposal of the national government which it may not be able to shift from one function to another. May I say that I would be in perfect agreement with the gentleman from Pampanga in showing doubts as to the wisdom of special funds if in creating special funds what we are doing is merely increasing responsibility of the national government for certain functions. But what we are doing here, Mr. President, is the opposite. While we are creating a special fund we are at the same time not increasing the responsibility of the national government but on the contrary we are decreasing the responsibility because we are decentralizing three functions, taking them from the national government and placing them under the responsibility of the provincial governments. Therefore the special fund which is now being created, instead of endangering the position of the national government by depriving it of the mobility of resources while at the same time increasing its responsibility, does the opposite. It does of course deprive the national government of the disposal of these resources, but at the same time, it also decreases its responsibility because, henceforth if this bill is passed, it no longer has to provide for the three services that we are decentralizing under this bill.

SENATOR PUYAT: That is clearly understood, but the point is, in transferring these activities, you intend to finance these activities by transferring certain revenues now being collected by the national government and which go into the national revenues as a special decentralization fund. That is why I raised that point because it is possible that although we transfer these activities to the provincial governments, it is possible to finance these transferred activities not necessarily by transferring outright these revenues from these sources. It may well be that we could discover another formula by just increasing the allotments of the provincial governments, because once you make this outright transfer you take out from the jurisdiction and control of the national government the management of these funds. Suppose in the future we discover that as a matter of national survival it will be more important for the national government to perform other functions more urgent with this special fund, the national government will have no right, unless we amend the bill, to touch these funds. You take away from the national government that much flexibility in the management of public finance. And I am preparing now another formula, because here is your position, Mr. Senator. The allotment of the national taxes to local governments from these different sources — income tax, estate, inheritance and gift taxes, residence taxes, taxes on agricultural products, franchise tax, tax on mines, based on the 1963 figures — is about P86 million. Now, taxes subject to regular allotment — allotment to the provinces to be increased from 10 to 12 per cent — go up to about P68 million. And from these sources that you specify the expected collection will be around P157 million. In other words the provincial or local governments will have a total revenue of P312 million. Now, my fear is: when the national government loses control over that P157 million, you take away from the national government that flexibility in the management of public finance which is so important, for without it the national government will be lost.

SENATOR MANGLAPUS: Mr. President, I welcome the thoughts suggested here by the gentleman from Pampanga. As a matter of fact I would like to state that the basic intent of the bill has to do with the decentralization of functions. The matter of financing is not of the essence of the bill but it becomes necessary because of our desire to decentralize. The manner of financing you are suggesting to us may not be the only manner of doing this, and we would welcome suggestions, especially from the gentleman from Pampanga, who is recognized as an expert in financing. I would like to state the position of the Committee here with respect to the choice of this method of financing. In the first place, we thought that these functions are so basic that it would only take an absolute national emergency in which there will be complete dislocation of government activities to justify the relocation of the special fund. When such a national emergency is declared, our laws are, by one stroke of legislation, suspended, and all these funds restored to the national government for ,its own disposal. Secondly, we felt that by segregating specific taxes, our people, the people who pay these taxes, knowing exactly where these taxes are to be expended, would be best inspired to pay the taxes in the full amount, rather than evade them. This will help speed the process of decentralization, and the success of our decentralization program. However, I would reiterate that the method is not of the essence. What is of the essence is that there be some way of financing, and this may well be according to the formula of the gentleman, who is experienced in this matter. If he would suggest an alternative proposal, the Committee would be very happy to entertain it.

SENATOR PUYAT: I raised these points because of the result of our collection of all taxes. It has been discovered that the law has been very lenient. 'It has been discovered that if you leave the collection of these taxes to local agencies, there is greater evasion. We have discovered in many provinces that many stores operate even without the benefit of a license. Now, when you leave the collection to local governments, there is that propinquity between the collector and the payer. And you will find that the net result is greater tax evasion.

SENATOR MANGLAPUS: May I have those last few words again?

SENATOR PUYAT: I say that the net result is that there is more propinquity between the collector of the tax and the payer, and this leads to greater evasion in the payment of taxes. If we leave the collection of these taxes to the local governments, I anticipate that the revenues may decline.

SENATOR MANGLAPUS: Now, Mr. President, I have just one comment on that statement of the gentleman. We are not radically departing from the present procedure. In the past, it has always been the municipal treasurer who collects these taxes anyway, and under this bill he will continue to do so. So, there will be no basic difference in the manner of collection. What we are establishing here is the segregation of the taxes, but the collection system will be the same.

SENATOR PUYAT: I know that. It will be different when these taxes are finally remitted to the national government. What check do we have on the local officials if the revenues start to decline?

SENATOR MANGLAPUS: May I correct the gentleman?

There is a misapprehension here. The decentralization special fund is essentially still a national government fund. The money collected by the municipal treasurer would not be retained in the municipality. It would all go to the decentralization special fund, which is essentially in the nature of a national fund, except that it is for the exclusive expenditures of the provincial government.

SENATOR PUYAT: This is the special fund that the national government cannot touch? Anyway, in my amendments, I would propose that whatever collections are made, should accrue to the provincial government. I would give the provincial government the power to retain, instead of sending all these decentralization fund to the national government and giving opportunity to the national government to make use of this fund in the meantime to the detriment of the local governments. I would give the local governments the right to retain. Properly, that will belong to them. Under the law, that would be more expeditious.

SENATOR MANGLAPUS: Well, if we can harmonize this desire of the gentleman with the mechanical problem involved, I believe that such step would be more in step with decentralization as envisioned in the bill. But I would say that in evaluating the manner in which these funds are to be deposited, certain mechanical problems are involved. Of course, the Committee has its own solution and it is as it is in the bill. That is to say, it will be necessary to put the special revenues together first, in order that there be established a sound basis for distribution. Unless this is done, the fear is that the situation may result in a province not deserving everything that it gets, or deserrving more than it gets, in which case, there would be need for reapportionment. Therefore, we felt that the best way would be to put. the funds together first, and have these redistributed later. However, if these mechanical difficulties could be overcome, the steps suggested by the gentleman will be more in keeping with this bill.

SENATOR PUYAT: Now, I will proceed along the line. As I said, our problem with regard to the financing of our public school system is until now unresolved, and the needs of our system of public education are not increasing arithmetically; they are increasing progressively, geometrically. Suppose, after earmarking these funds, you find that the funds are not enough to finance these activities? Unlike the national government the provincial governments cannot go to the Central Bank for an advance, or issue bonds. The provincial governments do not have this authority. Suppose, you estimate that we will have so much in your hands, and then your estimate does not materialize, as our experience in the past has shown, what will now be the remedy? The national government has the power to go to the Central Bank, borrow money from the PNB, issue bonds, issue registration certificates, and the provincial governments will not have that power. How will you remedy a situation like that?

SENATOR MANGLAPUS: Mr. President, that is the reason we choose these three taxes, because they are the most stable. May I just read for the record the performance of collection of these taxes? There has been a steady increase in the collection of these taxes. Starting from 1958-1959, the figure is P7 million; and then from 1959-

1960, P13 million; 1961-62, P18 million; 1962-63, P23 million; and 1963—64, P23 million. We felt that this performance in collection is a strong basis for concluding that these funds will steadily provide for an increasing reservoir of resources for the provincial governments to carry out these functions. I think it is safe to conclude that other taxes may suffer in collection, but these taxes would be the last to be affected by any radical change, even in the aggregate collections of the national government. It is not possible, of course, to say that this will always be. Some calamity may occur, so that even these taxes which are found to be the most stable may fall in collection. But in that case, we hope Congress will have the opportunity of restudying this matter and provide for the proper remedy. But we feel we are legislating now for a situation which is permanent. As a matter of fact, in adopting only the decentralization of three functions, we are taking a cautious step, not an all-out decentralization program, but a cautious step, and perhaps after a performance of three or four years, Congress could review the situation and improve or supply the remedy if certain defects have been found in the collection of these taxes.

SENATOR PUYAT: My fear, Mr. Sponsor, was not in the regularity or in the stability of the amounts to be collected. No. My fear was on the other end. The needs, for example, of education, of rural health, are growing so fast that revenues may not be sufficient to cover those requirements.

May I tell Your Honor that if we implement the law, our appropriation for rural health is just a fraction of what the entire program would call for, and that if we properly implement the law and the Constitution, our requirement of financing for our intermediate schools would be even bigger. But this is my bigger misgiving, that even with these revenues earmarked, you might find the services of the government so big that you do not have the revenue to cover adequately and to perform effectively and efficiently these functions that you are transferring to the provincial governments.

SENATOR MANGLAPUS: I share the desire of the gentleman from Pampanga in wishing to strengthen this bill in such a way that this unforeseen development as he envisions may not result in the collapse of the decentralization program that we are envisioning. However, I would like to state here that the Committee, while sharing his desire, has to act on the record. The record shows a pattern of expansion in the services that we mentioned which forecasts a situation which would be well within the provisions that 'we are putting on in this bill for the proper implementation of the decentralization program.'

Now, the gentleman makes reference, for instance, to rural

health. The figures on rural health as found from the expenditures of the national government show these increases: from 1961-1962, P4,693,000; 1962-1963, P2,890,000; 1963-1964, P1,953,000; 1964-1965, P166,000. This is rather small.

In evaluating this situation, we find that we are providing a margin beyond the expected expansion of services. The total amount that will come from these three taxes will on the average be P20 million to P30 million more than those required in the projections of the requirement of the services. We felt that we were providing a sufficient margin so that any unforeseen expansion of' services would be provided for until the local need may be viewed in the light of an abnormal situation.

It is correct for the gentleman to state that many times there are complaints that the rural health program, the education program and the agricultural extension program are never carried out to the full. I quite agree, but I think the gentleman will find upon close examination that always the basic reason for this is lack of funds, which by law are supposed to be available for these particular projects. What we are doing in this bill is assuring that the funds will always be there, from these stable taxes, so that. there will be absolutely no doubt at all in the minds of the people that these three functions will be carried out by the provincial government and that the provincial government cannot excuse itself on the ground that there are no funds.

Today, since there is no segregation of funds and there is no pinpointing of the financing of these functions, the people have no recourse when they find that the rural health unit, for example, which should be operating in their locality is not operating there, because the big, large national government can always excuse itself by saying that it does not have funds to carry out the basic projects. What we are providing for here is to insure that this excuse will not again be used by the national government.

SENATOR PUYAT: Mr. Sponsor, I think the figures that Your Honor has are those appearing in the budget, or were they taken from the figures of the joint Executive-Legislative Tax Commission?

SENATOR MANGLAPUS: These figures, Mr. President, according to our technical staff, are budgetary figures.

SENATOR PUYAT: Budgetary figures. Now, may I call attention to the fact, Mr. Sponsor, that what you see in the budget is just a fraction of the real situation. What is the budgetary practice in our country? Our different heads prepare the budgetary requirements; the directors of the bureaus send their budgetary requirements to the department heads; the department heads send their budgetary requirements to the budget commissioner; the budget commissioner prunes these requests; then the Lower House acts on the present budget, prunes this budget, and when this budget comes out of Congress, it is just a fraction of what the services will need. So that those figures are not safe to use. I am calling attention to this because when you place these activities in the hands of your local governments, there will be closer proximity between the people's service and those servicing the people. You will be receiving all kinds of complaints: why is this not being done; why is that not being done. The provincial government will not be able to say, "Well, this province got only P300,000 for rural health last year; although our requirement is P4 million. When we send our request to the budget commissioner, the budget commissioner prunes it. And when the budget, reaches Congress, Congress prunes it.

I am calling attention to this because at the same time while we are decentralizing these functions, we would like to approximate the real situation as much as possible; and when you place this problem in the hands of the people to whom the people's service are so close, you will develop a situation where that provincial official will find himself so exposed. You may generate much discontent. That is why I am providing a situation where funds are not adequate to provide a formula that will enable, let us say, the provincial government to supply the deficiency in the funds, in much the same way that the national government has this power.

SENATOR MANGLAPUS: Well, Mr. President, I thank the gentleman for his observations. 1 would want to state that I agree with him that we should try to approximate as much as possible the actual requirements, and it is for this reason that the figures that we are using are not just those provided for specifically in the budget for these sources. The figures that we are using are the actual expenditures which, in many cases, as the gentleman will probably agree, exceed the specific amounts mentioned in the budget, because there are possibilities of re-allocation of amounts specifically mentioned in the budget. Therefore, what we are basing on are figures that have actually been spent on these services. Now, the gentleman says that even these figures may not be accurate, and I quite agree that, perhaps, the rural health unit, instead of having P5 million should have P10 million. Well, this is precisely the reason we want to make sure that at least the requirements, as accepted by the national Departments of Health and Agriculture today, as manifested in the actual expenditures that they have made, that at least these should be guaranteed to the people by providing for this special fund and providing for decentralization. And we have no other basis, Mr. President, for determining what the gentleman would refer to as the actual requirements. Perhaps, it would be pertinent to say here that it is possible that no department of this national government is ever satisfied in any fiscal year because its full requirements are met, either in the figures in the budget or even in the actual expenditures allowed by the President and the budget commissioner. But until we arrive at a better basis, well, the Committee is content that it is proceeding on reasonable assumptions here when it takes actual expenditures as the basis for its estimates.

SENATOR PUYAT: Well, the answer of the sponsor would just further emphasize the need for resolving the point that I raised. Mr. Sponsor, invariably, in practice, you will find the actual expenditure even less than the amount appropriated. Can't Your Honor see that we estimate the revenues, and then you go to the budget commissioner for a certification of the funds available, and what does the budget commissioner do? He certifies only to the amount available which, in many cases, is not equal to the amount appropriated. So that if Your Honor now tells me that the figures you quote are actual disbursements, then offhand I can tell Your Honor that those figures would, be less than the amounts appearing in the Budget Act. That has been the practice.

SENATOR MANGLAPUS: Yes. Now, Mr. President, may I refer the gentleman to page 44 of our little red book? It shows that, accepting the position of the gentleman that the budget figures are generally more than those actually expended, we have used the budget figures here as the basis for our computation to show that the amount that we are enumerating for this fund is far in excess — far in excess — of those amounts required for these three functions. The figures that we have put down, for instance, in the first column to reflect the requirements of agricultural extension, rural health and intermediate school, namely, ?9 million, P33 million, and P80 million are taken from the budget. So, these are the authorized funds.

SENATOR PUYAT: And may I know what have been the disbursements on these?

SENATOR MANGLAPUS: Well, I read out one breakdown.

SENATOR PUYAT: If these are figures appearing in the budget, I would like to know now what have been the actual disbursements certified by the budget commissioner.

SENATOR MANGLAPUS: The General Auditing Office has not been able to provide us with the. actual and final figures on the disbursements in 1963 on this point. But as the gentleman pointed out, it is possible that the expenditures were less than the appropriated amounts.

SENATOR PUYAT: Are we agreed, Mr. Sponsor, that you will entertain an amendment to this point?

SENATOR MANGLAPUS: Oh yes, yes, by all means.

SENATOR PUYAT: So that in case this contingency develops, whereby there would be inadequate funds that will enable these provinces to discharge these functions, there would be that safety valve.

SENATOR MANGLAPUS. I believe that such an amendment would strengthen this bill immeasurably.

SENATOR PUYAT. I would like to remind the sponsor that once upon a time, when I was a small boy, there was such a saying that the most stable and the most valuable thing in the world was gold. Now, we find that that statement is no longer true because the gold mining industry in our country, if it were not subsidized, would be a losing industry. So, there is nothing permanent and continuing in this world. We must be ready for the contingencies as we can perceive them reasonably.

SENATOR MANGLAPUS: The Committee would welcome the suggestion of the gentleman at the proper or appropriate moment.

SENATOR PUYAT: Now, Mr. Sponsor, I would like to announce that my interpellation on this bill will cover two important aspects: the financing and the management, because, to me, this bill is both a question of financing and of management, and the two factors are very, very important. But let us proceed with the other details, and I will end up with a summary of these two important factors. Will Your Honor kindly refer to page 11. Section 14, subsection a)? (Reading): "Each province shall receive an amount equal to its authorized appropriations for the three transferred functions for Fiscal Year nineteen hundred and sixty-four: Provided, That such provincial allotment shall include the corresponding authorized appropriations of all municipalities and municipal districts within the province." What does this mean— "Provided, That such provincial allotment shall include the corresponding authorized appropriations of all municipalities and municipal districts within the province"? Aside from the appropriation. . . I suppose these are the funds being transferred to the provincial governments, that Your Honor referred to.

SENATOR MANGLAPUS: Yes, may I state here that the year 1964 may have to be updated, depending on when this bill is passed or takes effect. That is merely the latest year that we could arrive at as the basis for the figure or the amount that we want to be transferred.

SENATOR PUYAT: Is Your Honor satisfied with this amendment as being safe, knowing that in the allocation of funds, a certain amount of politics has crept in — that some provinces have been exaggeratedly benefited and others have been prejudiced?

Would the author entertain a provision so that we set up a system of priorities? So that whoever — whoever — the governor may be in that particular province. if we set up a formula establishing our guiding principles and a system of priorities, whoever that governor may be he will not be able to prejudice certain towns, especially if those towns do not belong to the party to which he belongs.

SENATOR MANGLAPUS: Well, as a matter of fact, Mr. President, the Committee has been considering a committee amendment, not especially on this point but on the point of the distribution of public works appropriations as contained in Section 17. It may be possible to make such a basis, which we would make applicable to Section 17 and also to Section 14. On that point, may I point out that there is some kind of a safeguard here in paragraph b), line 4, on page 12 —that 97 per cent of the balance will be distributed among the provinces and three per cent among cities on the basis of population as shown in the latest official census. That might cushion a bit whatever political preferences may have been carried out in the past. It may be a little difficult to correct these preferences in the past, but I agree with the gentleman that if we could arrive at a formula which would be more equitable, we could make it applicable not only to Section 14 but also Section 17.

SENATOR PUYAT: Yes, applying to all releases — applying to all releases — rural health, agricultural productivity and education. Because you may want to take into account not only the population; you may want to take into account, for example, the contribution of these different towns to the other revenues collected; you may want to take into account, for example, the area. There are some provinces of extensive areas where the revenues are small, and yet We have to recognize the fact that we have to serve the people in these provinces that have extensive areas like Cotabato and many provinces in the South.

SENATOR MANGLAPUS: As a matter of fact, Mr. President, if the gentleman will look at page 14, line 24, he will find that in the matter of releases of public works appropriations, there has been an attempt there to do something very close to what he desires, and that is in providing a basis for the distribution of public works funds —— three-fourths in proportion to population and one-fourth in proportion to area.

SENATOR PUYAT: Yes, but this provision does not take into account the contribution, the difference in contributions of the different areas which, I think, is very important.

SENATOR MANGLAPUS: I think an amendment will be entertained by the Committee. As a matter of fact, as I said the Committee was considering its own amendment so as to harmonize this provision with Section 14 and provide perhaps for a more equitable basis for distribution. But I think the gentleman will see that the bill does not attempt to approximate a basis enumerated here.

SENATOR PUYAT: I was only suggesting that perhaps that provision could be further improved so that other factors could be taken into account. Now, let us go to the highways special fund. To what extent does Section 18 amend the existing law on the highways special fund?

SENATOR MANGLAPUS: Well, to the extent that under this law the fund will now accrue directly to the Road and Bridge Fund of the province.

SENATOR PUYAT: Of the province?

SENATOR MANGLAPUS: Of the provinces and also the cities.

SENATOR PUYAT: So that instead of being a national fund, it now becomes a provincial fund divided up into different groups, including cities.

SENATOR MANGLAPUS: It will be directly a provincial fund although the tax is still a national tax. It will accrue directly to the provincial funds specified herein.

SENATOR PUYAT: I have serious misgivings about this provision because in our Road Building Program the concept is on a national basis and when you divide this fund this way you are going to lose this national perspective so important in a program of this kind. I have grave misgivings over this provision.

SENATOR MANGLAPUS: The answer to the doubts of the gentleman may be found both in this section and in the section on programming of activities, but particularly this section which says that "the Secretary of Public Works and Communications shall prescribe the standards in the construction and improvement of roads and highway projects."

SENATOR PUYAT: The present law governing this highway special fund provides for the disposition of this fund part for the construction of new roads, part for maintenance, part for the purchase of heavy equipment. Now, are you amending that portion or are you keeping that?

SENATOR MANGLAPUS: Well, such funds as those you mentioned which now pertain within the territory of the province would now be carried out by the provincial government using funds that accrue to the road and bridges fund.

SENATOR PUYAT: So all these different provinces now would be buying their heavy equipment. You will have 55 engineering depots.

SENATOR MANGLAPUS: No.

SENATOR PUYAT: How would it come out?

SENATOR MANGLAPUS: May I refer the gentleman now to page 16. We are providing for the creation of the positions of public works supervisors. These gentlemen will collaborate in the carrying out of the public works and public highway projects which are financed out of local funds. The district engineer, the highway district engineer and the city engineer shall continue to undertake public works projects and public highway projects financed out of national funds. The coordination can be found in the last proviso which says that the "Secretary of Public Works and Communications shall prescribe the standards in the prosecution of public works and public highway projects by the provincial engineer and the city Public Works supervisor." Under this scheme unless the gentleman feels that certain additional proviso may still have to be added, we feel that there could be coordination in such a way that equipment may be borrowed or rented by the local government. I understand that this is the usual practice even today —— that when a certain local unit of government would like to use national equipment, the national equipment is lent or more specifically rented out to the municipality or to the province. Therefore, there would be no need of duplicating purchases of highway equipment Since it is obvious that a provincial government could undertake to borrow or lease equipment from the national government.

SENATOR PUYAT: Mr. Sponsor, don't you think that it would be necessary to go over this law, Republic Act No. 901, and point out specifically which are the provisions that will be affected by this provision? I maintain that unless you do that the provision with regard to the disposition of funds will be affected by this provision of the bill which makes it mandatory on the government to spend these funds — so much for the construction of new roads, so much for maintenance, so much for equipment, and I think there is a certain amount for overhead. Are we going to follow the same provisions when we transfer these funds to the provincial governments?

SENATOR MANGLAPUS: Mr. President, the Committee has had an extensive discussion with the Department of Public Works and Communications officials on this matter, particularly on the point of R.A. NO. 901, and the Public Works officials are satisfied that R.A. No. 901 will be amended in so far as the accrual of these funds is concerned; and that functions, which heretofore have been performed by the national government, that may conflict with the functions we are transferring to the city and provincial governments will cease to be performed by the national government.

SENATOR PUYAT: That is what I maintain. Following that interpretation, these provincial governments will now be forced to use these funds in accordance with the provision of this law — so much for construction of new roads, so much for maintenance, so much for equipment. Now, is it the sponsor's intention to have an engineering depot in all of the provinces of the Philippines? Will that not to be too expensive? Where now you have regional depots where there is a project being undertaken, for example in Bicol — I do not know where the engineering depot is —— what I know is that the national government requisitions equipment in that area to be sent to the province where the project is being undertaken.

SENATOR MANGLAPUS: I do not see how we can conclude that simply because we are making the funds accrue to the provincial government that we will be forcing the provincial government to provide itself with all the facilities even in duplication of national government facilities. Obviously, this is what the gentleman refers to as management. Good management would dictate that the provinces do not go into expenditures that are duplication of facilities already provided for by the national government. There is nothing in this law which will oblige the provincial government to establish its own elabcrate depot. What it merely gives to the officials are funds and the responsibility to carry out the functions.

SENATOR PUYAT: And unlike R.A. No. 901, Your Honor is not indicating here how that fund will be spent. We saw fit to put in that provision under R.A. No. 901 because previous to the enactment of R.A. No. 901 we found that a great percentage of that fund was being spent unnecessarily for overhead. That is why Congress put into the law a certain percentage. If we do not provide for that we may have the same problem which we had several years ago with the national government.

SENATOR MANGLAPUS: Mr. President, may I recall here the exact words of the provision. It says:

All shares of provinces, cities and municipalities
from the Highway Special Fund, to which they are
entitled. . .

In other words, we are not removing from the national government any part of the share to which it is presently entitled under the law.

SENATOR PUYAT: Yes, and I am referring to that share that the province will get.

SENATOR MANGLAPUS: All that is going to happen is this: instead of waiting for its share to be distributed magnanimously by the national government, the province will get its share automatically and directly.

SENATOR PUYAT: I am afraid there is no meeting of the minds. That share will go to the province; does not Your Honor want to specify in this law how that share will be spent, in much the same way as does the provision under R.A. No. 901? Does not Your Honor think it would be wise?

SENATOR MANGLAPUS: It would seem to me that will all depend on how detailed the gentleman would like this construction to be. Offhand, I would like to say that the Committee would have confidence in the provincial government since this is the basic philosophy of this law —— that the officials will soundly spend, that they will soundly administer. Now, if the gentleman wishes certain guidelines to be included in this bill, if these guidelines are not so minute as to go against the philosophy of this bill, the Committee will be very happy to entertain them.

SENATOR PUYAT: Mr. President, it will be our hope— not only hope but also prayer — that if this bill becomes a law it will be implemented satisfactorily. But, Mr. Sponsor, in our experience with the government in the many, many bills we so nobly conceived in Congress, what have we found out? The implementation has been so different, the implementation has been so disastrous, that we have come to the conclusion that in approving laws we better express in these laws the thinking of Congress. Instead of delegating these powers to the implementing officials without guidelines, Congress has to give these guidelines.

SENATOR MANGLAPUS: I would like to say that I have no disagreement with the gentleman in this regard. I'd merely emphasize that the Committee in drafting this bill would like to express confidence in the ability of the provincial government to administer these funds Without undue and unnecessary direction from the national government. However, if the guidelines that the gentleman would like to offer do not conflict with this desire of ours to express confidence, we will be very pleased to accept them.

SENATOR PUYAT: Now, may I refer to another point. We will be transferring these functions to the local governments. When I say this, I do not want to be misunderstood. I am not casting aspersion on anybody. My only objective is that when and if this bill becomes a law and it is implemented, it shall redound to the benefit of the people. So, we must take all precautions so that in the interpretation and in the implementation of the law, all possible loopholes are covered.

Now, we entrust these functions to the local officials. Suppose we find that the performance is sub-standard; suppose we find that there is lack in technical preparation, is there anything in the law which will provide for a remedy? I am among the foremost exponents of decentralization here because in business nowadays you no longer centralize powers in the hands of your chairman or your president — you delegate power, and that is how business has grown in the past 20 years. But after delegating powers, that man delegating those powers still retains some sort of supervision and control so that the power delegated is properly used. Is there any provision to that effect in this bill?

SENATOR MANGLAPUS: I would like to state, Mr. President, that perhaps there is a misapprehension about the practical effects of this measure so far as the personnel of government is concerned. The bill very clearly states that all appointments under this bill will be under the civil service rules, that as a matter of fact whenever in each instance a province takes over functions heretofore carried out by the national government, the province will absorb the personnel that are already discharging these functions in the name of the national government. In other words these functions will be carried out with exactly the same competence on the technical level that they are now being carried out by the national government. The difference is that the responsibility and the power of appointment in some cases, instead of being placed in the hands of the national government, is being placed in the hands of the provincial government. But technical competence and managerial ability insofar as they may exist today under the aegis of the national government will continue to exist because the same people who would carry out these functions are carrying them out today. Therefore, I feel this Committee is confident that managerial problems will not seriously arise because there is absolutely going to be no change at all in the complexion, for instance, of the civil service requirements that will be imposed on appointments made by the provincial governor. May I add that political pressures may be minimized and responsibility at least pinpointed when we give the power of appointment to the provincial governor. Instead of so many appointive and elective officials from the President down making their influence felt on specific appointments, now we shall be able to pinpoint responsibility on the person of the provincial governor and the provincial board which will have to act to ratify the appointments of the provincial governor. I hope we are clarifying these doubts about the managerial problems that may arise.

SENATOR PUYAT: These are very important points to consider because, when you start delegating authority you have to be sure that you are delegating authority to people who will make use of' that authority soundly and efficiently, otherwise the purposes that we seek may be negated. Now, while your reply is correct that the civil service rules will apply, that by and large the same persons will handle the program, I maintain that when these same people now will become responsible to another set of leadership you change the situation, and that is very, very important. These same persons who feel that they are technologically qualified answering to persons whom they feel not as qualified as they are, you create there a problem of management.

SENATOR MANGLAPUS: Mr. President, I think this is a very important point and I would like to make a few remarks about it to correct the common belief that if we give the power of appointment to the provincial governor, we may automatically reduce the efficiency of the service. May I say this: We held hearings here for those Officials representing the departments affected by the decentralization of the three functions concerned. Not one of the officials who attended here denied, to put it in the negative, that appointments to the civil service today when the power of appointment ultimately rests with the national officials — not one of them was able to deny that a political influence isfelt in these appointments. As a matter of fact Undersecretary Gaffud appeared in one of these Committeé hearings and he admitted that whenever a teacher is appointed, it is not necessarily true that since his appointment is supposed to be a technical one there is no political influence brought to bear when there is a vacancy in a particular province to be filled by the division superintendent in the name of the Secretary Of Education. Who are the sources of political influence that is brought to bear on these appointments? The governor himself, any mayor who may have his own recommendee, even the senator of the area, the congressman. SO that in the end who is appointed may be the recommendee of the congressman or senator, and it cannot be said that the actions of this teacher in the future will be completely divorced from political considerations. The problem is that today it is sometimes difficult to pinpoint the responsibility for an appointment of this nature. Why? Because there are so many going to the President and going to the division superintendent. But now if we place the power of appointment in the hands of the provincial governor, and when we find out that this teacher or this official is acting under political influence, we will know whose influence he is acting under and the people will have recourse, come next elections, to hold the proper official, the governor and his administration and his party, responsible for whatever politically influenced actions this appointee may have performed. But today, Mr. President, it is not possible in every case to do this because it is not easy to trace the political loyalty of someone appointed even to the civil service. He may be qualified, but we all know that whenever an appointment is made, there is a list of civil service eligibles that are available for choice. And so in the choice of the eligibles political influence comes in. What we are doing'under this bill is pinpointing responsibility and reducing the possibility of excessive political influence and giving the people immediate recourse in case they feel that such appoinments have not been good ones.

SENATOR PUYAT: Well, I appreciate your reply on that point, but I still want to add that in the present system we must recognize that politics creeps in. In those cases you mentioned you are right, although I can say that in my own particular case, in spite of the fact that I am the chairman of the Committee on Education, I have recommended something like 20 teachers in the list of eligibles and not one was appointed. So that in spite of the fact that while we can recommend, the appointing official there can still refuse us. But when it is the provincial governor, so close to the electorate and so exposed to political pressure, who is the one that receives the recommendation, how well and how effectively can he resist political pressure? I call attention to that because, Mr. Sponsor, our intentions are good but in practice We may be sorry for some of the things that we do. I only hope that the results will be good because, as I said, even we in business first recognize the validity of decentralization. Business cannot prosper unless we know how to delegate authority and this, in essence, is delegation of authority. That is why I believe in and support your theory, but we must be careful. In delegating authority we must provide some safeguards.

Thank you, Mr. Sponsor, and I would like to thank also the gentleman from Quezon for ceding to me part of the time allotted to him.

SENATOR MANGLAPUS: Thank you.

2 - Decentralization and Responsible Politics

(From the Senate records, February 2, 1965.)

SENATOR ROXAS: May I refer, Your Honor, to Sec. 7, the last paragraph on the page, which states that the Municipal Treasurer shall be appointed by the Municipal Mayor.

SENATOR MANGLAPUS: The last paragraph on page 4?

SENATOR ROXAS: That is correct. The point that I would like to submit for your consideration, Mr. Sponsor, is the fact that, much as I quite agree with the objectives which Your Honor seeks to attain by this bill by granting local autonomy to local officials, I cannot as yet see the wisdom of having our municipal treasurers appointed by our mayors for the following reasons: First of all, it is well known and it is a matter of law that the municipal treasurers are the custodians of ballot boxes in cases of elections. We also know that to a certain extent municipal treasurers do wield a certain degree of influence especially with reference to elections. When a municipal treasurer owes his appointment to a mayor, I feel that the relationship which may be established by reason of the debt of gratitude Which a treasurer may owe to a mayor may bring about a situation that will subvert, even only temporarily, the will of the electorate in that particular municipality. The other reason is that one of the major sources of revenue in a municipality — if I am notmistaken it is actually the largest source of revenue — is the real estate tax which is collected by the treasurer in that municipality. Now, it is well known that many times these taxes are not collected, to put it bluntly, for political reasons. As a matter of fact, a survey was conducted in this regard and the survey revealed that one reason or one cause the real estate taxes have not been collected in the municipal level is simply because the local officials are hesitant to exercise their authority, simply because they fear that if they were to do so the landlord would not extend support to them in the coming elections. And so, for these two practical reasons, I would like to submit for your consideration the thought that the municipal treasurer should not be appointed by the municipal mayor. May we be informed, Mr. Senator, of the stand of the Committee with regard to this particular point.

SENATOR MANGLAPUS: Well, Mr. President, I appreciate the fact that the distinguished gentleman is in a position to evaluate the performance of municipal treasurers in the collection of taxes and so I share with him the concern that he has expressed here over the misuse of the office of the municipal treasurer during election time. As a matter of fact, we are all aware, I think, that one of the main forms of abuse of the office of the municipal treasurer during election time is the shifting of treasurers, whether provincial or municipal, from province to province or municipality to municipality. The word for that which is often used in *rigodon* of treasurers, also used for *rigodon* of PC commanders, etc. You see, the reason stated is that if the municipal treasurer is to be appointed by the mayor, this municipal treasurer will be under the political influence of the mayor. Frankly, I see no difference insofar as subversion of the popular will is concerned —— the municipal treasurer being under the influence of the mayor and the municipal treasurer being under the influence of the national government for purposes of national election. The philosophy of this bill is to pinpoint responsibility without getting away from the Civil Service principle. The gentleman will note that we are not giving the municipal mayor here absolute freedom in the choice of the municipal treasurer. We discussed this matter yesterday and I pointed out that in all these appointments to be made by the provincial governor and mayor, a list of eligibles are to be made available to the appointing power and that, therefore, the municipal mayor cannot come in and just sweep people out of office as the President would do on the national level. It is not really a Cabinet that we are giving him. It is merely a power to appoint someone within civil service regulations. So that, therefore, a municipal treasurer appointed by a former mayor cannot be removed on that ground by the next mayor because he would be protected by the civil service regulations. It is really the fundamental issue that faces us — national politics or local politics? Perhaps, we have too long proceeded, under the premise that national politics is better than local politics, that local politics is more destructive than national politics. I think the Barrio Charter and other instances have shown that this is not necessarily so, and when we bring down politics to the local level we may be creating problems, yes, but we are also allowing incentives and initiatives. Local treasurers are not the officials that are expected to check on the financial activities of the mayor. The municipal treasurer, as far as we view the system, is part of the management arm of the local government. The man that is supposed to check on the finances is not the treasurer but the auditor. The gentleman Will note that we are not giving any local official here, whether provincial or municipal, the power to intervene in the appointment of the auditor because we respect the system which will keep the auditor strictly independent of any other administrative arm so that he may perform his auditing functions properly. But the treasurer is a member of management in the local government and he is not expected to be the check against any abuse of the management of the local government because he is part of that management. It is the General Auditing Office that does that. Therefore, the municipal treasurer should know that since his appointment is local his loyalty is to the municipality. And because he survives in spite of the results of the election, he will continue as treasurer if this bill is approved into law even if that mayor, who appointed him, ceases to be mayor. By developing this feeling of loyalty to the municipality, we feel that we can improve the managerial level. I hope that will satisfy the gentleman insofar as the municipal treasurer is concerned in. relation to elections. We want to reiterate that the office of the treasurer may be used as an instrument during the elections, but it is also true that if there has been any such abuse by the municipal treasurer it has not been without the knowledge and intervention of national officials who influence the result not only of local but also of national elections. So I do not see how this situation can be improved by keeping the power of appointment in the hands of the national officials, a power which rightly belongs to the local officials.

SENATOR ROXAS: May I reply. First of all in respect to the so-called shifting and transfer of assignments of municipal treasurers, I feel that the records do not bear that out. It is true that these transfers have been done with respect to provincial treasurers and city treasurers, but I do not feel that there has been a large number of change of assignment on the municipal level. And so, as far as this particular instance is concerned, I do not feel that having the treasurer appointed by the mayor will resolve this particular problem.

Now, the second point. Actually the treasurers, even as they are appointed today, do already have security of tenure of office, and there is nothing additional to be gained by having them appointed by the mayor. Whether appointed by the national government or by the local government they do enjoy security of office. There is nothing to be gained there. The most important thing to consider is the relationship which may be brought about by the debt of gratitude which a treasurer will owe to a mayor who appointed him, especially so- when they both reside in the same municipality. That relationship may be temporary but I feel that even if it be temporary there might be collusion between the mayor and the treasurer which may bring about subversion of the will of the people in that municipality during elections, and I think that we should try to avoid this. I feel that the present system of having the treasurers appointed by the national government is better in this regard than having him appointed by the mayor.

Another point which I submit for your consideration, Mr. Senator, is the thought that if today our treasurers are not efficient enough in collecting real estate taxes due the municipality which is the main source of revenue of the municipality the situation will become worse if the treasurer is appointed by the mayor. Also, by having extended to the mayor a list of 10 from the most eligible available to enable the mayor to choose himself whoever he pleases to fill the vacancy, that thought of limiting the choice to the 10 eligibles does not cure the fact that the treasurer will owe his appointment to the mayor. It is for these two reasons: Firstly, that collusion may exist and, secondly, the finances of the municipality will not be benefited anyway that I feel that the present system of having the treasurer appointed by the national government is better.

I heard yesterday that Your Honor is willing to concede the fact that the chief of police in a municipality should be appointed by the choice of the mayor because of certain circumstances which exist and which require that the chief of police enjoy the confidence of the mayor for purposes of cooperation and for purposes of knowing the situation of the people living in the municipality. I think that the same reason exists with respect to municipal treasurers, and it is for this reason, Mr. Senator, that I would like to submit for your consideration the thought that out of the five which are enumerated in this section — the municipal treasurers, provincial treasurers, city treasurer, the provincial assessors and the city assessors —the municipal treasurer be eliminated from the list and said treasurer continue to be appointed by the national government.

Now I would want to submit another thought for your consideration which is in respect to seniority and in respect to opportunities to serve in larger municipalities and, perhaps, in cities and in first class provinces now that I have already expressed my views with regard to the conclusion which may exist and with regard to the fact that the finances of the municipality may be adversely affected if the treasurer is appointed by the mayor.

SENATOR MANGLAPUS: I would like to clarify that point. The gentleman will recall'that a few days ago I delved on the pinpointing of responsibility and on the existence of politics even in the matter of appointment by national officials. The Committee cannot see that we should accept the proposition that a national appointment is necessarily more free from politics than a local appointment, and that local appointments will necessarily result in lesser efficiency and more collusion. The gentleman will recall that I cited the instance of the appointment of teachers by the division superintendents of schools. We came to know from the very answers of the Officials of the Department of Education that politics play an important part in the appointment even of teachers by the division superintendents of schools, with the added problem that the political influence in this regard is very difficult to trace since, when a teacher is' appointed nationally, all kinds of politicians — not only the congressman, not only the governor, not only the mayor but even the senator — can influence the appointing power. As the distinguished gentleman from Pampanga admitted —— this is not a disgrace to us — we do submit our recommendations to the division superintendents of schools all over the Philippines. The result is that in the end, after a teacher is appointed, perhaps with all the influences and compromises that could be brought to bear on his appointment and he acts in accordance with political dictation, it is not easy to pinpoint responsibility for his acts. So the Committee does not feel that by merely keeping the power of appointment over municipal treasurers in the hands of the national officials, we will divorce from political influence his actions in the future after his appointment. It does not follow that merely putting his appointment in the hands of the local executive will necessarily lead to collusion between him and the appointing power. As a matter of fact we feel that by the very device of pinpointing responsibility — in the case of the province the provincial governor, and in the case of the municipality the municipal mayor— we are diminishing the possibility of collusion because then, there will absolutely be no doubt in the minds of the people as to who is at fault, if there should be found any irregularity in the funds of the municipality. The provincial governor or the municipal mayor cannot go to the people and say, "This is not my fault, this treasurer Was not appointed by me," or he is an appointee on the national level, blaming the national government. The result is that the people are left without recourse, and being left without recourse, then there is more encouragement for the officials to enter into such collusions.

Now, it is true that the gentleman from Capiz correctly stated that in the case of the chief of police, the Committee yesterday, upon interpellation by the gentleman from Iloilo, signified it had an open mind. May I say that in the case of the chief of police, there is no parallel because in the first place, there is no auditor, there is no corresponding official who will check on the actions of the municipal police, as the auditor checks on the actions of the municipal treasurer? I also realize that the chief Of police is the man who handles the armed section of the administration of the municipality, and naturally, when We speak of a section that handles firearms, etc., we will be even more lenient in making exceptions, so that the end of confidence is better achieved. But in the case of the municipal treasurers, we feel that enough safeguards exist in the person of the auditor, and we feel that the urgency is inadequate as it would be in the case of the chief of police, the urgency of self-confidence and of remedy. So, therefore, Mr. President, with due respect to the distinguished gentleman, the Committee, as of now, subject to further presentation of arguments by the gentleman from Capiz, we do not see any ground for changing the provision that the municipal treasurers are members of the executive offices appointed by the municipal mayors.

SENATOR ROXAS: Well, Your Honor mentioned teachers. In this particular respect, I would like again to submit for your consideration the fact that I do not feel that the teachers should be appointed by the mayor, even from the list submitted by the supervisor or by the principal teacher.

SENATOR MANGLAPUS: No, we are not decentralizing on the municipal level, only on the provincial level.

SENATOR ROXAS: As far as the teachers are concerned?

SENATOR MANGLAPUS: Yes, because the teachers are subordinate officials. We are devolving the educational function to the province, not to the municipality. In this case, they will be appointed by the governor, upon recommendation of the division superintendent of schools. Again, that is a subject which we discussed as early as last year, when Senator Osias presented his position. The Committee expressed an open mind to any way by which a member of this body may seek to improve the bill.

SENATOR ROXAS: With regard to the teachers being appointed by the governor, Mr. Senator, again I feel that this should not be the case, because I have been a congressman for two terms, and I know how these things are done, and I feel that if we were to place education under the influence and authority of local officials, more so, than on the national level, I feel that we may hamper the educational system. Let us just give Your Honor one example, which is perhaps, the most common example with regard to teachers. Here is a temporary teacher. He is in Barrio A, and perhaps, because he incurs the ire of the local officials, he is transferred to the Barrio B, which is 10 miles away, where he has to walk everyday. This is a very common occurrence with regard to teachers, these transfers. You have a competent teacher who is, let us say, in some barrio. And he never gets a chance to come to the poblacion to teach in the elementary school, simply because he does not see eye to eye, or he has not won the favor of the governor. In this respect, Mr. Senator, I can cite to Your Honor, many many examples with regard to teachers. I feel that we should dissociate the educational system, at least in so far as their appointments are concerned from the provincial government.

SENATOR MANGLAPUS: Mr. President, the examples cited by the gentleman from Capiz are examples that have already happened under the present system where the teachers are appointed by the national government.

SENATOR ROXAS: That is correct.

SENATOR MANGLAPUS: And I think that the explanation for this is that it is difficult to pinpoint the responsibility for the arbitrary transfer of these teachers, because as I have stated earlier, by the very admission of the department, certain political influences are brought to bear. So, in other words, the instances that have been cited by the gentleman from Capiz are instances happening today, where the teachers are appointed nationally. Now, this is one of the things, I think, that will be cured, and perhaps, if not completely, at least it will be minimized, by pinpointing responsibility. Today, the teachers are transferred; it cannot be immediately resolved whether they are moved because the congressman or the mayor or the governor asks that they be moved. Why? Because it is the national government which in person appoints them. That is ultimately the source of the authority in moving these teachers, and these things are subject to all kinds of political pressures from top to bottom. But by pinpointing responsibility — this is not only true in the case of teachers —— but in the case of other officials whose appointments we are putting in the hands of local officials. . .

SENATOR ROXAS: I can see Your Honor's point.

SENATOR MANGLAPUS: (Continuing) In pinpointing responsibility, at least the people can say that this would not have happened if the governor had not approved it, or had not initiated it. In the proper time, the governor can be held responsible. Today, everybody washes his hands from all kinds of political influences, such as are felt in the province Where nobody gets to be blamed because everything is so vague that there is no pinpointing of responsibility.

SENATOR ROXAS: I think your whole point revolves around the thought that these mistakes are being committed today, because the appointing power is lodged in the national government; that perhaps, the solution is in giving the appointing power to the local government. I think that is the whole purpose here.

SENATOR MANGLAPUS: Let us say, that that would be a result. Let us say that the primary consideration for our placing the power of appointment in the hands of the local official is our expression of confidence in the local official and those chosen by the people themselves to carry out the functions which have heretofore been carried out on the national level.

SENATOR ROXAS: There is no question as to that.

SENATOR MANGLAPUS: Now a result of this would
be one of the things that I mentioned here, pinpointing responsibility which I think would make the situation better, not worse, than that which exists today.

SENATOR ROXAS: There is no question as to the confidence which we have with regard to local officials. As a matter of fact, with regard to all other appointees, there seems to be no question. It is only with regard to the teachers and the municipal treasurers where there is a certain doubt, whether this is now the proper time, or whether this is the proper remedy or whether this is the proper procedure to adopt insofar as granting the power of appointment is concerned, because there is, for example, a half-way measure.

Let us take the case of teachers. There is the View that if the appointing power is in the governor there will be more funds. On the other hand, there is the other view perhaps, as Your Honor stated: by pinpointing the responsibility this may cure the defect which is occurring today. But there is a little doubt. Supposing we grant the provincial governor the right and the authority to recommend 10 out of which the Department of Education may choose anyone rather than give to the provincial governor the outright and ultimate authority to make the recommendation —

SENATOR MANGLAPUS: Is Your Honor referring to the treasurers or to the teachers?

SENATOR ROXAS: I am referring to both. I feel that as of this moment, we are experiencing this error. We may feel that by granting the authority to the local official this may be the remedy. On the other hand, it is also quite possible that it may turn out to be worse. So I feel that we should adopt an intermediary step before going to the ultimate one which is to grant full authority to the provincial and local officials.

SENATOR MANGLAPUS: As a matter of fact, the necessary device was suggested last year by the gentleman from La Union, Senator Osias, insofar as teachers are concerned, and the Committee at that time expressed an open mind on the matter. Of course, the gentleman from La Union is not here today. The Committee merely wants to state that as much as possible it would like to preserve the original intent of the bill, that is, that devolution of power is an expression of confidence in the local officials.

The half-way measure that is being suggested may not actually be a half-way measure at all because while we are giving the local official the power to submit 10 recommendees, still in that list of 10, there could be political influence from many sources that would come in in the matter of choosing one from the 10.

Let us say that you have one recommendee and the governor submits 10 recommendees which after all he cannot arbitrarily choose because these recommendees according to the basic provisions of this law would have to come from the civil service commission. The situation today is that, as a matter of fact, civil service regulations are followed in the sense that the appointee is a civil service eligible. But in the final choice which civil service eligible is to be appointed? That is Why today we have this proliferation of political influence which causes the blurring of responsibility that I referred to earlier. And if we make the provincial governor submit 10 names coming from the list of the civil service commission anyway, over which he has no control, and if we give these 10 names to the division superintendent, or in the case of the treasurer or whatever official may be concerned, to the secretary of finance, the result is that we are not changing the situation.

SENATOR ROXAS: Certainly it would be a forward step, because, as it is today, while that may be the result, it is not actually as clear and as definite as it would be if we were to provide in this bill that the appointing power will only elect one from the 10 names submitted by the provincial governor.

SENATOR MANGLAPUS: That might, Mr. President, on the other hand be a deceptive step. We may be deceiving ourselves into thinking that we are enlarging the powers or even enlarging the intervention of the provincial official in the matter of appointment; whereas, as a matter of fact, what we are doing really is preserving the status quo for the reasons that I have already pointed out.

SENATOR ROXAS: That is not the case of the status quo at this moment. At this moment anyone can be appointed not necessarily from the first 10 names submitted by the governor.

SENATOR MANGLAPUS: But he is still a civil service eligible.

SENATOR ROXAS: Yes, but not from the 10 names submitted by the governor. At this moment you can choose anyone who has a rating of 7 8% as against» somebody who has a rating of 89%.

SENATOR MANGLAPUS: That is true, but when you have submitted the 10 names, you still have a range for the 10 politicians to be fighting for one.

SENATOR ROXAS: From the highest 10.

SENATOR MANGLAPUS: That is correct, but it is in the range of 10, so that politicians could come in and make their influence felt which of these 10 could be appointed.

The gentleman has raised legitimate points here, and if the gentleman wishes to submit them depending on how close or how faithful they are to the spirit, to the essential objectives of this bill, ,I can assure him that the Committee will be open minded.

SENATOR RODRIGO: Mr. President, may I express my thoughts on this political influence? I admit, Mr. President, that under the present setup there has been and there is and there will continue to be political influence in the appointment and shifting of government officials. This is unavoidable and this happens even in the best of democracies, even in the United States. Now, I beg to disagree, however, with the observation that if this power is transferred to the local officials there will be less politics. First of all, the power will be transferred to the local officials—to the provincial governor and to the municipal mayor. They are politicians, and I think that politics will be most intense if the power is given to the municipal officials. I would like to make it clear that I have confidence in our local officials. However, my observation is this: Let us take the case of the appointment of teachers. I suppose this will include the power to appoint even supervising teachers in the province which is given to the provincial governor. The provincial governor is either a Liberal, a Nacionalista or in very few cases independent, but he belongs to either of the major parties, usually. Now, first of all I would like to state that it is my experience — since I have dabbled very much in local politics— that politics on the local level is more intense, more passionate than politics on the national level. It is more personalized, more direct. The approach is more personal, the fights more intense, and as you go from the province to the municipality you will find out that the amor propz'o is terrifc in municipalities. The people go to the extent of even killing; relatives not talking to one another. And when you go to the barrio, politics even becomes more passionate and more intense. This is said without any reflection on the personality of anybody; it is not the person but the situation that I am considering. I would like to state that it has been my experience that now that the appointment of teachers is done by the district superintendent of schools who is a career man, who is not a politician and who has served under several administrations and will hope to serve under several administrations more, we get less politics than if the appointing power were to be given to a local politician. As a matter of fact it has been my experience that I have been recommending very strongly several names to our district superintendent, but I admire him for telling me frankly: "Mr. Senator, I am sorry but there are some teachers who are senior to your teachers. And so, I see, Mr. Senator, that you will not want me to violate the seniority rule." And invariably I follow him. And so my point is —— this was brought up during the interpellation by Senator Roxas — that while I admit that there will be politics in cases of appointment of teachers by the district superintendent, there will certainly be more passionate politics if this appointment is given to the provincial governor.

SENATOR MANGLAPUS: Mr. President, the arguments of the gentleman bring to light the vicious cycle which we are faced with in this country. Basically the arguments of the gentleman have reference to the social attitudes of our people, that our local politics are influenced by deep-seated, family feuds, that in local politics there is no real issue involved except personalities. As a matter of fact this is the reason. we are trying to decentralize the government. We see that the reason these social attitudes remain is that our system has perpetuated these attitudes. It has perpetuated these attitudes because the paternalistic atmosphere in which our people live today does not permit them to think in terms of. one idea against another. It merely permits them to think of one temporary leader against another temporary leader, and the philosophy of this bill is to bring down responsibility in their hands, for them to begin to realize that politics is not just the kind of thing that the gentleman is referring to but a matter of serious import and responsibility and meaning to their lives. The impact of the Barrio Charter on our barrios is evidence that this can be done. In the implementation of the Barrio Charter we are encountering conflicts with the family systems in the barrios, but this is not an argument against the Barrio Charter. It is an argument in favor of it because the Barrio Charter is beginning to cut across the family lines. NOW, the gentleman would like to prevent the devolution of power to the lower level and in preventing this devolution he uses the argument that these people are not ready socially for it because politics on the local level is of such personal intensity. Then what we are doing is succumbing to an argument which is a vicious circle. Our people are not ready, but why are they not ready? Because they have not tasted the experience. They have not tasted the experience because we have not given them this taste, but we do not want to give them this taste because they are not ready. Now, where do we begin and where do we end? I believe, Mr. President, that the proper beginning is to give them responsibility, to give them the feeling that we are trying to give power to as low a level of official as possible in order that they may feel the responsibility close to them and get over these social attitudes that they have, otherwise we will never have a beginning and we will be going around the circle, in the same way we are going around today.

SENATOR RODRIGO: May I clarify one point. I would not want anybody to misunderstand that we who are interpellating and expressing our apprehension regarding certain aspects of this bill, we are against the fundamental idea of entrusting power to our local officials—n0. It is just a matter of procedure and timing. This matter of a vicious circle, I understand it. Somebody who does not know how to swim cannot learn how to swim unless you put him in water. But if you don't put him in water because he does not know how to swim, he will never know how to swim. However, let us not throw him in deep water right away, because, he is going to drown. It is just a matter of degree. As the gentleman himself said, even the provincial governors themselves, when they saw the original draft of the bill, saw that there were certain provisions in the bill which were too extreme. And so, that is our stand. It is not that we are objecting to the general idea, but to certain aspects, in certain provisions, as regards certain officials, who, according to this bill, should be already appointed by the provincial governor. When we express certain misgivings I beg of everybody not to misunderstand our position. We are not against the bill.

SENATOR MANGLAPUS: Now, may I state that the gentleman from Bulacan made the statement that politics on local level is of such intensity that it may be inadvisable to bring down the power of appointments to that level. I made this fundamental observation. This goes to the core and philosophy of this bill.

SENATOR RODRIGO: You notice, Your Honor, that I have limited my interpellation to the provincial treasurer, municipal treasurer and the teachers. I have not touched the provincial assessor. That is shallow water, not, too deep to teach them how to swim. I have not objected to the provincial agriculturist being appointed by the governor. But I have my misgivings about the provincial treasurer and the school teachers, as well as the municipal treasurers being appointed by the municipal mayor. So, this makes my position clear. I am not against giving them the power. It is just the degree of power that we will give them at this stage.

3 - Decentralization and the Senate

(The following is taken from the Senate records of February 22, 1965, when all senators present during the session voted in favor of the Decentralization Bill.)

SENATOR MANAHAN: Mr. President, may I explain my vote?

THE PRESIDENT: The gentleman from Manila and La Union has the floor.

SENATOR MANAHAN: Mr. President, as I vote Yes for this measure I would like to make the observation that the Senate has traditionally fathered many of the autonomy bills that we have presented. I recall the first one introduced by Senator Cabili, an act providing for barrio improvements, which was passed by the Senate but which, unfortunately, did not pass the Lower House and was not subsequently re—introduced due to the death of Senator Cabili. I recall also the bill which later on became Republic Act. No. 2259, fathered by Senator Cuenco,

AN ACT MAKING ELECTIVE THE OFFICES OF MAYOR, VICE-MAYOR AND COUNCILORS IN CHARTERED CITIES,
REGULATING THE ELECTION IN. SUCH CITIES AND FIXING THE SALARIES AND TENURE OF SUCH OF-FICES. I recall too R.A. No. 2264, AN ACT AMENDING THE LAWS GOVERNING LOCAL GOVERNMENTS BY IN-CREASING THEIR AUTONOMY AND REORGANIZING PROVINCIAL GOVERNMENTS;

this was also initiated here in the Senate. In the Fourth Congress, the Act granting autonomy to barrios sponsored and passed by the Senate, Senate Bill No. 82 which was later approved as Republic Act No. 3590, an act amending the Barrio Charter was also initiated and passed by the Senate.

If I rise today, it is not only to give my thanks to my colleagues for their traditional recognition of the need for greater autonomy for our provincial, city, municipal and barrio governments, but also set on record the fact that while it is true that Senator Manglapus and myself originally authored this bill, it can be truthfully said that this is no longer authored by the two

of us alone; but by many who contributed. to it in the course of more than 32 public hearings in different provinces, cities and municipalities of the Philippines and in seven public hearings in the Senate and by the more than three weeks of debate, which some people interpreted as opposition to it. We felt, however, that a bill well debated will turn out to be a better law. So, therefore, with this statement I vote Yes, Mr. President.

SENATOR MANGLAPUS: Mr. President, as one who has had the privilege of having been the sponsor of this bill, I feel that I must rise in spite of the fact that Senator Manahan has already expressed what I feel towards the members of this body. May I just express my appreciation as sponsor of this bill to the members of the Senate for their statesman—like cooperation in making this bill what it is today—a very workable piece of legislation which is full of promise for the future of our local governments. I will not mention specific names for fear of committing the sin of omission; but I will say that in the deliberations on this floor and in the executive Session, the members of this body showed their patriotism and statesmanship when they proposed improving amendments and resisted the temptation---in spite of some doubts that they may have had about certain sections of the bill—to weaken this bill to such an extent that it may not have provided the experiment that we would like to see undertaken in giving our people in the rural areas and our local officials a larger share of the political power of this country.

4 - Decentralization and the House of Representatives

(The following is an excerpt from the Senate records of February 5, 1965. The Senate had not yet voted for the Decentralization Bill; how, in the end, the bill would fare in the Lower House is the subject of the discussion below.)

SENATOR ROY: Now, we will discuss the practical aspects of the provisions of the bill. Your Honor will have to admit that the measure under discussion, especially with reference to the transfer to the provincial board or to the provincial government of the powers of appointment is something which the congressmen do not like. You have to admit that. The congressmen always feel —— perhaps I may call it jealousy — that any power granted to the provincial board or to the provincial governor deprives congressmen of some of their powers. The congressmen will have the natural feeling that they have nothing to do with the appointment of intermediate teachers, and later, with the maintenance of intermediate education for the simple reason that they have nothing to do in the way of appointment, in the way of recommendation for teachers in the intermediate schools. I am talking now as a practical politician, and I have been talking to several congressmen regarding this bill. The congressmen believe that if we give this power of appointment of intermediate teachers to the provincial board or to the governor, the congressmen may lose interest in providing funds from the national government— let us call it the pork barrel—for buildings in the intermediate schools. If such will be the attitude of members of Congress, can the local or provincial government provide funds for the maintenance, construction, reconstruction, or repair of intermediate schools? These to me may be a serious problem, Your Honor.

SENATOR MANGLAPUS: Mr. President, may I again remind the gentleman that this bill does not provide that buildings and textbooks of the elementary schools be provided for by the local government? Those functions remain in the hands of the national government.

SENATOR ROY: When we speak of national government, we refer to Congress, because Congress appropriates the money.

SENATOR MANGLAPUS: Yes. Now, let us refer to section 17 on page 14. Mr. President this action was the subject of discussion yesterday when the sponsor was interpellated by the lady from Albay, and we clarified this point yesterday, and I think the lady was convinced that we were not preventing the congressmen from intervening in deciding the specific items of public works to be undertaken on the local level, but what we are providing here is a guarantee that all congressmen, no matter to what party they belong, will have the opportunity and equal voice indeciding the items for their congressional districts, and they be entitled to automatic and immediate release of funds once the plan or program has been agreed upon. If the gentleman will look up line 31, supra.

SENATOR ROY: Yes. line 31.

SENATOR MANGLAPUS: Page 14, I think this is very clear from the terms of this paragraph. We have done our best, Mr. President. The Committee has seen to it that within the framework of decentralization, we do not take away too much from what the congressmen would like to retain, but it is not possible to maintain the status quo. It is not possible to clear from the terms of this paragraph. We have done our best, changed the status and still gave the congressman everything that he is enjoying today. It is possible that national interest may require that the congressmen and the senators give up some of the prerogatives they are enjoying today, in order that we might arrive at the objective that we are seeking through this bill, namely, the political awakening of our people.

SENATOR ROY: Your Honor, may I call your attention to the first part of section 17 of the bill, page 14, which provides that:

> Within 10 days after the start of each quarter, the
> Budget Commissioner shall set aside Whatever amount
> is available from the general fund for public works
> projects.

That is presuming that there will always be appropriations or money appropriated from the public works acts. That is presuming that since public works projects are passed by Congress, the members of Congress are the sole architects in the apportionment of public works projects and funds. I have my serious doubt as to whether a congressman or a senator would be cooperative on that point of providing money for the maintenance of schools for intermediate grades when they are not given the right in the way of, say, recommending teachers for intermediate classes which is given exclusively to the provincial board or, should I say, the provincial government. Then the congressman would rather distribute their public works allotments to the primary schools.

SENATOR MANGLAPUS: Mr. President, if we proceed on that basis, then we will not decentralize any function because this argument that the gentleman is using regarding public schools is also applicable to rural health and other matters which may involve projects which will require public works. But the gentleman will see readily that we just cannot satisfy everyone in this bill if we are going to devolve powers to the provincial level. Some men in the national government have to give up power, and we have to appeal to their sense of public service. I hope that the members of Congress may be willing to give up some of their powers.

SENATOR ROY: I wish the members of Congress would really take an enlightened View on this point.

SENATOR MANGLAPUS: Well, I already see an enlightened view in the Senate, and I hope it will be found in the House of Representatives.

5 - The Groundless Veto

The basis of veto message challenged

(Excerpts from extemporaneous privilege speech delivered on the Senate floor by Sen. Raul S. Manglapus, April 12, 1967.)*
*See Appendix for Marcos veto message on bill

Mr. President, the inevitable has arrived. The veto message which we all feared is at hand. In spite of the obvious merits of the bill it has been vetoed by the President of the Philippines.

The veto message, Mr. President, contains additional confusions, contradictions and unfair abbreviated quotations from our bill in support of its disapproval.

Public opinion

You will recall, Mr. President, that when the campaign to arouse public opinion against the bill began, one of the spokesmen of the President practically charged the authors of the bill with trying to introduce the- Federal System of government in the Philippines. In effect, he was confusing Federalism with decentralization. It will be recalled that in answer to that charge the attention of the spokesmen of the President was invited to the fact that there is a difference between Federalism and decentralization. The mere fact that a country is federalized may not mean that it is more decentralized than a country under unitary form of government. I cited the instance of Russia which, although more decentralized than We are, is federalized but less decentralized than Japan which is unitary. In other words, a nation may be federalized but it may be more centralized than a unitary government.

Veto message

And now, Mr. President, the veto message begins with another confusion. It reads:

"The learned framers of our Constitution, some of whom still sit with that august body, has decided upon the establishment in this country of a unitary or centralized system of democratic government. . ."

In other words, according to this message there is no difference between a unitary and a centralized government. If a government is unitary, it must be centralized.

Mr. President, it is very clear that there is a difference between a unitary form of government and (a decentralized form of government. A government may be unitary but it may be at the same time decentralized. It is true that many of the stable governments of the world today are federalized and at the same time decentralized like the United States of America, United States of Mexico, Australia, Canada and India. But it is also true that other democratic and progressive countries of the world today are both unitary and decentralized. In other words, they are unitary in that they consist only of one state, not divided into several autonomous states but are decentralized in that they are local government enjoying powers that render them effective and strong and not just subservient to the central government. Examples: The United Kingdom, Israel, Italy, the Scandinavian countries. One only has to travel a few miles to Japan to see that Japan has a unitary government like the Philippines. But it is a decentralized government. The prefectures and the municipalities of Japan enjoy powers beyond the dreams of the governors and city mayors of this country, even those dreams that they dreamed when they hoped that this decentralization bill might eventually be passed.

Basis is false

Therefore, the very basis of the veto message is false. It accuses the bill of trying to go against the Constitution which sought to put up a "unitary decentralized government." All that the Constitution sought to do was to put up a unitary and centralized system of government. The veto message proceeds to warn against imperium in imperio, quoting the late distinguished Justice, former Senator Laurel.

Before I go to the analysis of the Laurel opinion, I will proceed to show how deceptive the veto message is. If the gentlemen have copies of the veto message on hand, I will refer you to page 2 of the veto message. The veto message on page 2 in the paragraph on the lower half of the page reads as follows:

"On the erroneous assumption that our system of government is still 'overcentralized,' the present bill declares it to be the policy of the state 'to transform local governments gradually into effective instruments through which the people can, in a most genuine fashion, govern themselves and work out their own destinies,' and in accordance therewith, seeks to transfer to local governments various powers and functions, essentially national in character, in order to enable them to operate as autonomous self-government units."

Policy of the hill

The idea that is sought to be conveyed by this paragraph, Mr. President, is that in the declaration of policy of the bill, it is stated that we are seeking to decentralize functions that are essentially national in character. Of course, if one did not read the veto message carefully, one will not notice that the quotation ends in the word "destinies." The quotation insofar as it goes is correct; but it leaves out the very important portion of the declaration of policy which contradicts the impression that is sought to be created by this paragraph where it says:

"To this end, local governments henceforth shall be entrusted with the performance of those functions that are more properly administered on the local level and shall be granted with as much autonomous powers and financial resources as are required in the more effective discharge of these responsibilities."

In other words, the bill says that it is devolving to the provincial level functions that are better discharged by the provinces, and are not necessarily "national in character."

National character

Mr. President, what are these functions that the President says are national in character which are violations of the Constitution and which we are trying to decentralize? The veto message says that we are trying to implant a system of local government rejected by the Constitutional Convention. We seek to decentralize rural health and agricultural extension. And it is charged that by decentralizing agricultural extension and rural health, we are, in the words of the President, trying to establish a "system of local self—government which was precisely rejected by the Constitutional Convention."

Mr. President, I think we should remind the President and his advisers that these two functions until the middle of the 1950's were in fact operated on the provincial level.

Rural health

Rural health, since the beginning of the operation of the Constitution, in fact, since the days of the American occupation was carried out on provincial level. Before Republic Act 1081 was enacted in 1954, and since the days of the American occupation, there was a pr0vincia1 health fund, 5 per cent contributed from the municipal general fund and matched by the province, this health fund was budgeted by the provincial board. The salaries and traveling and other expenses of health personnel Were paid out of this fund. The provincial board organized sanitary division. Sanitary inspectors, as they were known then, were appointed by the municipal council.

It was only after Republic Act 1081 in 1954 that the rural health service in its present centralized form was "nationalized" on the principal excuse that the provincial governments did not possess the proper financing to continue discharging this very important function.

Agricultural extension, Mr. President, until 15 years ago, was operated on the provincial level.

Extension service

You will recall, Mr. President, that before the creation of the Bureau of Agricultural Extension there was no such thing as a centralized agricultural extension service. There was the agricultural fund from the municipalities and provinces budgeted by the provincial boards. The subordinates in field agricultural work were appointed by local officials in the provinces and municipalities. It was only when it was seen that the provinces did not have the proper financing to carry out this function that the Bureau of Agricultural Extension was organized 15 years ago.

All we are doing, Mr. President, in this bill is to return these two functions to the provincial level with the assurance to the provinces that they will now have the financing with which to carry out these functions. How then, Mr. President, can the President of the Philippines say that this bill is trying to establish a system of local government rejected by the constitutional convention when for many years under the American regime and under the Philippine Constitution these functions which we are decentralizing were already operating in decentralized form?

City level

As a matter of fact, even public school education was once conducted on provincial and city level. Until Commonwealth Act No. 586 was enacted, with the exception of the four primary grades which according to the Constitution must be conducted by the State, everything was conducted on the provincial level. Again lack of funds obliged the provinces to give this up and caused the centralization of our public education, although even that centralization is not complete because we still have provincial high schools existing today.

Let us look at England, Mr. President, which is known to be

now a democratic-socialist society under the Labor Party, and which is known for its very efficient health service. One would think that socialized medicine could be carried out only on a centralized national level. But, no, the health service of England is the most decentralized of all democratic countries in the world today.

Let us look at Israel, which is a small spot of earth compared to the Philippines, whose wonders of agriculture have become the model not only for Asians but even for Europeans. In that small country of Israel agricultural extension is decentralize .

Contradictory grounds

Mr. President, because of these contradictory grounds the President of the Philippines would now say that if you want to decentralize his government you first must amend the Constitution. Yet in the same breath and in the same page, Mr. President, the President of the Philippines says that it is a fact, attested by recent legislation, that Congress has already granted greater independence or autonomy to local governments. In other words, you can reduce the power of the President as in the Local Autonomy Act and in other subsequent Acts, without violating the Constitution. You need not amend the Constitution in order to reduce the power of the President.

Ah, but the President would say we must draw the line somewhere so that we may not establish an *imperium in imperio* that Justice Laurel warned, us against his opinions in the Supreme Court. Where do We draw the line? The Local Autonomy Act of 1959 fathered by the distinguished gentleman from Cebu, Senator Osmena, when he was in Congress provided for budget autonomy. It limited the power of the President to his budget commissioner and his secretary of finance to control the budgetary function of the province. It authorized the provinces to carry on projects which heretofore the provinces were not authorized to carry on without clearance from the national government.

Republic Act No. 558 granted powers of appointment to local government, which heretofore were not given to local officials, and each city charter that has been enacted has taken from the President the power to appoint some officials.

What is unconstitutional, therefore, Mr. President? Where does President Marcos want us to draw the line? Is there any line drawn in the veto message? All We find are vague generalities! He does not tell us where we shall stop. He just said, after misquoting or under-quoting our bill, that we are going too far.

Appointments

He does not say just how far is too far. Is it in the matter of appointment? May I ask, Mr. President, do we establish an *imperium in imperio* in the province simply because we give the provincial governors, the power to appoint heads of offices created by the provincial governments? In fact, this is repeated in the so-called compromise bill of the President and in the bill which is under consideration in the House today.

Do we create an *imperium in imperio* simply because we give the provincial governor the power to appoint the provincial assessor and the provincial agriculturist? We have excepted from this application judges, auditors, fiscals, division superintendents, supervisors, principals, provincial treasurers, provincial health officers and district engineers. All of these would continue to be appointed by the President of the Philippines!

Where then, Mr. President, is the *imperium in imperio* that we are creating in the province and city government? Is it in the power to suspend and remove local elective officials? Most of these less important provisions are repeated in the compromise bill now pending in the House.

We look everywhere, Mr. President, and we cannot find any power that we are granting to the local governments that could cause so much alarm. First, I will repeat, in the matter of decentralization of functions, we are only decentralizing functions which used to be exercised already by the provincial governments under the Constitution of the Philippines. Second, the power of appointment that we are giving is so limited that the governors would appoint the provincial assessor and the provincial agriculturist — nothing more. The rest of it is repeated in the compromise bill now in the House.

Vague grounds

Mr. President, after vainly trying to impugn the constitutionality of the bill on vague grounds, the President would now make broad and sweeping statements that the bill is prejudicial to the rice program. Mr. President, what is the rice program of President Marcos? Until now we have no definite indication delivered to us directly from Malacañang as to What this rice program is; but I think we can glean it from various publications that have come out with quotations from the President.

It would seem that the rice program is at least a P150 million affair participated in by such agencies as the Bureau of Plant Industry, the Agricultural Productivity Commission. The International

Rice Research Institute, the University of the Philippines College of Agriculture, the National Irrigation Administration, the Irrigation Service Unit, the Agricultural Credit Administration, the Land Administration, the Land Authority and the Land Bank, and the Philippine National Bank.

Now, all we are doing in this bill, Mr. President, is transferring field agricultural extension, which costs P14 million to the provincial level —- a function which was already practiced or exercised by the provinces before. How does the transfer of field agricultural extension workers, involving P10 million, affect this tremendous program—rice program—of the President?

The field agricultural extension worker is there to inspire the farmer to plant more and to plant better. Does the farmer get inspired more by the thought that the field agricultural extension worker is a national agent instead of a provincial agent?

As a matter of fact, the records will show that the more centralized a function is, the less responsive the people are. Why is it that private organizations like the Philippine Rural Reconstruction Movement can claim greater successes than the PACD? Because they are not in the barrios carrying the image of the National Government to the people— the handout image; they are there, having convinced the people that they are there to show them how to plant better and to live better. And the reason for this circumstance is because the PACD suffers from the image that they are there to give out handouts to the barrio people, the Philippine National Bank has been harnessed for the rice program. It is now going to give an additional P200 more per hectare for loans. I ask, what possible dislocation of the rice program could the decentralization of field agricultural extension create? Let me remind the President that when field agricultural extension was being handled on the provincial level, the rice situation was never as serious as it is today — perhaps because field agricultural extension was under the responsibility of the provincial government and the people could pinpoint responsibility, and there was greater *rapport* between the men in charge of the extension service and the farmer that the extension service is supposed to help.

Deceptive message

Mr. President, the veto message says deceptively: "In addition to this fragmentation of efforts, there is the primary question of funding. Since under the bill the source of the funds for the transferred services, estimated to cost about P53 million annually, is the general fund, to that extent therefore the national government will be deprived of the finance necessary to support the rice program envisioned."

Now, this is a masterful piece of deception, Mr. President. Let me remind the President of the Philippines that when he voted for this bill in 1965, it was very clear — and it is still clear in the bill today — that the money that we are devolving to the provinces will be used to discharge the functions that heretofore had been exercised by the National Government. Therefore, if we are giving money to the provinces and taking it away from the National Government, we are also taking away from the National Government those functions for which this money is being spent.

And what are those functions? Rural health, amounting to P35 million; and agricultural extension, amounting from P10 million to P18 million, depending on the extent of field extension service required. What connection Mr. President, to begin with, does rural health have to do with the President's rice program? He wants to make the people more healthy and less people to die. We would need more rice if less people died in this country.

Point of issue

But seriously, the point at issue here is that he is deceiving us and deceiving the people when he says that when we remove P53 million from the National Treasury and devolve this money to the provincial level, we are depriving him of the finances necessary to support his rice program. Because, as I have shown you, there is absolutely no relation between his rice program and this P53 million. If we left this P53 million in the hands of the National Government — as it is going to be left now because of his veto, unless this veto is overriden — if this money remains now in the government as it will remain in the National Government, I ask President Maroos: Is he going to be able to use it for his rice program? No, because this P53 million will have to be used for those functions which we have failed to decentralize; namely, rural health and ffield agricultural extension.

The message goes on to say that we are disrupting his public works program. It says, to begin with, that we are transferring to parties other than those that have prepared and started to implement the program the power to expand public works. There is no provision in the bill, Mr. President, which takes away from the secretary of public works, in conjunction with the budget commission and the district engineers, the power to expend public works. All we are providing for here is that justice be rendered to every province in the disposal of public works that, under present conditions, are supposed anyway to go to local governments.

Community project

Much is made by the President's Office of the fact that in one provision of the bill we provide that 60 per cent of the public works should go to community and related projects and national projects and 40 per cent will be at the pure disposal of the Public Works Secretary. But, Mr. President, this is the reality today. If We examine the public works project today, the public works law and outlays passed by this body, we will find that 60 per cent of them are supposed to go to this type of community projects; 40 per cent is for national projects. All we are asking is that when that 60 per cent is expended, that the President is not given the opportunity again to abuse this power by releasing public works only to those provinces whose leaders are willing to surrender their principles and their convictions in exchange for that which, after all, belongs to their people as citizens of this Republic.

We listened yesterday and the day before and last week during the hearings of the Blue Ribbon Committee on the $34 million scandal — and we heard the Secretary of Public Works tell us that the public works program of the President is not going to depend mainly on the available public works funds. As a matter of fact, they seek to justify the $34 million purchase as a loan. They seek recourse in public borrowings.

In other words, the public works program of the President—if we are to believe the Secretary of Public Works — is not going to be carried out entirely out of public works appropriations because there just isn't enough. That is why they are eager to borrow, buy on credit in that particular case —financed by an American company, the Continental Ore Corporation. That is why they issue bonds.

Mr. President, if we put together the funds appropriated, bond funds, reparations funds and public borrowings, we will find that only 20 per cent of the total funds that are used by the government for public works go to community projects and 80 per cent go to national projects of the type included in the President's carrying out in his public works programs. Even this 20 per cent for community projects Mr. President, under our bill is programmed by the national government. The Budget Commissioner, Mr. Sy-Changco, made the very misleading statement, which was played up in the press, that by this 60 per cent provision we had passed a gigantic pork barrel fund. Why? He combined that 60 per cent figure with the fact that we are allowing the congressmen to be consulted on the local level. This was a compromise that we agreed with the House" The congressmen are only to be consulted. They are not to be followed if the national government feels that their advice is not for the good of the country, but they are going to be given the chance to have their way so that there should be a more equitable distribution of community projects and national government projects.

Major change

The major change that we introduced was the simultaneous release. Last night, Mr. President, when we were discussing Senator Antonino's bill on the distribution of funds amounting to P1500 to the barrios, there was mention that these funds should be simultaneously released. I believe this was an amendment going to be proposed by the gentleman from Cebu. It is the same thing that we are asking for here, that whenever public works funds are to be released, they must be released simultaneously so that even if the governor of the province does not belong to the party of the President, that public works funds will go to that province together with the public works funds that go to the other provinces. How does this disrupt the public works program of the President?

The veto message says that we are depriving the Executive of the power to create new offices which would take over or supplement the functions of agricultural extension, rural health, or public works. We are not, Mr. President, abolishing the Department of Health; we are not abolishing the Department of Public Works, and we are not abolishing the Department of Agriculture. They will remain as national offices.

What We are taking away from the Department of Agriculture. which annually spends hundreds of millions of pesos, is P10 million for agricultural extension, which used to be performed by the local government.

All we are doing with public works is not to abolish the Secretary of Public Works or even the district engineer. All we are making sure of is that there be equitable distribution of public works funds among other provinces.

Health department

We are not abolishing the Department of Health. We are merely stating that rural health which used to be carried out by the sanidads before, the sanitary inspectors, when our towns were cleaner than they are today and more healthy, be devolved again to the provincial level with the proper funding to come from the taxes that we are levying on our people.

Mr. President, there are now in the House of Representatives two bills which are purported to be compromise bills "that will fulfill our aspirations for decentralization of government. Let me first analyze for you the more simple bill, which is, the residence tax. You have heard that there is a bill in the House which would provide that the residence tax henceforth be retained on the city and municipal level.

Mr. President, today, 50 per cent of this amount is already devolved to provinces and cities. So, let us not deceive ourselves into thinking that the entire amount of the proceeds from the residence tax will constitute the benefit that will go to the local governments. Only one-half, because the other half already goes to the local government.

Now, the second half will devolve in such a way that it will decrease the share of provinces which will further aggravate their financial positions since unlike cities and municipalities, provinces do not enjoy regional powers of taxation. As proposed, the provinces will get only 10 per cent instead of 25 per cent, and at the same time, they will not share in the 1.50 increase should that 1.50 increase come.

Now, how much will the barrios receive from this magnanimous bill that is now in the House, assuming that there are only 25,000 barrios? But we all know that there are more than 25,000, barrios in the Philippines about 29,000, in fact, but we are using as a quick basis 25,000. If there are only 25,000, the berries would be getting P68 each minimum to P500 maximum. This magnanimous bill is going to give this tremendous figure to the barrios in compensation for the veto of the decentralization bill.

Compromise bill

Mr. President, I have'here the copy of the compromise bill called Decentralization Act of 1967, which is now in the House. Let me state to begin with, that this Decentralization Act Of 1967 now in the House submitted by the resident originally, this decentralization bill does not decentralize any functions. Therefore, the title itself is a misnomer.

What does it do? It gives powers to local governments that are already in the hands of the local governments. Section 1 in so many words says. that a province or a municipality may create a new office and, having created this office, they may then proceed to "appoint the heads of these offices. This is in lieu of our provision which would permit the provincial governor at least to appoint the assessor and the agriculturist. Now, we all know, Mr. President, that under the Local Autonomy Act this power is already granted provided that the provinces and the other local governments have funds. They can create offices, if they want to, but the point is, they haven't got the funds. So, the whole of

Section 1, Mr. President, grants a power that is already in the hands of the local governments.

Section 2, well, these are the repetitions of the less important provisions of our bill regarding vacancies in the office of the vice-governor or vice-mayor.

Section 3, the vacancies occurring in the board or council. As against our bill, they do not abolish the special funds which would increase the income of the local governments tremendously. They have reduced the duties and powers of local chief executives that we have listed down that would no longer be subject to review by national officials.

Tax collection

They have provided a very deceptive provision regarding the apportionment of excess of income tax collection. Under our bill, there is a provision which would allow that the excess of the proceeds from annual collection of income taxes shall devolve 20 per cent to the municipality, 10 per cent to the province and 30 per cent to the city. But by cleverly changing the base from that of 1959-1960 to the last three preceeding fiscal years the result is, that there is a decrease in the share of the local government instead of an increase.

Finally they repeat a section of our bill very magnanimously. Section 9, program of activities and implementation. Mr. President, you will remember that we put in this program of activities and implementation requiring the national officials to program their activities every year in consultation with local officials, because we were decentralizing functions. But now that we are not decentralizing any functions, what is the purpose of programming and coordinating the national with the local officials since everything will be conducted anyway on the national level?

Mr. President, they have eliminated from this bill the important provision on the simultaneous release of public works.

They have eliminated from this bill the automatic retention.

They have eliminated from this bill, in fact, the truly important provisions that we provided for in our Decentralization Measure.

Today we mourn.

Mr. President, it was said to me this afternoon that the authors of this bill are now probably mourning the death of the Decentralization Measure. I think that is not quite true. I think what we could say now in Congress is not that we are mourning the death of the Decentralization Bill, *but that we are mourning the death, not of the President, but in the President of that fire of concern that once glowed in his heart for local governments. The fire which he showed when he voted so eloquently in 1965 for our Decentralization Bill and accused the then President of not carrying out the promises of his administration, the fire that glowed as late as March, 1967 when he submitted to this Body proposals for the revision of the Administrative Code containing those provisions copied verbatim from our Decentralization Bill which he now would reject as unconstitutional.*

I hope that in the future this fire will be revived not perhaps by the overriding of the veto (we here in the Senate voted unanimously for this bill) and I do not see Why we should override this veto. But I hope that this fire will be revived by public opinion, by the people whom President Marcos has deprived, by his unreasonable veto, of that power which he promised them years ago and which I hope he will restore to them in the future when at last he sees the light.

BARRIO CAPTAIN'S 0DYSSEY*

* Manglapus' verse was originally published in The Daily Star.

I

Today in our barrio, if we'd like our thinking nimble
We must imbibe the mixture that is now the status symbol;
A bottle of beer we pour into a half a glass of tuba
And we would then feel strong enough to sing the "missa luba"!

II

Now every time we open a beer bottle from Manila
We start the vicious process, of initiative the killer;
The tax on every bottle comes to almost twelve centavos,
A reasonable sum, if it were not all sucked above us!

III

The money goes so far away to fill a central treasure
Releaseable only at one man's capricious pleasure,
That man who is all-powerful and by the Pasig resident
Who by the constitution is all the people's President!

IV

According to the statutes, every province, town or barrio
Should get its share of revenue without praying the rosario,
The law has fixed this sharing, the law may e'en increase it
But only the executive can graciously release it!

V

And so our barrio captain must to Manila travel,
And spend for fare the money for our feeder roading gravel,
(He can not bring much baon, so he can't be tempted
wayside,
Not e'en to culture centers, like the late lamented Bayside!)

VI

He goes straight to the busy man who lives inside the palace
(His luck will be sufficient if he sees Paeng M. Salas!)
But if he's even luckier he'll see the señorito,
Perhaps in the act of signing another shocking veto!

VII

He then must kneel and tell him: "I do not come to quarrel,
I come about the matter of our delayed pork barrel,
Oh please be kind and merciful — and kindly do not block it,
Please give us some of the money that comes from our
pocket!"

VIII

And then the chief executive will show his generosity
He'll say: "I will release this sum, I will with great velOcity
But first please raise your hand — and while it's up there,
Mistah,
Repeat after me quickly: "I'm now a Nacionalista!"

IX

Our captain has no choice, he joins the President's Party.
Returns to us with the money — to a barrio welcome hearty;
How long will he retain his new political affections?
It all depends on who will win the '69 Elections!

Collected speeches by Raul S. Manglapus

Introduction

In the following pages, we reprint the recent speeches by Mr. Manglapus in the Social Revolution.

The first, entitled "Social Revolution," was delivered on the floor of the Senate during the debates on Vietnam on March 24,1966.

The second, entitled "Asia: Revolution and Ideology," was delivered at the Twentieth Annual Conference of the World Affairs Council of Northern California, Asilomar, California, U.S.A. on May 7, 1966.

The third, entitled, "The Tragedy of Philippine Isolation," was delivered before the Rotary Club of Manila on June 9, 1966.

We are also reprinting his article "Christianity and Social Democracy," originally published in the *Philippines Free Press* on February 4, 1967.

1 - SOCIAL REVOLUTION

BEFORE ANYONE in the Philippine Congress was ever pro-Vietnam, I was pro-Vietnam.

It was my unmerited privilege and my task, 11 years ago, as the Undersecretary of Foreign Affairs of President Magsaysay, to defend publicly and in contention with distinguished senators, his recognition of the Republic of South Vietnam.

Recognition and Consensus

We recognized it quickly so that it might live in freedom. Those who opposed us did not think the new Republic viable. We maintained that it was.

And it lived. By transfusion, byintravenous nourishment, by utter tenacity, by splendid achievement and in spite of dismal error—it lived. . .

Through it all, grave doubts were cast on whether its government was supported by popular consensus.

The test was to come by ballot in 1956. It never came.

Instead, the Vietcong began to test it themselves—by terror, by pillage, by murder, by striking at the tenderest spot in the armor of the republic, namely, the absence of intimacy between governor and governed and the collapse of what promised to be a determined campaign to transform Vietnamese society.

It is in this context that the issue of assistance is now brought to Congress.

Not Conventional War

Many a clev'er reason has been given to drive us to send armed troops marching to Vietnam. One of the most clever has been this:

"How would we feel if, at a time when the Philippines is the target of armed aggression, we ask the United States for soldiers, and she sends us Peace Corps volunteers?" (Privilege speech by Sen. Rodrigo, March 1, 1966)

A devastating *reductio ad absurdum*, indeed, but I fear only useful were we faced in that broken land with a conflict that conformed to the conventional patterns of war.

Yet our own military have produced maps, charts, figures and statistics, to show that this is not such a war.

Maj. Gen. Edward Landsdale, the American expert who has been returned to the Vietnamese scene because they have found, we hope not too late, his ideas to be valid, has asked America and the world to stop calling it such a war if what is desired is victory. He has asked the American people: "Do you understand revolution ?"

Revolutionary Warfare

In the most prestigious American publication on foreign affairs, he told his countrymen just before he was recalled from retirement:

"Some believe we should plainly identify the struggle as a war and make use of our military proficiency to force the Communist regime in Hanoi to cease its adventure in the south. Some believe we should continue along the present course, but greatly increasing the quantity and effectiveness of what is done so that it eventually smothers and kills the Communist insurgency. The anomaly in these reactions is that each falls short of understanding that the Communists have let loose a revolutionary idea in Vietnam and that it will not die by being ignored, bombed or smothered by us; Ideas'do not die in such ways.

He then points to the road to victory. Fight revolution with revolution. Establish a political base State political goals founded "on principles cherished, by freemen, which the Vietnamese share.' Then secure "the aggressive commitment of organizations and resources to start the Vietnamese moving realistically toward those political goals."

In essence, he says, "This is revolutionary warfare."

Vietnamese Patriot

He then quotes with approval the Vietnamese patriot Don Van Sung who in July, 1963 told the nationalist leaders of Vietnam:

"By emphasizing anti-Communism rather than positive revolutionary goals and from lack of a better adaptation to the local situation, the United States has reduced its anti-Communist efforts in Vietnam to the maintenance of an administrative machine and of an army... The way out, to our mind, is not by an, abandonment but, on the contrary, by going deep into every local revolutionary problem and helping solve them, using principles of justice and freedom, and perhaps in fusing them with the revolutionary spirit of 1776." (id.)

Social Revolution
1Foreign Affairs, October, 1964

Have these ideas prevailed? On February 8, 1966, the American and Vietnamese leaders finally gave them legitimacy before the world. The Declaration of Honolulu gave" them a ringing summation: Social revolution, to be fought with land reform, agricultural productivity, rural credit, rural health, medical logistics, electrification, technical education, constitutional change, free elections.

President Johnson said the war was of two fronts. One was the military; the other the struggle "against social injustice, hunger, disease, ignorance, political apathy and indifference."

"They know and we know," he told the American people, "that this revolutionary transformation cannot wait until the guns grow silent and the terrorism stops."

And so, he was to send to Vietnam, to dramatize and concretize the American impatience for this social change, John Gardner, his Secretary of Health, Education & Welfare, his field general in his own local fight against poverty in the vision of the Great Society.

Humphrey Mission

He was to send his Vice President, Hubert Humphrey, who had just returned from Asia, back again to Asia. Humphrey understood his mission. In his response to Johnson, he said, "I shall try to do my best as your representative and the representative of this country to work with the brave people of Vietnam in helping them to rebuild their country; and going on, as you have indicated, to other capitals to carry-the message of America's commitment to the building of human resources and of social and economic progress for all mankind."

This is the way the world understood this grand announcement. As the German paper, *Frankfurter Allgeneine Zeitung* said, "Social revolution, self—government, the fight against hunger, illness and ignorance. .. America seems determined to make great efforts... in this direction—but [she] needs partners for this purpose—a broad cross-section of trained and energetic people. These partners are largely missing."

Revolution Forgotten?

And yet, the same Vice President Humphrey then returned to Manila, said nothing of the social revolution and proceeded to praise the Philippine commitment to ship 2,000 engineer troops.

Why? Was it because he could see that our President was so committed to the military front and did not wish to embarrass him by emphasizing the social revolution?

Or was it because, as the British weekly *The New Statesman* lamented, as early as February 25, the "social revolution" half of the Declaration of Honolulu "does not seem very important"?

If the reason is that America did not mean what she so, solemnly declared, then it is time we reviewed the value that we place on her word.

If the reason is that our government had forestalled an emphasis on the true mission of the second Humphrey visit, by insisting so stubbornly on the sending of engineer troops, then it is time we reviewed the justifications that are invoked for this insistence.

Whose Decision?

It is first argued that we must send engineer troops because that is What the Vietnamese want and, as Senator Rodrigo has warned us, "It would be presumptuous on our part. . to determine the kind of aid" that Vietnam needs.

I am not ready to admit that we are so bereft of genius, of resources, of experience and of sophistication as to be unable to decide for ourselves on the most effective means by which we can help our neighbors in need. Let us listen to the suggestions of the Vietnamese, of the Americans, of our friends and allies. Let us sit down with them—but having sat down and deliberated, let the choice be ours.

Many of the problems of Vietnam we have faced and continue to face in our land today. We have known of the spirit, the soul, the psychology of the Vietnamese from the lips of our own people who have lived and worked with them over the last 12 years.

We, and no one else, can tell What part of our experience can be of value to Vietnam and what is irrelevant.

This insistence on the sending of engineer troops is at best unimaginative. It is too ready "and too flat a response to the magnificent, albeit tragic, challenge that is Vietnam today. It does no justice to our capacity to be original, to be discerning, to be creative.

May I ask, if any attempt has been made to bring together the experts from all Departments of government—Foreign Affairs, Defense, Education, Health, Agriculture, Finance, Community Development, Labor, Commerce, the National Economic Council, the Land Authority—4:0 sit down with our young civic and entrepreneural leaders so that an effective, rounded, efficient and Filipino form of aid to Vietnam might thus be devised?

We asked the Department of National Defense and the answer was no. The Departments of Justice, Finance and Defense have indeed met—but only to savor and justify the pre-cooked and pre-digested formula of an engineer battalion.

And yet, the Vietnamese themselves had, as early as June of last year, given us the cue for this c1rcumspect approach.

The Latest Request

I am now ready to dispute the assertion that an engineer battalion is, in fact, the only or the latest request of the Vietnamese.

In the official record, the genesis of the Vietnamese request runs as follows:

On July 15, 1964, Maj. General Nguyen Khanh, chairman of the Military Revolutionary Council of Vietnam, wrote to President Macapagal requesting "all the support you deem possible and opportune" without defining the kind of support preferred.

On April 14, 1965, Dr. Phan Hay Quat, the Prime Minister of Vietnam, wrote President Macapagal another letter, this time specifically asking for engineer troops "for peaceful and constructive tasks."

This was the request which, according to President Marcos, was reiterated to him verbally by the Vietnamese Ambassador on February 2 of this year.

However, on June 10 last year, the Vietnamese Minister of Foreign Affairs had delivered to our Ambassador in Saigon a note containing "the new requests for assistance submitted by the Government of the Republic of Vietnam."

"These requests," the note states, "divided into two groups, are destined to help Vietnam meet the urgent needs for its national reconstruction and defense. The blue-cover group includes all requests for aid adaptable to a satisfaction comparatively rapid while the yellow-cover group is reserved for the requests of which the satisfaction demands a long range study."

No Action

The note was referred by the Secretary of Foreign Affairs to the Department of National Defense, which, through its Undersecretary, replied on August 28, 1965 that "this is a matter mainly pertaining to the Department of Foreign Affairs."

On September 28, 1965, the Acting Secretary of Foreign Affairs endorsed the note to Malacañang with this annotation:
"The Department notes that the materials and equip— ment enumerated therein fall under the following catego- ries:

1. Public Works and Communications	6. Labor and Social Security
2. Rural Affairs	7. Security and Pacification
3. Public Health	8. Information and Psychological War
4. Social Affairs	9. Rallying
5. Education	10. National Defense

The Department endorses, in principle, the sending of additional aid to South Vietnam. Although it may be desired to extend other kinds of aid aside from medical and technical assistance we are at present giving, the Department believes that only Congress and the Office of the President can decide the kind of aid that may be sent to South Vietnam."

On February 11, 1966, the Department of Foreign Affairs wrote Malacañang as follows:

"Reference is made to our 1st Indorsement, copy of which is attached for ready reference, dated September 28, 1965, concerning the request of South Vietnam for additional aid.

"It will be appreciated if the Department can now be informed of the action on the matter by that office."

No answer has come from Malacanang.

Is it not strange that neither the past nor the present administration has bothered to act on this Vietnamese request?

The New Direction

In their obstinate drive to send troops, they have failed to examine new requests carefully and to realize that the Vietnamese had in fact caught the first chills of the fever of revolution as early as the middle of last year and had moved their emphasis in this direction.

The introduction to the blue cover reveals this fresh approach in clear terms.

It is written in French but the Department of Foreign Affairs, for lack of will and not of French translators, failed to translate it officially. I must now do it for them.

Mais le succés d'une telle entreprise erige de sa part une double condition:

—parvenir a démonstrer a l'ennemi que la guerre ne paie pas, et par des victoires militaires décisives, montrer a l'ennemi que sa politique belliqueuse fondée sur la force et la subversion le conduira fatalement a sa propre destruction.

—realiser des réformes sociales et économiques de grande envergure afin de relever la niveau de vie de la population ét de mettre fin aux injustices et oppresions sociales susceptibles d'etre exploitées par l'ennemi dans sa propaganda subversive."

"But the success of such an enterprise requires on its part a double condition:

"Success in demonstrating to the enemy that war does not pay, and by decisive military victories, show to the enemy that its war-like politics based on force and subversion will conduct him fatally to his own destruction.

"Realization of social and economic reforms of such a breadth asto raise the standard of living of the population and put to an end social injustice and oppression which can be exploited by the enemy in his subversive propaganda."

In this request the Vietnamese ask for support in such things as fiscal reform, labor unionism, school hygiene, social security studies.

Non-Military

Ninety per cent of the requests have nothing to do with the direct pursuit of the military offensive. As the Vietnamese Ministry put it:

"The requests for aid formulated correspond to urgent needs for a series of programs of high priority whose realization should permit the intensification of ef= forts for pacification and for the promotion of the social, cultural and economic development of the country."

In brief, their target of high priority is the hearts of the people—which they hope to win by reconstructing Vietnamese Society.

To Avoid Discovery

It will now be demanded, if this indeed was the new Vietnamese request, why did the Vietnamese Ambassador not stress it when he called at Malacafiang on February 2, 1966? Why did he reiterate the request for troops?

The answer is manifest. It is the same reason why Vice President Humphrey must have decided not to push social reconstruction in his second visit; It could not be done without discourtesy to our government which had already plunged headlong into a commitment on troops.

And so the government must justify this commitment *ex-post facto.*

And so it .must search for some compulsion that will explain why we should refuse to heed these new directions offeredld by the Vietnamese themselves and insist on dispatching soldiers.

We are compelled to do this, we are now told, because of our sacred obligation under our collective security arrangements.

We must not, we are admonished, seek to enjoy security without responsibility.

The Southeast Asia Collective Defense Treaty is invoked as the source of this responsibility.

Is SEATO Invoked?

But the Government of Vietnam has not sought assistance from us with the framework of this treaty.

Not one of the Vietnamese notes makes reference to SEATO, even if Vietnam is entitled to do so under the Protocol to the treaty.

In May 1965 the SEATO Council heard a report from a Vietnamese observer. There was no specific request for aid and so the Council merely noted that at its last meeting in Manila the members had agreed only to "remain prepared, if necessary, to take further concrete steps within their reSpective capabilities in fulfillment of their obligations under the Treaty."

Had Vietnam come to SEATO with specific requests, however, what would our obligations have been under the Treaty?

The distinguished Senator Tanada was a signer of that treaty. I had the privilege of acting as the Secretary-General of the Manila Conference of 1954 at which that treaty was drafted, discussed and signed.

We listened and participated in every deliberation of that meeting.

There was never any intention that each member would be obliged to render exactly the kind of assistance specifically requested.

Extent of Treaty

The words of the treaty are clear. Under Article IV, each member, "recognizes that aggression by means of armed attack in the treaty area against any of the Parties or against any State or territory which the Parties by unanimous agreement may thereafter designate, would endanger its own peace and safety, and agrees that it will in that event act to meet the common danger in accordance with its constitutional processes."

Measures so taken are to be immediately reported to the United Nations.

On September 21, 1954, two weeks after the treaty was signed, I had occasion to explain the inclusion of the phrase "in accordance with their constitutional processes" in a speech before the Manila Jaycees. I said that the same phrase is carried in Article XI of the North Atlantic Treaty. And I said that both the Philippine and the United States delegations to the Manila Conference, having in mind the constitutional prerogative of their respective Congresses of declaring war, insisted on including this phrase in order to re-assure their Senates that by ratifying the treaty they would not be divesting their legislators of this right.

Respective Capabilities

This is why the SEATO Council in its London communique last May stressed that the members should be prepared to act only "within their respective capabilities" in fulfilling treaty obligations.

And what are these "respective capabilities"? They are those that the treaty itself suggests—not only military aid—but also, as in Article III, "technical assistance, designed both to promote economic progress and social well—being and to further the individual and collective of governments toward these ends."

Recapitulotion

I hold, then:

That our collective security treaty commitments are not legally pertinent in this issue.

That were they pertinent, it would be our obligation and our prerogative to render assistance of the form and extent that are consistent with our capacities and our constitutional processes.

That, therefore, even our treaty commitments do not dictate to us that our assistance in every case be military in form or in substance.

That what is happening in Vietnam is not normal war. It is revolution, and our response to itmust be the firing of a superior, peaceful, social revolution that will place the hearts of the Vietnamese beyond the reach of totalitarian deception.

That we cannot fire this revolution by sending our army engineers motorcading through Saigon so that for some fleeting moments they might, with bands blaring, flags waving and helmets dazzling in the sun, "lift the morale of the Vietnamese."

That we can fire this revolution by stubbornly emphasizing its priority, by bending our talents to it, by tapping the mind and muscle of this republic and producing our own peculiar fuse for its igniting.

We can fire it and keep it alive by dogging the Vietnamese and the Americans, and all who seem at least to have caught a glimpse of its promise, so that they may never lose sight of it again.

Continuing Revolution

Indeed, social revolution, the fight against injustice, the production of wealth, the shortening of the breach between those who enjoy it and those who do not —— all this must continue if the world, not just Vietnam, not just Asia, is to survive.

America in all her opulence has had to keep it alive in this century—through the New Deal, the New Frontier—and now the Great Society.

Russia, her arms already reaching far out in space, must ever remind her people that the day of pure communism is not yet and that the social upheaval must not stop.

The end of the Diem Republic began when the spirit of revolution was replaced by the spirit of "business as usual."

The revolution of love that began 2,000 years ago has had to be renewed. Luther renewed it in the 16th century and in our time John XXIII and Paul VI renewed it again, renewed it so thoroughly that there are those who are now led to wonder whether the Lutheran protest continues to be valid.

We are now asked in this world of change to shut our minds and keep the winds of change away.

In a golden hour where we might, for our own sake, affirm our subscription to revolutionary goals, we are asked to remain conservative, to dismiss this unique occasion for bold ingenuity and succumb to the trite and the convenient by dispatching a uniformed expedition that will have no decisive bearing on victory.

I say it is for our own sake for we, as much as the Vietnamese, require this affirmation.

When our poor ask for rice and our unemployed ask for work—what is it that we shall give them?

Bread and Circus

What is now suggested is that, like the decaying, debauching Roman, we follow the road to ruin. Failing to give the people bread, let us give them a circus, entertain them, send a battalion of men that will provoke the drama of battle—so that daily the curious anticipation for glorious headlines or the anxious wait for casualties may divert a hungry people and cover up for the failure to act on social change.

I have been warned by friends not to shock our complacent society by stressing social revolution. It is advised that we must have evolution not revolution, for revolution connotes violence, and evolution is more in keeping with the peaceful ways of democracy. It is counseled that "social" is too radical—too close to "socialism" and this, of course, we are reminded, is a grievous "sin" against democracy, ignoring that the parties in power in Britain and the United States today are those that follow the democratic socialist ideal.

It is time that we broke away from our self-knotted bonds of isolation from the movement of world revolution. It is time that we entered into dialogue with men of other and all beliefs so that we might begin at last to distill our own ideology from the ferment of ideas that the best minds of men can offer.

Far too many souls are being born on this and other lands, far too many injustices and far too many pressures are upon us, for us to persist in relying on the slow, traditional, turn over in the social conscience of democratic man.

What I seek, indeed, is violence—not the violence of arms—but the violence of sudden and jolting indignation that will startle our citizenry with the realization that freedom must permit not just some men but all men to have dignity, or else it must perish.

Commitment vs. Improvisation

For thus far the answer of those on the side of freedom has always been to improvise, to wait for a crisis and then to meet it, first by the quick shedding of young blood—and only second by a hurried look into the basic social causes.

All this while, there is no improvisation on the other side—only a determined, uniform, sustained commitment to revolution that is deceptively exciting to those who seek a better life.

Let us not leave this moment that God has given us to pass by—to impress upon ourselves, upon America and upon the world, the continuing urgency of revolutionary change, so that, after Vietnam, never again may we have to seek achievement of justice by the force of arms.

Let us tell Vietnam, let us tell America that we are ready to assist in a mode that is our own.

As we help our farmer plant his feet on his own plot of land, we can spare some of our resources to help the Vietnamese peasant to stand on their own acres.

As we liberate our farmer from the alien usurer, keep him in health, educate his children, light up his house, increase his produce, make his future secure, we can aid the Vietnamese in duplicating these endeavors among their people.

As we seek to give our freedom meaning, we can show the Vietnamese the meaning of freedom.

As we amend our fundamental law, we can collaborate in rewriting theirs.

As we innovate our archaic methods for suffrage, we can demonstrate to the Vietnamese how to hold their first free elections and, indeed, in what manner these should not be held.

Our own house is not in the best order—but we can spare a

moment to help our neighbor build his own and in this fashion learn to strengthen ours.

This, I think, is bayanihan. Call it that. Call it also collective security. Call it what you will—it is the way that may yet take us, straight and unswerving, to our absolute goals—the heart of Vietnam and the peace of the world.

2 - ASIA: REVOLUTION AND IDEOLOGY

THE FIRST RELEVANT TRUTH about Asia today is this:
Asia wants revolution. Asia needs revolution.
There was, indeed, a time when it did not.
There was a time when Asia was in a state not of revolution but of equilibrium.

Asian Equilibrium

Asian society is agrarian and it once relied for its survival on a delicate balance between land and population.

Land suitable to rice culture was limited and concentrations of rice-eating populations struggled to extract from it a bare existence. The result was that the masses of Asia had neither the time, the ability, nor the energy to think of governing themselves or even of participating in government. And so this chore was left to the few, the small specialized class of scholar—officials whose business it was to govern the many, whose business in turn it was to labor and obey.

Thus developed the centralized state, strong enough to protect these precarious balances from the natural or artificial forces that were always threatening them, skilled enough to undertake the control of the flow of water that was the life-blood of their staple production.

In the centers of Asian cultural development, in Java, Cambodia, Japan and most especially in China, this was the structure of society. In China, this was the pyramid: the peasants at the bottom, the land-owning gentry above them, still higher the scholar-administrators and at the summit the emperor, the divine maintainer of the equilibrium between land and population, man and Nature, heaven and earth.

Confucius gave this stable society a philosophical base which sanctified harmony and reverence for authority.

If the balance was disturbed, if the emperor could not control the avarice of landlords, the corruption of officials, the looting by invading barbarians, if, therefore, the masses starved and the sacred work-cycle stopped and there was chaos, there was yet a remedy — a Chinese formula adopted with modifications throughout East Asia.

The ruler ceased to be divine. Rebellion was permitted, nay called for, and the successful rebel was by his victory *ipso facto* vested with divine power. A new dynasty was born and the balance was restored.

This equilibrium was to last for 4,000 years until one day Western man arrived.

Western Impact

Western man arrived bringing with him ideas more explosive than the powder that the Chinese had invented originally for firecrackers at the harvest festival but which later Western man himself would use more profitably by shoving it into the mouths of cannons.

What were these ideas?

There was Christianity, proclaiming human rights superior to those of the state.

There was science, substituting immutable laws for the capricious will of the gods.

There was parliamentary government, with the governors responsible to the governed.

There were new techniques for mass production and for the control of disease.

Southeast Asian society was shaken at its roots. The indigenous rulers were replaced by the European governors. The land, once tilled only for the subsistence of the population, was now made to produce raw materials for the colonial power.

Equilibrium Gone

When the Manchus fell in China, there was no other dynasty to take its place. The cluster of Western ideas which the Europeans never bothered to knit together into one harmonizing force to replace the old Asian divine maintainers of the equilibrium, fell separately on Asian soil, breeding at once hope and despair, expectations that could not immediately be fulfilled, mass populations, their growth unchecked by the old natural levellers of epidemic and plague, plantation economies, which, upon liquidation by the departing colonial, left country sides unproductive of food because geared to export crops whose markets had faded away.

There is now more ambition and less fulfillment, more people and less food.

The equilibrium is gone. And it no longer suffices to follow a new rebel so that he might assume the divine mantle and restore the harmony.

The Asian, persuaded by the ideas of the West, would now like to control his government and his destiny and not leave these to the mere successors of the colonial master to the native aristocrat or the comprador.

Though he may still be at the base of the old pyramid he wants dignity for himself — not just for the emperor, the potentate or the scholar-official. *1*

This is why Asia is in revolution. And this now is the question: is America ready to face this truth?

Understanding Revolution

In discussing Asian-American relations I think I am entitled to two assumptions: first, that all is not well with these relations; second, that Americans do not seek to be comforted with pleasant half—truths. I know they expect the truth and I am honored if they should allow me the presumption of knowing it.

Are Americans ready to face a revolution in Vietnam, in Asia and in Latin America? Do they, as their own countrymen have asked them, understand revolution? *2*

And I suppose that many of them would shoot back:

"Do we understand revolution? But of course we understand revolutionl Are we not the first revolutionaries of the modern age?

"Is not our Declaration of Indepedence a ringing revolutionary document for men of all time to invoke in the cause of justice and equality?"

And they would, indeed, be entitled to this retort.

But recalling .one's own revolution may not be enough to understand another's hunger for revolutionary change.

It becomes even less sufficient, when one's original revolution and its "ideological underpinnings" no longer seem to be relevant to the deep current of human events among those who now need revolution most ——— the masses of the developing world.

In another era, in an era of limited population and pure libertarian motives, they may have been and they were indeed relevant ——— so much so that when America snatched the prize of independence away from the first Philippine Republic, William Jennings Bryan, in 1900, was able to say in answer to the imperialist justification of "educating the Filipinos":

> "Some argue that American rule in the Philippine
> Islands will result in the better education of the Filipi-
> nos. Be not deceived. If we expect to maintain a colonial
> policy, we shall not find it to our advantage to educate
> the people. The educated Filipinos are now in revolt
> against us, and the most ignorant ones have made the
> least resistance to our domination. If we are to govern
> them without their consent and give them no voice in
> determining the taxes which they must pay, we dare not
> educate them, lest they learn to read the Declaration of
> Independence and Constitution of the United States and
> mock us for our inconsistency." *3*

----

1 Cf. Horacio de la Costa, S.J., The Background of Nationalism and
Other Essays (Manila, Solidaridad Publishing House, 1965) pp. 10-15.
2 Cf. Maj. Gen. Edward G. Landsdale, Viet Nam: Do We Understand
Revolution (Foreign Affairs October 1964, p. 75) and George C. Lodge,
Revolution in Latin America (Foreign Affairs, January, 1966, p. 173).
3 Cf. American Forum (Harper & Brothers, New York, 1960) p. 364.

Ideology vs. Improvisation

But today the philosophical reasoning of John Locke and the scientific precepts of Isaac Newton, which were the well-springs of the principles of the American Constitution and Declaration of Independence, may no longer suffice to meet the pressures of population, to shorten the breach. between rich and poor, to hasten the demolition of the barriers on race and creed.

Equality is good. But there is now in the newly emerging nations too much equality in destitution.

Dignity would be better. But where in the "rockets' red glare" of the American revolution are there the brilliant directions that point to the way by which his dignity might be achieved by the multiplying millions of this age?

In a world where men are in search of firm ideology that will bring this dignity, where even America's own young would seek a "national purpose," Americans seem to offer only the promise of pragmatic improvisation, meeting crises on a "case to case" basis, espousing or rejecting ideas because of associations that are either imprecise or no longer applicable.

Capitalism

For instance, capitalism was once for Americans the rallying cry of private initiative against government ownership; and who will deny that private initiative is an attribute of a man of dignity?

Yet, to many, a capitalistic society is one in which the rich are in full political and economic control, in which ownership indeed is private but in the hands of a few who have no interest in measures for the welfare of the many.

Free Enterprise

America is a monument to the genius of free enterprise, and American propagandists abroad would like to credit their unabated economic growth to completely free initiative almost in the classic sense of "laissez faire" liberalism.

This is the usual American retort to the young Filipino entrepreneur who, inspired by the American example, schooled in the American tradition, and seeking to build his enterprise in the image and likeness of the American industrial god, seeks Philippine government assistance in competing with the giant American firms who are free to enter and operate within our decontrolled economy.

Yet, no mention is made of American government restrictions and controls, subsidies and supports that enable its free enterprise economy to fit into its ambitions for national welfare. No mention is made of the fact that within the American "free enterprise" society, sporting blood will not allow putting a heavyweight and a lightweight in the same ring and will make the pleasures of tournament golf available to all by a system of handicaps.

Socialism

Americans are proud to be known as alert opponents of socialism, so alert that they will sound the alarm if it should so much as try to creep into the fabric of their economy.

Yet, their own statisticians and poll takers will tell them that there is a "high middle ground" in the world of political and economic thought, where millions of Western Europeans, Asians, Africans and Latin Americans think of themselves as "socialists" in terms which even the conservative American need not condemn since they believe, not in full government control of production, but in a government with a social conscience, in a mixed economy where the supreme consideration is social justice for all. *4*

Communism

Americans are proud of their crusading anti-communism. For

being against communism most people in most countries side with them.

Yet to many in the uncertain world, communism is merely opposed to capitalism and not democracy.

Allies of the United States and her other non-communist friends are beginning to tire of negative anti-communism.

As early as 1963, Don Van Sung, the Vietnamese patriot, warned that: ". . .By emphasizing anti-communism rather than positive revolutionary goals and from lack of a better adaptation to the local situation, the United States has reduced its anti—communist efforts in Vietnam to the maintenance of an administrative machine and of an army. . .The way out, to our mind is not by an abandonment but, on the contrary, by going deep into every local revolutionary problem and helping solve them by using principles of justice and freedom and perhaps in fusing them with the revolutionary spirit of 1776." *5*

----

4 Cf. Ralph H. White, "Socialism" and "Capitalism" (Foreign Affairs,
   January, 1966 pp. 216-228).
5 Quoted in Viet Nam: Do We Understand Revolution, supra.

To Eduardo Frei, the Christian Democratic President of Chile, "the anti-communism of fear, of preservation of 'order,' and of forces manifested in military coups, are doomed to failure and are constantly in rout. They have nothing to say to youth or the people." *6*

Pragmatism

But Americans will ask, what need is there of ideology when pragmatism is sufficient? Did it not cure the ills of America?

Has it not been said that "the reform movement in the early years of this century — that revolt of the American conscience which was kindled by Theodore Roosevelt, the elder La Follette, and Woodrow Wilson," resulted in the fact that "through a combination of patchwork revisions of the system —— tax laws, minimum wage laws, subsidies and guarantees and regulations of various sorts, plus labor union pressures and new management attitudes," Americans "had repealed the Iron Law of Wages"; they "had brought about an automatic redistribution of income from the well-to-do to the less well—to-do"; they "had discovered a new frontier to open up: the purchasing power of the poor." *7*

Is this not "the essence of the Great American Discovery?" *8* And is not this its corollary: "that if you thus bring advantages to a great lot of previously underprivileged people, they will rise to their opportunities and, by and large, will become responsible citizens?"*9*

Has not the American "new social and economic regime given the lie to the forecast of Karl Marx?"*10* Did not the American system come about "not by virtue of some kind of inner necessity in the evolution of capitalism which Marx had overlooked, but by virtue of the freedom and spirit of man, namely by virtue of the American mind and conscience, and of the American collective effort of imagination and creation?"*11*

To most of this I could agree.

American spontaneity

The histories of other nations are always to be divided into periods — periods of rise and decay — of benevolent kings and lecherous kings, of the ascendancy of reason and of the fall of faith, of the prevalence of groups that propel to progress and groups that retard it.

----

6 Cf. Religion, Revolution and— Reform, edited by D'Antonio and Pike (Frederick A. Praeger, New York) p. 36.

7 F. L. Allen, The Unsystematie American System (Harpers Magazine, June, 1952, p. 21) as quoted by Jacques Maritain in Reflections in America (Charles Scribner's Sons, New York, 1958) pp. 114-115.

8 Ibid-.

9 Ibid.

10 Reflections on America, p. 114.

11 1bid., pp. 114-115.

I have read American history and found it singularly lacking in these periods. I have found it, in this respect, monotonous.

Ask the Englishman who put his country on the road to industrial power and he may answer: the non-Conformists. Ask the Japanese who built his nation and he may answer: Meiji.

Ask the American these questions. Will he answer, perhaps, George Washington or Abraham Lincoln?

If he does, then I would dare to suggest to him that he is wrong. Indeed, one of these men led America to freedom; the other gave that freedom substance. But neither of them built America. No, not Jefferson or Edison, not Adams or Wright. The unique, consistent and gloriously monotonous context of America prescribes that every minute an American be born free, free in every sense —— to develop himself and his country according to his own will and initiative.

I say of America that there never was and I prophesy for America that there will never be one single man known as the builder of America.

This is important to Americans because this might just 'be their guarantee for greatness without end, for escaping that cycle of rise and fall which dismal historians would predict of great civilizations.

What shall we call this guarantee? I shall not call it capitalism. I shall not call it free enterprise. I shall use the word which a hard-headed monk of the 13th century once associated with freedom. Thomas Aquinas said that "freedom is the spontaneous obedience to law."

Spontaneity. As America built herself spontaneously, so also could we build Asia.

Asia Not Ready

But is Asia ready for spontaneity? I do not think so. I am not optimistic about any immediate Asian enthusiasm over the example of American spontaneity.

For it is now evident that patchwork democracy is based on assumptions that are not verified in the developing world.

What are these assumptions?

Frontiers

There is the challenge of the open, Virgin, boundless frontier — a challenge the response to which was the beginning of the great American miracle.

There are no such frontiers to challenge Asian societies. The Asian peasant must respond not to the heartening call of the rich wild but to the demoralizing prospect of having to make productive two hectares of unowned land, the tenancy on which he has inherited over the centuries, emanating from some unwritten ancestral contract or some royal decree which his ancestor could not read.

This absence of Asian frontiers has moved practical theologians like the Celenese Oblate Father Tissa Balasuriya to urge that the developed white countries abounding in virgin land, such as Canada, Australia and the United States, voluntarily respect the demands of "macro-justice" and open up their frontiers to the land-hungry millions of Asia.

"If I were born of white parents," he laments, "almost the entire underinhabited world would be open to me to settle down and reproduce my kind. Australia, Canada, South Africa, Southern Rhodesia, etc., would not speak of unemployment and other difficulties. Yet these same countries generously give non-whites arms to fight the communists to make the world safe for political democracy and Christian civilization. And they blame us when we are not enthusiastic."

"The present policy," he says, "of 'increase and multiply and stay where you are, for we have filled the earth' cannot, humanly speaking, last." *12*

This may sound extreme to some and I will not now discuss the finer points of "macro—justice" that are here raised. But this will at least explain why most Asians will not find inspiration in the squirrel-capped figure of Daniel Boone.

Dissent vs. Conformism

A second American assumption not verified in Asia is the tradition of dissent.

The very act of crossing the Atlantic by original settlers to America was one of dissent — dissent from oppression, dissent from tyranny, simple dissent from opposing opinion.

No such tradition of dissent motivates the Asian. The waves of Malays and Proto-Malays that landed on the shores of Luzon, Visayas and Mindanao, my ancestors, who drove the Negritos and the Igorots away from the lowlands and into the mountain fastnesses, just as American ancestors were later to drive the indigenous population eventually to reservations — these men were no fugitives from tyranny. They came in groups of families, in *barangays*, and their tradition was conformism —— conformism to the will of the chief, the datu and further up, the sultan, just as in India there would be conformism to the rajah, in Arabia to the sheik and in China to the emperor.

Soon it would be conformism to the white colonial governor. But whether the supreme will was indigenous or foreign, non-conformism would not be a right and, the penalty for it would invariably be death.

There is a third unverified assumption — the richness of the land.

---
12 World Apartheid (Commonweal, December 24, 1965, p. 364).

Resources

Pilgrims found on the American continent a prodigious wealth of resources —— forest, soil, minerals, coal, water power— in quality and quantity no other nation can claim to possess.

Indeed there are pockets of great natural wealth in parts of

Asia, not excluding the Philippines.

But for most Asians work must be done on barren land, and superstition must be overcome before the fertilizer that will fatten the soil is put to use.

No wonder then that Asia is not yet ready to understand spontaneity.

No wonder that Asians, having almost always been servants, have developed the habits of the servant, unwilling to change, willing only to obey the gods of superstition that continue to exist even in Christian societies such as ours, deified, as in Latin America, in the syncretizing process of Latin Evangelism.

No wonder that when the Asian is told: "Go and be free. Develop yourself. Face and overcome each problem as it comes with your own genius," he does not understand.

Chinese Responsiveness

Yet it would seem that something akin, though not identical, to American spontaneity can come from other antecedents.

The noted Filipino writer, Nick Joaquin, after a visit to Red China recently, has reported that "responsiveness to challenges is the spirit that is Americanizing the Chinese."

He says the party line this year in New China sounds, in translation (and the translation is by a Chinese), like Babbitt at a sales pep talk, like Madison Avenue at its campiest:

"Go all out, aim high, get results! Think big, do big!

"What could be more Damn Yankee? If you bumped into it in the dark, could you guess this was Chinese, not Rotarian; that this was Slave State, not Rugged Individualism?

" ..... There's the same dynamic taste for the big figure, the boom term, the comparative graph... The Faustian drive in the Chinese, once expressed in the pagoda, is currently bursting forth in secular skyscrapers.

"The vertical spirit shows in the women. . ... They drive buses, tend machines, are elected to Congress. A superb road—paved, laned, tree'd and gardened — that runs from a Shanghai suburb to a factory town is popularly known as The Highway The Housewives Built. Before it was built those housewives' husbands howled about getting to work on time at the factory town; so the housewives got together and completely on their own, laid out that primrose path for their lords and masters. The kind of thing one hears about the American pioneer women who built the Great West.

"Everywhere that very American obsession with growth, with progress, with colossal figures." *13*

Responsiveness without freedom. Is this paradox really possible? If it is, it is the result of an upheaval whose premises have been so much easier to understand, so quickly to be verified in the context of Asia.

Simple Premises

It is the simple dichotomy of the rich and the poor, the oppressor and the oppressed, the master and the slave, capital and labor, the few and the many. The rich are the few, the poor are the many. Let the many rise in revolution and redistribute the fruits of the earth.

This is something that Asians may understand.

It is a revolution that an Asian may indeed find easy to join, because he knows of its premises—the poverty, the inequality, the oppression and all the rest of it. It is at least easier to join than that complicated revolt-against retarding tradition, that rebellion against self through which an Asian would have to go before enjoying the privilege of pragmatic spontaneity.

I am not saying that Americans are incapable of spectacular performance, of magnificent response to challenge that excites other men and other nations. The whole history of the United States is a sequence of such performances, like the brilliant improvisation in a jazz band played by individualistic instrumentalists, each going his own way, but somehow, as with Turk Murphy at Earthquake McGoon's, making a totality that is a smashing success.

But in the eyes of Asians what chance has such a sequence, however brilliant, against the sustained, persistent, unequivocal panorama of revolution projected from other capitals?

Torches and Beacons

In brief, Americans are perfectly capable of lighting torches, and men will at times follow them but, as Jacques Maritain has put it:

"You are advancing in the night, bearing torches
toward which mankind would be glad to turn; but you
leave them enveloped in the fog of a merely experiential
approach and mere practical conceptualization, with no
universal ideas to communicate. For lack of adequate
ideology, your lights cannot be seen.

----
13 Philippines Free Press, April 11, 1966, p. 3.

"I think it is too much modesty." 14

Call it modesty, call it indifference, call it over-confidence.

Whatever it may be, it is not suggested that Americans stop lighting torches, for even though they may not last, torches are always useful in the dark.

What is suggested is that besides, over and way above these torches they also light a beacon.

It is suggested that they project a permanent beam to suffuse all others, that will, without blinking, proclaim what they stand for and inform the world what it is that from their leadership they might gain for the elevation of each human life.

This may involve putting most of American running traditions in sudden reverse. For I understand that their forefathers came from Europe precisely so that they might flee the oppressive glare of the old continental beacons and light their own individual torches in peace. And Max Lerner says that the American Constitution for 150 years was looked on as a way of fighting the "imported European philosOphies." *15*

In brief, they are organically averse to continuing ideology.

Need for Ideology

But analyze this aversion and you will find that it was entirely proper to the early American — the American settler, the American pilgrim, the American pioneer.

How proper is it to the modern American — the American with his global commitment to leadership?

No, I fear that this American, unless it is his desire to withdraw into isolation, must put together his bundle of brilliant improvisations andpfrom them distill an ideology, his ideology, that will be relefant to the problems of this age and the lives of those who are touched by his commitment.

If I should now be dared to say what exactly this distillation should be, I would decline. I would not take up such a dare because I am not an American and only an American can fathom the ideological possibilities of his pragmatic experience.

But, as an Asian, I will here venture a few expressions of hope.

Human Dignity

I will here venture to hope that when that beacon is lit, it will bear, somewhere at the core of its message, the promise of human dignity.

I will venture to hope that the path to that dignity will be illuminated with the incandescence of a sustained, social revolution that will lift men everywhere to a level where they might begin to enjoy the freedom and privilege to be spontaneous.

---

14 Reflections on America, p. 118.
15 America as at Civilization (Simon and Schuster, New York, 1963)

I will venture to hope that the American revolutionary ideology will enable Americans to give better reasons than those which they so far have given for some of the changes that are required for this lifting.

Why must land be redistributed? _

"It is the absolute right of the proletariat," says Dos Kapital.

"Because of the social character of property," says *Quadragesimo Anna.*

Will Americans limit themselves to saying:

"Because without land reform American aid is wasted?"

In San Francisco, Louis Kelso is seeking to diffuse the ownership of industry among all citizens, and from Korea down to the Philippines his ideas are being debated.

We may find the Communist Manifesto applauding these ideas as a step towards the "abolition of bourgeois property, based on class antagonisms, on the exploitation of the many by the few."*16*

We may find ideological support for them in *Mater et Magistra*, where John XXIII has said that "it is not enough to assert the natural character of the right of private property, productive included. . .but its effective distribution among all social classes is to be insisted upon" including that of- "shares in middle-size and large firms."

If America should accept Kelso, shall it again be just an— other part of the "patchwork-revision," with no message for the non-American, save that of another successful make—shift improvisation?

Marx and Teilhard

And will Americans wonder why men like President Senghor of Senegal, rejecting the scientific socialism of Marx, now turns not to Thomas Jefferson and "life, liberty and happiness" but to Pierre Teilhard de Chardin and his humanistic, optimistic Christ-centered synthesis of all races evolving irresistibly upward toward a transcendent God -— as the hope for Negritude, for Africa, and for mankind ? *17*

If Africans now turn to Teilhard instead of Jefferson, it is not because the Jeffersonian Declaration was not valid. It is perhaps because it was so valid and so successful within the context of America that the young vibrant civilization'that it engendered never bothered to review its relevance to the world;

---

16 *Manifesto of the Communist Party, 1846', by Karl Marx & Frederick Engels, Chapter II.*
17 *Cf. Thomas and Margaret Melady, Teilhard de Chardin and the Afro-Asiom World (The Catholic World, November, 1965, pp. 102—106).*

Maritain has said that among the vulnerable points in the American people is that they are "anxious to be loved; (they) need to be loved."

He adds that they "will never see such a need in an Englishman" and that "as to Frenchmen, they are so sure in advance that everybody loves them that they don't feel any particular anxiety about the matter." **18** 18 Reflections on America, p. 43.

An English friend of mine put it in another way: "The trouble with Americans is that they want to be on top of the world and still expect to be loved. It simply can't be done, you know."

True? Yet, who knows. When Americans shall have shown the world how they have leapt over barriers of race, of creed, of poverty, not "case to case" but on propulsion of ideas so universal, so understandable and so consistent that they reach the hearts of all men, who knows, they may yet manage to remain on top of the world and *be loved.*

Yet, it is not the important thing. It might even be the wrong and the vain thing to expect affectionate returns for the work of world leadership. There is enough inherent urgency, essential value and prospect of historical recognition to this task — that of flinging in the teeth of those who would create an anonymous and faceless class, the coming of a world of men, each endowed with individual dignity.

Do we hear the stirring of an American awakening to this task?

Vietnam and Revolution

I think we do. And it is not without reference to these stirrings that I have stood against a bill in our Senate which would send a Filipino battalion of engineer troops to Vietnam. I feel that the Declaration of Honolulu should not go unheeded — that resonant call to the world by the American President and the Prime Minister of Vietnam — assigning to social revolution a priority equal to, but not less than, the military effort.

I feel that we Filipinos should come to the aid of that broken land by sharing with it our own experience in social reconstruction.

We would thus be stressing the long-term vision that may yet enable America to forego in the future such costly stop-gap military reflexes to crises abroad.

Let there then be social revolution. Let it give hope. Let it fight injustice. Let it produce wealth but let it close the gap between those who enjoy the wealth and those who do not. Let it not surrender to the deceptive simplification that the only problem in Asia is productivity, "the enlarging of the pie" and that the exploitation of man by man will resolve itself 'with this enlargement.

Let it release the millions of Asia from the bonds of retarding tradition, of feudal tenancy, of heavily centralized government power.

Let America help to fire it, but let it not be an American revolution. Let it be so universal in meaning, so pregnant with optimism for all races that each nation will accept it as its own.

Nationalism vs. Paternalism

For the first false god that must be smashed in this revolution is that of paternalism. The family of young nations will have no more of the father image. Lerner reminds us that in the early days of the shaping of American nationalism the Americans had first to slay the European father so that he could then without inhibition use his European heritage in his own drive to greatness.[19]

[19] America, as (1 Civilization, Supra, Vol. 1, p. 23.

This is what the Asians must do. 'The Indian has had to slay the British father image so that he might work his own destiny through British constitutional traditions. And in my country, there is the young Filipino already known to Americans, an entrepreneur, who must slay the American father image, or at least cut it down to brotherly size, so that he might collaborate with him or compete with him on equal terms using techniques of the Harvard Business School.

There is also in my country the Filipino leader who must slay the American father image so that he might lead his country, with no self-consciousness, through his own version of Ameriican constitutional democracy and negotiate claims and treaties with America on the basis of mutual respect.

I am told that one need not worry that the American will resist this slaying for it ill befits the American to play the role of international father: a leader among equals, yes, but not a father — not him with his passion for brotherhood, not him with his sporting blood that will keep him from taking fatherly advantage.

I am aware how versatile the sword of freedom can be. It can cut the bonds of slavery, it can slay the father image, it can hack at the jungle of injustice to make way for social revolution — and it can also be used for self—destruction.

May God show Americans and all free men the way to wield it, so that mankind may survive — in freedom, yes, but also and above all —— in dignity.

3 - THE TRAGEDY OF PHILIPPINE ISOLATION

I have come for my annual visit to Manila Rotary.

I do a few good things once a year.

Once a year I visit the dentist and go on retreat.

And once a year, to give vent to those of my ideas to which nobody else will listen, I come to Manila Rotary.

I first addressed you in 1954, in my maiden speech as a public servant. I spoke On "The Case for the Little Squirrels." The squirrels were the small nations of Asia, and I ventured the opinion that they were entitled to group together among themselves and with bigger nations in order to protect their Security.

Collective Defense

Six days later, the Southeast Asia Collective Defense Treaty was signed in Manila. SEATO was born. The concept of collective security was introduced to Asia.

It was not all that new a concept. Five centuries before Christ, the Greek city states had banded together to stem the growing power of Sparta and Persia. The Holy Roman Empire was in fact a collective security organization "bound by laws of restraint above the states which composed it." The Concert of Europe has been called a "perverse" kind of collective security because it sought to keep the peace by freezing the status quo.

In our time NATO preceded SEATO and by being thus compared to NATO, SEATO until recently has been under attack from two directions: for being a tool of nee-colonialism on the one hand; for not giving enough automatic security on the other.

It is now becoming evident that what is wrong with our being with SEATO stems from neither assumption.

What is wrong is not that we signed the treaty, not that we subscribed to the concept of collective security.

What is wrong is the way in which our official policy later came to regard the treaty.

The Realistic View

When the Greeks drew up their Pan-Hellenic union, they may have been rallying to the highly emotional call of unity of race, but they never lost sight of the reality that had made it necessary, namely the extrication of Pericles from a difficult situation where the Athenian autocrats were succumbing to the ideological appeals of the Spartans and the Persians.

The Holy Roman Empire, for all its claim to being "holy," was viewed by Pope, emperor and allies as a measure at times to maintain the balance of power in Europe, at others to nurture budding German nationalism.

The members of the North Atlantic Treaty Organization, have not been content to huddle under the umbrella of NATO power. They have gone about, each his own way, to make their own assessments, and take their own steps in the context of world politics.

And so it is with all the members of the Southeast Asia Treaty Organization — all, that is, except the Philippines.

Our False Approach

There is a unique quality about the manner in which we have approached our position in SEATO. It is what would accurately be characterized in our language as *"talagang pambihim."* It coincides with our approach to our relationships with other nations and with our entire outlook on foreign affairs.

While other nations, interlocked in all kinds of "bilateral and multilateral military, commercial and cultural treaties, have never lost the perspective of the realities of the national interest, we have somehow always given up what George Kennan would call "the feeling for reality" in foreign. relations.

What takes its place is not just "idealism" or "morality." I am one who believes there is still a place for these in our dealings with foreign nations. It is more than these. The closest thing I can think of to describe it is "romanticism."

Our Romantic Policy

We have become incurably romantic in our view of the outside world. In the pursuit not of reality — not even of ideals or morals — but of a make-believe world, a fairy land where there must always be the good angel to protect us and the monster to be slain, we have created false images of others which have distorted our own outlook and in the process we have succeeded only in being unfair to these others and to ourselves.

There is our image of America and Americans. It is one which would credit each American with wings, qualifying him for angelship — a divine protector, the impeccable dispenser of international charity. When a Filipino diplomatic negotiator, a Filipino entrepreneur, or a Filipino labor leader, emerging from dealings with the American, reports that he has looked hard and has not found any wings — only a hard-bargaining American, warm at heart, but warmer still in the pursuit of his own company and national interest — in brief a very human being such as we might want to — we are shocked. And refusing to accept reality, we seek to dismiss the report as "subversive."

There is our image of Communist China. Heretofore we have simplified it in terms of a monster—a huge monster eager to swallow up all those around her. And then when our own fellow Filipinos go to visit her and report that if she is a monster, there are in her bowels some very real human beings who believe they are rebuilding the lost greatness of the Middle Kingdom and repairing indignities of the past, we are hard put to balance the report with statements of refugees and figures of crop failures.

The irony of it all is that Americans themselves are embarrassed with all this, for they have never in their history truly intended for themselves the role of ministering angels set apart from evil by international alliance or unilateral proclamation.

No Real U.S. Isolation

In the days of their strictest isolation as well as in these days of global commitment to the defense of democracy, Americans have never isolated themselves from reality as tightly and as ludicrously as we Filipinos have managed to lock ourselves up in our own little unreal world.

In our rush to deify America, we have missed the useful lessons of American history which could have prevented our own false imitation of American policy and assisted us in formulating a real one for our own.

In 1793, George Washington issued the Neutrality Proclamation. In 1796, he reemphasized its principles in his Farewell Address. In 1823, the Monroe Doctrine elevated those principles to that of a unilateral declaration to the world, which the European powers, busy with the industrial revolution, did not bother to challenge.

The Doctrine declared that "the United States would keep out of the territories, wars, alliances, spheres of influence and politics of the world outside the Western Hemisphere, but in return non-American powers would be expected to stay out of the political affairs of the Americas. Non-American countries with colonies in the Western Hemisphere could keep them, but they were to acquire no more colonies and refrain from expanding those they had." *(William Carleton: The Revolution in American Foreign Policy; Random House, N. Y., 1964; 17. 18)*

In carrying out the Doctrine, the United States soon demonstrated that it was not to be an act of self—denial. While warning Europe to stop expanding in the Americas, she began her own expansion in 1803 with the purchase of the Louisiana Territory. She continued to expand across the continent at the expense of France, Spain and Mexico. In the war of 1812, she tried in vain to conquer Canada while England was busy keeping Napoleon from upsetting the balance of power in Europe.

The most important lesson in U.S. continental expansion is her sending of American settlers to adjacent territories to stir up the cry for joining the union.

American Realpolitik

The noted American historian, William Carleton, says that the "use of fifth column American settlers in Florida, Texas, Oregon and California to prepare the way fer annexation was worthy of the most sagacious European Realpolitik." (id., p. 20)

This lesson was all but lost on Philippine diplomacy. In 1956, the British took the initiative in negotiating with us a labor agreement over North Borneo. It was my privilege as Undersecretary of Foreign Affairs to direct the negotiation on our side. The British wanted the Philippines to send thousands of families to settle in NorthBorneo. The British negotiator gave me this broad hint:

"Sooner or later Britain will have to leave Borneo.

To whom shall we leave it? If you've got enough Filipinos over there, we might jolly well leave it to you."

This was before 1960, the year in which the idea of Malaysia was conceived in the fertile mind of. British diplomacy.

We signed the agreement containing as its first condition, at the instance of the British, that Ilocanos would be given priority in the settlement — a step which was less an attempt to split the Solid North than a tribute to the diligence and trustworthiness of half of my ancestors.

Unfortunately legalism reared its unwanted head. The insistence of other Departments of our government on the observance of technical details of our laws prevented the implementation of the agreement. Otherwise, we might have achieved, by observing Realpolitik not as in Hitler's Sudetenland, but as in America's California, what our self-righteous diplomacy has thus far failed to get us in Sabah.

There is yet another truth about America's "isolationist" Monroe Doctrine that is of even more immediate relevance to our current posture.

Ideology and Trade

A few years after its declaration, the United States made it clear that she did not mean it to be any kind of economic isolation. In 1844, she acquired trading rights in China, taking advantage of the British action in the Opium War. In 1853, she sent Commodore Perry to open Japan to trade. She never found this incompatible with her post civil-war, high tariff policy of economic nationalism.

It is this same Spirit which guides America's foreign policy today. In spite of criticism by her own senators that she is straying far from reality, America continues to distinguish ideology from power politics and refuses to confuse a firm stand against communism with economic self-abnegation.

While America fights communism in Vietnam, she sends massive aid, including military assistance to Communist Yugoslavia.

While America rings the accepted centers of potential aggressive power with multilateral pacts like NATO, SEATO, and CENTO, and with bilateral agreements like the Philippine Mutual Defense Treaty, she maintains diplomatic relations and trades heavily with Russia and the communist countries of Eastern Europe.

This is true with all her allies in all Of these collective defense arrangements.

In our own SEATO, Australia recognizes Russia and Yugoslavia, and trades with communist countries including Red China and East Germany.

New Zealand recognizes Russia and all Eastern Europe except Albania and East Germany and trades with Red China, Czechoslovakia and Poland.

Britain recognizes Red China, Russia and all Eastern Europe except Albania and East Germany, has consular relations with North Vietnam and trades with all communist countries except North Korea.

France recognizes Red China, Russia and all communist countries except East Germany and North Korea. trades with all except North Korea, but including North Vietnam.

Pakistan recognizes Red China, Russia and Yugoslavia, trades with Russia, Red China, Yugoslavia, Rumania and Poland.

Thailand, the headquarters for SEATO, recognizes and trades with Russia and Yugoslavia.

Outside of SEATO, West Germany, the new bastion .Of Western democracy, recognizes Russia, trades with Red China, Russia, Hungary, Poland and Rumania.

Japan, the new Asian democracy, the northern anchor of the American line of defense in Asia, recognizes all communist countries except North Korea, North Vietnam and Red China and trades with all except North Korea, but including Red China and North Vietnam.

All the countries of Latin America, except two or three in Central America, recognize and trade with communist countries.

Catholic Spain, Catholic Portugal, Catholic Ireland trade with all communist countries, except North Korea and North Vietnam, but including Russia and Red China.

Meanwhile, our own republic, afraid of its own shadow, has kept blissfully away from the current of world thought and world events.

Shield, Not War

Instead of making a collective defense, as others have, a shield to hold with the left hand while the right is free to shake hands, to negotiate, to trade, to maneuver freely in the maturing experience of international politics, our republic has made it a wall, so high, so thick and so non-porous, as to keep away all persons, all thoughts, and all ideas that will disturb the stale, complacent atmosphere of our stagnant society.

Our diplomats are forbidden to deal with anyone but our "truest" friends, not allowed to break bread or drink cocktails with Communist counterparts except within the protective, collegial confines of the United Nations. The result is a kind of naive Philippine diplomacy which is headed for premature atrophy.

Our businessmen, our manufacturers, our agriculturists are told they must produce more, trade more, find new markets for our products, but they are limited to traditional outlets, denied access to Eastern Europe which annually imports millions of tons of tobacco, sugar, vegetable Oil, iron ore, copper, textiles, clothing, leather and rubber shoes, cement, furniture and wood products, all of which are high in our exportable list.

Our Tragic Isolation

Most tragic of all has been our isolation, from the current of world democratic political thought.

In our childish illusion that having crouched behind military pacts and having played along with an artificial one party, two-faction political system, we are then free to work leisurely towards a progressive society, We have not bothered to investigate what it is that has taken democratic countries to progress since the Industrial Revolution.

Liberalism and Conservatism

Modern democracies, operating on mass populations and marching towards industrialization, move forward on the propulsion of ideas polarized from left to right which are come to life in the ideology of freely evolving political parties or groups or coalitions Of parties.

The conservative party or group of parties representing the right, the urge for free and individual initiative, contends with the liberal or progressive party or groups of parties of the left that would use government power for the peaceful and democratic equalization of political, social and economic rights.

There will be a tendency for the independent businessmen, the independent farmer, the tradition-minded class to group together under the conservative banner. The progressive intellectual, the socially-conscious aristocrat, the younger entrepreneur and the workers' unions will find common cause under liberal or progressive leadership.

In the United States, the conservatives are the Republicans and the progressives the Democrats. In England they are respectively the Tories and the Laborites.

Democratic Socialism

In the Whole community Of Western democracies, the parties of the left will respond to the name Democratic Socialist, or simply Socialist.

The Americans may still pretend that they are germ-free of socialism and may loudly denounce the slightest suspicion that it is creeping into their system. But it was the frankly socialist revolution of the American conscience fired by Theodore Roosevelt, la Follette, Wilson —and fanned to dramatic heat by the millionaires Franklin D. Roosevelt and John F. Kennedy, that characterized the American patchwork solution to the challenge of the distribution of the wealth concentrated in the hands of the few by *laissez fairism* — patchwork and pragmatic socialism, but socialism just the same.

The British are more candid about the matter. The Labor

Party that came into power in the 1930s, riding on the alliance of the workers' unions with the progressive intellectuals of England's aristocracy, including the Fabian Socialists of George Bernard Shaw, Sidney Webb, Annie Besant, frankly calls itself Socialist.

So do the counterparts in France, Germany, Italy, Scandinavia, Japan, India, Malaysia, Australia and New Zealand.

By engaging in periodic peaceful struggles for political power on ideological issues, the socialists and conservatives have provided their electorate with a free choice of direction to follow at given moments in their history.

Socialism and Communism

It is often asked why in spite of the fact that the Communist Party is free in Britain, Western Europe, Japan, India, Australia, it has there never assumed power.

The answer perhaps lies in that very fact, namely that it is free and not driven underground and that its ideological drive is met not with frantic congressional investigations but with ideologies just as dynamic and just as promising to the citizen who has less in life and would like a little more.

The industry of post-war Europe was restored and made booming with the Marshall Plan. NATO deterred further Russian advances westward. But in the most important battlefield—the mind of the Western European—it was the healthy rivalry, the sparkling dichotomy of Christian Democracy and Socialism, with their own peculiar promise of a better life, conceived and executed in the image Of their respective ideologies that stemmed the ideological advance of doctrinaire Communism.

Socialism Not Class War

The Democratic Socialist movement has been characterized by an alliance of citizens that transcends class divisions and has therefore exasperated the orthodox Marxist-Leninist who has been hoping to achieve his end by pitting class against class.

The word "socialist" was first used in 1827 by Owen, and later by Saint Simon and Fourrier — men who *rejected laissez* faire in favor of a system where the rewards of the new industrialist would be shared by the many instead of the few.

In the Communist Manifesto of 1848, Karl Marx and Friedrich Engels condemned those socialists who did not believe in violent revolution.

"The socialist bourgeois," they said, "want all the advantages of modern social conditions without the struggles and dangers necessarily resulting therefrom. . .. They wish for a bourgeoisie without a proletariat. [They require the proletariat to] cast away all its hateful ideas concerning the burgeoisie." (Ch. III, (2))

With the rallying power of the manifesto the communists hoped to make exclusive use of the word "socialism" in Marxist revolutionary terms of hate.

Peaceful Revolution

To their dismay, however, Socialism continued to grow in another climate — that of peaceful, revolutionary democracy.

In 1900 the British Socialist Labor Party was born owing "far more," Giles Radice says, "to Christian ethical principles and to the gradualist philosophy of the Fabian Society than to the teachings of Karl Marx." (Democratic Socialism; Longmans, London, 1965; p. 12)

This was the development in Sweden and Germany Where the Social Democrats moved away from revolutionary Marxism as early as the 1910s.

By the early 1980s, while the Russians were decreeing purge after purge to purify the 1917 revolution, Ramsay MacDonald's socialist government was attempting to work out in Britain a peaceful socialist revolution.

His revolution was destroyed by the Great Depression because Radice argues "he ignored the advice of brilliant economists like Keynes and of trade union leader Ernest Berin and relied instead on orthodox laissez faire economic advisers." (id. pp. 21-22)

It is interesting that Keynes was recently featured on the cover of that remarkably non—socialist American magazine Time as the inspiration for the American economic boom under Lyndon B. Johnson and the guiding light for his fight against poverty in the Great Society.

Other things are also interesting.

The most Catholic branch of the German Christian Democratic Party is the Christian Socialist Party of Bavaria.

The Palm and Socialism

Pius XI began by accepting' modern socialism."

John XXIII went much further. "*With Mater et Magistra*," says the British author E. E. Y. Hales "we are, in fact, brought right into the world of the Welfare State. Gone is not only the semi-feudal world in which Leo saw the simple workman, surrounded by his family, settling down to his frugal but sufficient meal, the just reward of his labour. But gone, too, is the world of Pius XII, who referred, with evident alarm, to communal kitchen, free health services and free education. Now it is not only free education that is being claimed; it is further education for all those suited by their ability to benefit from it."

"The Pope is not merely accepting, he is embracing what many would call socialism, and he is acknowledging that a new concept of the duties of the state is involved. He calls it an increase in social relationship and 'a development of the social life of man.' " (Pope John and His Revolution; Eyre and Spottiswoode, London, 1965; 10. 1,5)

Socialism I n Power

Today, socialist parties, or parties committed to democratic socialist objectives are in power in Britain, India, Sweden, Kenya, Tanzania, Singapore and, like it or not, the United States of America.

We might say that they are all agreed on one thing — the pie must be enlarged, yes, but in the process of enlargement, more and more must be allowed to get in a bite. Otherwise, someone is liable to get a hold of that pie and throw it in our collective faces — and there shall be weeping and wiping — and there shall be loss of liberty and universal chaos.

One may not agree with democratic socialism. That is not the point. The point is that whether European or American, Asian or African, Christian or still remotely Marxist, it is one of the forces that is today determining the shape of the present and the future democratic society.

The point is that we in this country, persisting in our innocent view of the world from inside our cloistered walls, remain hopelessly unaware that such a force exists.

"Socialism" is, in this country, still a dirty word, and we experience an innate compulsion to rush to the confessional to admit to bad thoughts if we so much as allow our minds to wander in its direction.

Vision, Not Investigation

Our population is multiplying. Our resources continue largely untapped. Wealth is being produced but its fruits go to an even smaller portion of the population. There are rumblings of a Huk resurgence, and alarms have been sounded over the infiltration of labor and students.

What is our response?

Imprisoned in this "elect-me—first-I'll—think-'of—ideology-later-and-I'm—less—corrupt—than—thou" political system, all we can think of is to let loose the congressional investigators and prepare to pin the label of ,"un-Filipino" on anyone who, seeing no future in our system, would explore other possibilities for a society based on social justice.

Instead of offering our young, our peasants, our workers, our underprivileged, a choice of fresh directions and a vision of a better tomorrow, balanced, if you will, on the alternating but identifiable forces of liberal socialism and conservatism as other modern democracies have succeeded in achieving, we have persisted in pragmatic "case to case" politics which our society can ill afford but which is the only kind which our imprisonment will allow.

And will one blame these young, these peasants, these workers, these underprivileged, if, failing to see this choice, this direction, this vision, they turn to the promise, however Utopian, of those who would raise the banner of social class, stir hate and sow subversion?

Philippines Unredeemed

In the tenth stanza of his "Ultimo Adios," Rizal must have written with deepest feeling:

"Ora par todos cuantos muriero sin ventura;
por cuantos padecieron tormentos sin igual;
pom nuestras pobres madres, que gimen su amargura;
par huerfanos y viudas, por presos en tortura,
t ora por ti, que veas tu redencion final."

Pray for yourself, Rizal tells his country, that you might witness your final redemption.

And just what did Rizal mean by final redemption?

Some biographers have chided him for not supporting the violent revolution for political independence, for confining his crusade to revolutionary reform — reform in government, reform in traditions, reform in religion, reform in the mind.

For Rizal sought the liberation of the mind. He thought the Filipino mind should be open to the liberal ideas that were then sweeping Spain and Europe. He believed in the freedom to discuss all ideas. Once he wrote glowingly of the refreshing exchange of views he had had with a Protestant minister in Germany, a bit of news that was received with no little shock in the Catholic Philippines of the 18905.

Rizal and True Freedom

Has Rizal's dream of final redemption already come true?

I would answer with the first lines of Zulueta da Costa's "Like the Molave."

"Not yet, Rizal, not yet. Sleep not in peace:"

Not yet, therefore, Rizal.

Oh, the Church whose discipline you once challenged has indeed already redeemed you.

Last year, the successors of that Protestant minister were given places of honor at the Vatican Council and embraced with the Papal kiss of peace.

Last month, a priest at the University of San Francisco, of the same order as Sanchez, Balaguer and Pastells, who educated you but cautioned you, for fear of your safety, to mind your haste towards liberal ideas, proposed that the Catholic Church canonize Martin Luther because most of his protests has at last been validated by the Fathers of Rome, tardily but, they hope, not too late.

But, alas, your own country does not seem anxious to redeem herself.

She wanders about aimlessly in her fairy-land prison pretending to be free.

When shall she truly be free?

When shall her independence be real?

When shall she begin her march to greatness?

It shall be of course when her mind is free. Meanwhile:

"Not yet, Rizal, not yet.
The glory hour will come.
Out of the silent dreaming,
From the seven-thonsand fold silence,
We shall emerge, saying. WE ARE FILIPINOS,
And no longer be ashamed "

Let us speed the coming of that glory hour. Not tomorrow, perhaps, but sometime in this generation the redemption must come so that our childien may cease to grope in the darkness and begin to follow a vision of the greatness that we deserve.

4 - Christianity and Social Democracy

LAST NOVEMBER IN Washington a very high American official told me: "I have always felt that the problems of the Philippines are not to be solved in Washington. They can only be solved in Rome."

No true Filipino of course will accept that statement. The problems of the Philippines will obviously and ultimately be solved in the Philippines.

But the American simply meant that his country's appeal in the Philippines is to the stomach, to the senses, to an exaggerated sense of gratitude and a selective, wishful View of history. But the influence that Rome exercises is far deeper. It is in the soul — and as sociologists and socio-anthropologists are now agreed, it is the Filipino soul that must be revolutionized if we are to have social change and progress. It is the Filipino soul that must be asked to rebel against itself.

In 1963, a seminar of top Catholic clerics and lay leaders of Latin America was held at the University of Notre Dame. The record of the seminar, published in the book "Religion, Revolution and Reform" (Praeger, NY. 1964) is a devastating expose of Catholicism and its responsibility for the social problems in that area.

"Imagine the Church," says Bishop Mark McGrath of Panama, "in the paternal framework in which everything was in its place; God in heaven, the king in Spain, the governor in the province, the patron on the farm, the farmer in his house with his woman and children, the priest who came and attended spiritually to the needs of the people"

Fr. Roger Vekemans, S.J., ideological thinker of Chilean Christian Democracy, is quoted as hoping that: "Latin American Catholicism, influenced by the way in which the practice of the faith has evolved in Europe and the United States, will undergo a mutation and begin to foster value judgments that, when applied to the secular world, will be conducive to social change and economic development. If this mutation does not take place, Marxism may triumph throughout Latin America."

The Most Rev. Helder Pessoa Camara, leader of the Brazilian Hierarchy, charged that "Liberty is only a name, a sound, for two-thirds of mankind, without house, without clothes, without food, without a minimum of education and above all without human conditions for working. *Unfortunately our Latin American rich men talk very much about basic reforms, but then brand as Communist those who decide to make them real."*

Split-Level Christianity

These warnings could apply to the Philippines as much as to Latin America. The social problem of the Philippines are closer to Latin America perhaps than to problems of our Asian neighbors because of the type of Christianity which is the effect of the same kind of Latin evangelization that converted Latin America.

This type of Christianization was "synchretistic" i.e. it incorporated pro-Christian customs and practices into Catholic rituals and produced beautiful music, rites, art and architecture. Jazz in New Orleans, was a product of this synchretization, as is the Latin music of Spanish American. So, in fact, is Philippine music.

But this fusing process cannot be selective and so retarding traditions and superstitions were continued in the minds of the people, resulting in the "Split-level Christianity" now made famous in Fr. Bulatao's writings on Filipino psychology.

Destroy or Reform?

The "other worldliness" of Latin Catholicism and the early abuses and distortions of spirituality and doctrine (e.q. indulgences) have always provoked reformers and social revolutionists. To them there have been only two ways of dealing with the matter.

To Voltaire there was only one way: "Crush the infamous thing."

To Rizal the way was to liberalize the Church, to purge it just as Martin Luther and the protestant reformers sought, by separation, to reform it and as the Vatican Council has now brought it up to date.

In the past the Church has not always been quick reacting to the demand for change and in adapting itself to the requirements of progress and industrialization. These problems call for social change and a positive body of social doctrine.

The original position of the Church regarding the widening differences between rich and poor was a paternalistic one: "There will always be the rich and the poor. Let the rich be kind to the poor. Let the rich treat the poor like a good father would treat this son. Let the poor learn to respect the rich and learn to be satisfied with his poverty. He will be rewarded in the after life."

At the Notre Dame conference, a Mexican conservative was quoted by Prof. D'Antonio as explaining the social order in the following terms: "I was brought up to believe that God created the rich and the poor. The rich are supposed to take. care of the poor, and the poor, with their limited talents, are supposed to work as hard as they can according to the directions of the rich."

Justice Not Alms

The sum total of this attitude was a paternalistic view of charity. It meant the giving of alms to the poor and the showering of pity on the unfortunate without attempting any basic solution to the problem of social and economic inequality. But as Father Jordan Bishop in his book "Latin America and Revolution" (Sheed & "Ward, London, 1965; pp. 64—65) says:

"*Charity is not a substitute for justice.* Real charity should give us a deeper perception of human dignity, a new dimension in other men which is proper to a Christian world outlook. There is no condescension in it, no flattering benign image in oneself being kind to the poor, but rather an identification of oneself with him who is poor. And should it come to the giving to the poor one's own sufficiency, real charity will find a way to do this without paternalism, without despising the other, without deception."

"*Not that giving to the poor is charity.* It can be and indeed should be, but the word is often used to cover a condescending sort of animal pity which is a mean and degrading thing.

"*Justice is a basic value which must animate Christian social thinking.* The petty bourgeois notion of justice which prevailed in much of the 19th century was prefectly compatible with economic liberalism, with a theory which considered human labor as a commodity to be bought in a competitive market 'like any other commodity.

The Church and Cooperatives

In the Philippines, the Church has began to move away from purely charitable efforts to emphasize the role of justice and social reform in Christian attitudes.

With intense zeal but with no evident national co-ordination, Church groups, schools and mandated organizations have gone successfully into the stimulation of co-operatives in parishes, among fishermen, farmers and office employees. Some of the most successful credit unions in the country are built around parish organizations.

Xavier University in Cagayan de Oro has pioneered in agricultural cooperatives and the Institute of Social Order in Manila has been at work in urban unions. The Asian Social Institute in Manila which operates on scholarships for Filipino and Asian students, is gaining recognition as the center for Christian social instruction in this region.

"Labor Priest"

Catholic trade unionism and peasants' associations have survived on the foundations built by the "labor priest" who first fought for them in the early 1950's and who has had to move his operations abroad due to determined conservative opposition in this country.

The Church seems to be taking strong roots in the middle class but somehow it has managed, up to now, to project a national image as the Church of the conservative and the affluent, alienated from the poor and their problems of daily existence.

Church Lands Sold

In the days of Governor Taft, the Church sold its big estates to the Philippine government with the understanding that they would be resold to the tenants. The lands were sold instead to big landholders.

Later the estates of a religious order in Batangas were sold directly to the tenants. But lack of government credit and support forced the tenants to resell their lands to rich hacenderos. For want of government cooperation and of strong determination of its own, the Church missed an early opportunity to initiate a land reform program that could have precipitated a peaceful Christian Social revolution a generation ahead of the violent upheaval in Central Luzon.

The Church in the Philippines is today committed to social reform but planning and implementation have thus far been sporadic and uncoordinated and have not really changed its national image.

Faith us. Superstition

Most of the problems encountered in our efforts towards social change stem from superstitions and distortions of doctrine that are justified in the minds of our people in terms of religion mostly, of course, the Catholic religion.

In a 1966 study of the problems of land reform in Bulacan, (Philippine Sociological Review, October, 1966, pp. 262-263) UP sociologist Gloria D. Feliciano refers to the notorious spending during town fiestas which has been denounced by other sociologists and community development experts as a disease which results "in perennial poverty of our people." These fiestas, according to the respondents interviewed by Miss Feliciano, enable them to "demonstrate their gratitude to God and patron saint for the bounty of their fields, to show their' generosity by sharing food, ,fun and frolic with people in and out of the barrio, etc."

What Bishop McGrath says of Latin American Catholicism is painfully reminiscent of the Philippine problem: "A person cannot be expected to practice correctly his faith unless 'he knows what that faith really means. *There is in us, and we must shake ourselves out of it, an acquiescense to the external trappings of the Church —that is, to the signs, statues, amulets, scapulars, medals, blessings, and religious fiestas. Only a small number of the faithful receive the sacraments, and, therefore, the interior fruit of these sacraments is realized by only a very small number."*

Miss Feliciano thinks that the fiesta could, if properly reformed, become a change agent in the implementation of land reform. The Church, around which the fiesta is built, is in a splendid position to take the lead by instructing the faithful in [the true nature of the fiesta and de—emphasizing or stamping out the purely pagan, pre-Christian aspect of food offering which is what impoverishes the farmer. Other imaginative solutions could be attempted. For instance in China, the problem of feasts, whether pagan, Christian, or Buddhist, has been solved by obliging the people in each province (each of China's provinces is bigger than the Philippines) to hold their feasts on the same day of the year, thus preventing over—spending due to numerous visitors from outside of town. This could be done, without violence to doctrine and in the exercise of her disciplinary authority, by the Catholic Church in the Philippines.

Need for Ideology

The Church is not to drive blindly towards "improvement in living conditions" without ideological direction. As Bishop McGrath has said: "If we exclusively dedicate ourselves to working for an improvement of living conditions, without stressing the ideology that must go into our concept of life then we are merely promoting a desire for material progress greater than we will be able to produce in our time and this will push persons closer and closer to Communism." (Quoted by George C. Lodge, "Revolution in Latin America," Foreign Affairs, N.Y., January, 1966 p. 193) What Bishop McGrath means is that the Church must approach the people with the total view of progress in terms not only of material advancement but also of human dignity in keeping with the teachings of Christ.

What is required is a comprehensive Christian social program drawing its inspiration from social teachings of the Church. The Dutch Augustinian Fr. Robert Adolfs has said in his book "The Church is Different" (Compass Books, London, 1966, With Imprimatur; p. 138) "An active, socially concerned Christianity, drawing its inspiration from religion, but well organized, too, from a human standpoint, must show the meaning of love for one's neighbor on a world scale. The Catholic Church ought to be giving a lead anywhere in the world Where social injustice is occurring; and she must do this without hidden motives of proselytism. In a number of countries or areas of the world there is need for sociological studies designed to discover ways and means of detaching the Church from antiquated colonial or feudal systems with which in the course of centuries and in some territories (such as South America) she has come to be identified.

"Special attention must be paid to the developing countries; and this should take the form more of a concern for the human being and less of a desire to introduce an ecclesiastical system beautifully structured from a canonical standpoint. A programme of social action on a global scale and deriving from an authentically Christian inspiration (the depth dimension) is part of the essential task of true Catholicism."

Evolution of Social Doctrine

How much has Catholic social doctrine evolved? How far has it progressed from paternalism, to justice?

The noted British Catholic author E.E.Y. Hales in his book "Pope John and his Revolution" (Eyre & Spottiswoode, 1965, London, pp. 43-46) traces Catholic social doctrine from Leo XIII to John XXIII:

"(1) *Workers have a right to the Just Wage*, which means a wage that will keep themselves and their families "in decency."

"(2) 'Pure Socialism' (meaning Marxist Socialism, and especially the First International) is not compatible with Catholic teaching because it looks upon the material organization of human life, in this world, as the final objective of government. However, with Pius XI, "Moderate Socialism" (especially the Second International) is distinguished from "Pure Socialism," or Communism, because it has lost much of its doctrinaire Marxist basis, and is prepared to allow freedom to the Church, to acknowledge some parental rights, some right to private property, etc. and *its aims have become scarcely distinguishable from those of some Christian Democrats.* Pius XI is prepared to concede that some forms of property are best reserved to the State — 'goods which carry with them a power too great to be left to private individuals without injury to the community at large.'

"(3) In the structure of Trade Unions, Leo XIII hoped to see a revival of the medieval guild organizations, in which employer; and employee were combined in a 'vertical union.' But he came to accept the 'horizontal union' (or normal trade union structure) while hoping that the workers could achieve most of their purposes through cooperatives or mutual assistance associations, provided they were not run by anti—Catholic organizations, such as the Freemasons.

"(4) *Unrestricted Capitalism*, which takes no consideration of employees' welfare, thinking only of profit and power, and treating human beings, inhumanly, as though they were merely machines, is illicit. Employers must consider the human rights of their employees (and especially their need to fulfill their religious duties on Sundays). Pius XI speaks of capitalism (meaning unrestricted capitalism) in almost Marxist terms, as though it had killed itself by becoming monopoly capitalism, thereby eliminating the very freedom which had brought it to birth and given it vitality.

"(5) Pius XI developed the concept of the Subsidiary Function. This means that a greater body should never be used to perform a function which can be equally well performed by a lesser body: thus the state should not try to run what can well be left to a regional council, or a regional council what can be left to a local council, or any public body what can be performed by the family. (Author's note: this is the principle of decentralization which even Communist countries are beginning to adopt and which Senator Manahan and I have been pushing in Senate Bill No. 1.)

Welfare State; Socialism

"With Mater et Magistra we are, in fact, brought right into the world of the Welfare State. Gone is not only the semi-feudal world in which Leo saw the simple workman, surrounded by his family, settling down to his frugal but sufficient meal, the just reward of his labour. But gone, too, is communal kitchens, free health services, and free education. Now it is not only free education that is being claimed; it is further education for all those suited by their ability to benefit fnom it.

"The Pope (John XXIII) is notmerely accepting, he is embracing what many would call socialism, and he is acknowledging that a new concept of the duties of the State is involved. He 'calls it 'an increase, in social relationships' and 'a development of the social life of man.' 'It is an effect,' says Mater et Magistra, 'and a cause of the growing intervention of the State even in matters of such intimate concern to the individual as health and education, the choice of a career, and the care and rehabilitation of the physically or mentally handicapped." No longer is the State seen as merely the ultimate protector of the basic right to a minimum wage or, as Pius XII put it, of 'the right to the indispensable means of obtaining a livelihood,' but it is recognized as the active agent in promoting human welfare in a manner undreamed of by Leo XIII and deprecated, when they saw it developing, by Pius XI and Pius XII."

Early Christian Socialism

This odyssey of Catholic social doctrine from paternalism to social justice and Christian social democracy or Christian socialism was anticipated by the Fabian Society, the intellectual precursors of the Socialist (Labor) Party now in power in Britain. Some Fabian Anglican priests began to write tracts on Christian Socialism as early as the 1890's.

During my visit to the Fabian Society headquarters in London last October I was given a copy of "Fabian Tract No. 78" published in 1897 entitled "Socialism and Teaching of Chris " by the Rev. John Clifford, in which he laments that Leo XIII should condemn socialism in general and proceeds to justify socialism in Christian terms in much the same way that Pope John would later substantiate his socialist thesis in "Mater et Magistra" and "Pacem in Terris."

Much later, in 1950 but before Pope John XXIII, another Anglican priest, the Rev. John Groser, in a lecture entitled "Does Socialism need Religion?" quotes the Catholic philosopher Jacques Maritain's book "The Rights of Man" to demonstrate the connection between Christian socialism and the natural law and to show that socialism stands for values which are true whether we accept them or not but which have been conscious to us and deepened in meaning through the Christian gospel.

Maritain says! "The consciousness of the dignity of the person and of the rights of a person remained implicit in pagan antiquity, over which the law of slavery cast its shadow. It was the message of the gospel which suddenly awakened this consciousness, in a divine and a transcendent form, revealing to men that they are called upon to be the sons and heirs of God in the Kingdom of God. Under the evangelical impulses, this same awakening was little by little to spread forth with regard to ..the requirements of natural law, over the realms of man's life here on earth, and of the terrestial city.

"The political task," therefore, "towards which all this must tend is .... to procure the common good of the multitude, in such a manner that each concrete person, not only in a privileged class, but throughout the whole mass, may truly reach that measure of independence which is proper to civilized life and which is insured alike by the economic guarantees of work and property, political rights; civil virtues, and the cultivation of the mind."

Marx and Rizal

Catholic social doctrine must continue to develop in positive response to the injunction of Christ and not merely out of fear of Communism. In fact it is time to acknowledge that the development of Catholic social doctrine, as a body of doctrine, has come after and not before Karl Marx.

Fr. Adolfs in the "Church is Different" (Supra; pp. 125 et seq.) says that "19th century Catholicism was isolated and together with the main Protestant dominatio'ns, remained aloof from the great issues of the time including the social question."

"What did Christianity and the Christian Churches do in this situation?" he asks. "Here and there the voice of protest was heard. Charitable institutions were spurred on to even greater activity. Natural law was invoked to prove that the existence of master and serf, rich and poor, was prescribed by Nature and that the labouring classes must rest content with their lot."

Fr. Adolfs now asks us to turn what Karl Marx has had to say and "get an exact description of this so-called Christian attitude." In 1847 Marx writes:

"The social principles of Christianity proclaim the necessity for a ruling class and a subject class; and for the latter it merely entertains the pious wish that the formen may exercise beneficence toward them. The social principles of Christianity declare that heaven is the place where all injustices will be duly rectified; and therefore these principles justify the continuation of such injustices on earth. The social principles of Christianity explain every outrage perpetrated by the oppressors on the oppressed either as a rightful punishment for original sin, or something of that sort, or as trials visited by the Lord in his infinite wisdom upon his redeemed. The social principles of Christianity. encouraged dullness, lack of self-respect, submissiveness, self-abasement, in short, all the characteristics of the proletariat."

Does this not read like Rizal lampooning 19th century Latin Catholicism in "Noli Me Tangere"?

Communism: First But Inhuman

"What we really end up with here," Fr. Adolfs continues, "is a confrontation of nineteenth century Christianity and Marxism. Over against the feeble, prevaricating attitude of Christianity toward the great human problem of the time, Marx applied himself to working out a programme that would abolish this inhumane social and economic constellation. The misery was only too real; and *his programme, forged under the stress of it, is so radical that it falls into another extreme of inhumanity by seeking to eliminate everything and everybody standing in the way of a 'new world'."*

"But," he says, "there is no getting round it: the Church's isolation gave rise to a grave form of social blindness; and so it was Marx who fathered 'social thinking'."

"In the mid-nineteenth century — just when it was most urgently needed, in fact — no Catholic socio-political programme had been evolved — let alone a doctrine of property or a Catholic doctrine of labour that would have shown the concept–— one so central to the time — in a Christian light."

"Of course, the 'social idea' and way of thinking were not wholly absent from the Church; but at the start they were represented only by a few individuals, who often had to wage a heroic fight against a tide of misunderstanding and evil insinuations."

Father Adolfs minimizes the immediate effectiveness of Rerum Novarum. (The Catholic writer Barbara Ward agrees with him in her book "Faith and Freedom")

"Furthermore," he adds "this encyclical did not aim at social reform but was rather an attempt at accommodation within the capitalist social and economic order. The intention was to maintain labour relations on the existing basis of a 'two class' society and at the same time to improve wage-rates among the workers. *It is only with the encyclical Mater et Magistra (1961) that the basic concepts taken over from capitalism — ownership, capital and wage— agreement —are called in question and relatioized for the first time."*

Bishop Fulton Sheen in his early post-war book "Communism and the Conscience of the West" states that "the philosophy of Communism is on the conscience of the Western world." So also Fr. Adolfs says "we should not be allowed now, therefore, to forget that Marxism and also Communism in its later Marxist-Leninist form were (and still are) a terrible indictment of a 'churchified,' remote, middle-class, laisse-faire Christianity."

Catholicism and Human Institutions

Catholics need not despair over the fact that sometimes the Church is late or is anticipated by other forces at work in the world. As a matter of fact, the Church was not founded so that it might start everything that was new and good. It was founded so that it might incarnate itself in every civilization and infuse its spirit in existing human institutions.

The Church embraced Roman civilization, divested it of its pagan practices and made it the foundation of Western Christendom. For many centuries Catholic philosophical thought, the great scholastic system, was based not in any thing new but on the philosophy of the ancient Greeks.

In the sixteenth century, the Italian Jesuits, their influence reaching the top of the Chinese Empire, sought to make incarnate Christianity in Chinese culture by adopting non-dogmatic aspects of Chinese customs and rites into Catholic practice. Conservatives in Rome blocked their ventures at the time. Recently the Vatican vindicated them by declaring their purpose valid not only for China but for all cultures of the world. It is rather late for China but the decision is proving useful in many parts of Africa and may yet prepare the way for the acceptance of Christianity as a universal, not just Western, religion in Asia.

There are other important examples of how the Church has successfully "taken on" secular externals and infused its own spirits to reshape them for its own spiritual objectives.

'The Knights of Columbus was organized by: an Irish-American Catholic priest in 1882 with the hope (since spectacularly fulfilled) that by adopting the secret ritualism, the fraternal fellowship, the mutual aid activities, (e.g. insurance) of quasi-religious or secular societies such as the Masons, passion among American Catholic men for civic brotherhood could be directed to Catholic objectives.

"Cursillo"

Even more spectacular has been the impact in this country of the tearing away of the "spiritual retreat" idea from its traditional moorings of silence and self-contemplation and its launching into a more mobile course with the driving power of "group Dynamics" — a modern approach to spiritual renewal borrowed from up-to-d'ate psychological theory, traces of which are to be found in "Moral Rearmament" meetings. The Catholic adaptation — the "cursillo" — has produced stunning results in individual Christian renewal in the Philippines.

Were such intense "cursil-lista" dedication to be allowed to apply itself beyond personal Christian renewal to the diffusion and implementation of Catholic social doctrine, we could be witnessing in this country a genuine Christian social revolution sooner than might otherwise be reasonably expected today.

The Philippine Church Today

Fr. Adolfs says "the Christianity of our grandparents and great-grandparents was infused with a mystical *"Welt'flucht"* (a "fleeing from the world"), a strong *Jenseitigkeitserlebung* (cultivation of other-worldliness), that refused to contemplate in any way the injunction to build here and now a world in which all people might find it good to live."

That was the Church and the Christianity that Karl attacked and which Rizal sought to reform.

"How is the Church in the Philippines Today?"

The current meeting on Catholic Rural Reconstruction comes late but not too late, if it is to be followed with total action.

The recent joint pastoral letter of the Catholic Hierarchy must be received with great joy. In stressing agricultural cooperatives, the Bishops have placed a finger on the heart of the problem of productivity.

The Agricultural Land Reform Code, once implemented, would have to depend on cooperative purchasing, planting and marketing by the liberated tenants for final and permanent success.

Land Reform

The Vatican Council decisions, particularly those in the Pastoral Constitution on the Church in the Modern World ("Gaudium et Spes"), commits the Church to support land reform. It would be useful if the Church in the Philippines could come out with a clear statement squarely supporting the implementation of the government's Agricultural Land Reform Code in order to wear down some of the stubborn opposition of conservatives, most of Whom, of course, are Catholics.

The-Pastoral Constitution enjoins all "to establish a better social order and regulate the distribution of land with greater fairness." It decries the existence in underdeveloped areas of "gigantic rural estates" while "the majority of the people are either Without land and have only very small holdings."

Just as our Agricultural Land Reform Code would strike down tenancy as a social evil and not only as .a disincentive to productivity, the Pastoral Constitution laments the condition of "those who are hired to work for the landowners or who till a portion of the land as tenants," who "receive a wage or income unworthy of human beings who "lack decent housing" and who are "exploited by middlemen."

Philippine conditions were certainly in the minds of the

Council Fathers when, in the Pastoral Constitution, they spoke thus of tenants: "Deprived of all securiy, they live under such personal servitude that almost every opportunity for acting on their own initiative and responsibility is denied to them and all advancement in human culture and all sharing in social and political life are ruled out."

Property and Society

The same Pastoral Constitution speaking on the "Common Purpose of Created Things" says: "69. God intended the earth and all that it contains for the use of every human being and people. Thus, as all men follow justice and unite in charity, created goods should abound for them on a reasonable basis. Whatever the forms of ownership may be, as adapted to the legitimate institutions of people according to diverse and changeable circumstances, attention must always be paid to the universal purpose for which created goods are meant. And using them, therefore, *a man should regard his lawful possession not merely as his own but also as common property in the sense that they should accrue to the benefit of not only himself but of others.*

"For the rest, the right to have a share of earthly goods sufficient for oneself and one's family belongs to everyone. According to their ability, let all individuals and governments undertake a genuine sharing of their goods. Let them use these goods especially to provide individual and nations with the means for helping and developing themselves."

"By its very nature, the Fathers asserted, private property has a social quality deriving from the law of the communal purpose of earthly goods. If this social quality is overlooked, property often becomes an occasion of greed and of serious disturbances."

Because this social quality is overlooked, there are serious disturbances in Central Luzon. There will be more serious disturbances all over unless the government and leadership are awakened to their duty to emphasize this social quality.

Christian Social Democracy

Here then is the essence of Christian Social Democratic ideology.

It will redistribute wealth, in response to the spirit of Christian justice not by violence but by the democratic meaning of law.

This process will include the use of the police and taxing power of the State for, the redistribution of land, the spread of ownership of industry, the providing of housing, free education, free medical attention to all citizens who need it or who may not be able to afford it otherwise. "Therefore, there must be made available to all men everything necessary for leading a life truly human, such as food, clothing, and shelter; the right to choose a state of life freely and to found a family, the right to education, employment, to a good reputation, to respect, to appropriate information, to activity in accord with the upright norm of one's own conscience, to protection of privacy and to rightful freedom in matters of religions too." (Pastoral Constitution, Sec. 26)

Economic Planning

Christian Social Democracy will place economic development in the hands of the many and not of the few.

"Economic development must be kept under the control of mankind. It must not be left to the sole judgment of a few men or groups possessing excessive economic power, or of the political community alone, or of certain especially powerful nations. It is proper, on the contrary, that at every level the largest possible number of people have an active share in directing that development." (id. Sec. 65)

It will, therefore, pursue economic planning. Only a year ago, the Bishops of France, tiring of production with social justice, issued a document entitled "Reflexions Sur La Situation Economique Et Sociale Actuelle," which a report published in the Manila Daily Bulletin characterized as "democratic socialist."

Calling for more national planning, the Bishop decried "the inhuman consequences of blind competition based on the principles of economic liberalism and called for "economic initiatives" to be "organically integrated into a general plan. . . the definition of which is the responsibility of government... (with the) permanent cooperation of the various economic groups."

Self-Reliance

Christian Social Democracy will advocate, for developing countries like the Philippines, the acceptance of foreign aid only under honorable terms.

"Additional help should be offered by advanced nations, in the form of either grants or investments. These offers should: 'be made generously and without avarice. They should be accepted honorably. (Pastoral Constitution, Sec. 85)

But above all, it will advise developing nations that "progress begins and develops primarily from the efforts and endowments of the people themselves. Hence, instead of depending solely on outside help they should rely chiefly on the unfolding of their own resources and the cultivation of their own qualities and tradition." (id. Sec. 86 (a))

But traditions must be changed if they retard progress: "If, however, customs cannot answer the new needs of this age, an effort must be made to avoid regarding them as altogether unchangeable." (id. Sec. 69)

Revolt Against Tradition

Christian Social Democracy will lead in destroying superstition that passes as faith.

"The institutions, laws and modes of thinking and feeling do not always seems to be well adapted to the contemporary state of affairs a more critical ability to distinguish religion from a magical view of the world and from the superstitions that still circulate purified religion. . ." (id. Sec. 7)

Prodigality, improvidence, idolatrous excesses in the treatment of religious statues and processions, the cyclic view "gulong ng palad," the "bahala he," the "hiya," are all manifestations of pre-Christian superstitions and beliefs that retard progress and are explained in the mind of the Filipino as religious, and therefore Christian or Catholic in weight.

Minorities

Finally, Christian Social Democracy will revolutionize the treatment of political, ideological, cultural and religious minorities.

So far our attitude toward such minorities has ranged from condescencion and paternalism to "investigation," suppression and outright persecution. All believers in Christ, whether Catholic, Protestant or non-confessional are to be brothers and partners, not enemies in the building of a social democratic nation.

Muslims are not to be called condescendingly "non-Christians," the objects of paternal concern, pity or massive conversion at all costs. Their culture is to be treated as the equal, not the inferior, of the Christian, though they may have retarding customs that need as much change as some of those of the Christian Filipino.

Atheism is to be rejected — but atheists are not to be persecuted.

"While rejecting atheism, root and branch, the Church sincerely professes that all men, believers and unbelievers alike, ought to work for the rightful betterment of this world in which all alike live. Such an ideal cannot be realized, however, apart from sincere and prudent dialogue. *Hence the Church protests against the distinction which some State authorities unjustifiably make between believers and unbelievers, thereby ignoring fundamental rights of the human person.* The Church calls for the active liberty of believers to build up in this world God's temple too. She courteously invites atheists to examine the gospel of Christ with an open mind." (id. Sec. 21)

This means that Marxists, Marxist-Leninists, Communists, those Who may harbor beliefs close to these or those who may sympathize with their cause Will not be hunted down, persecuted or "investigated as criminals" merely for holding to their belief. They are rather to be invited to dialogue and the best of their doctrines, divested of their atheism, to be studied for the possible lessons that they may hold for all in the unending quest for social justice.

Dialogue with Marxists

Pope Paul VI dramatizes this attitude in receiving the President of Soviet Russia, in negotiating with the Communists in Eastern Europe, in expressing his desire for contacts with Peking, and in giving his approval to such organizations as Paulus Gessellscahft which in Germany is dedicated to dialogue with Marxists.

In the University of San Francisco there will be held next August a symposium on "Darwin, Freud and Marx" conducted by Jesuits, which Marxists from all over the world will be invited to attend. Catholics and Protestants recently were hosts to Roger Graudy, chief theoretician of the French Communist Party, in his lecture tour of the United States. Woodstock College, alma mater of hundreds of Filipino Jesuits including the present provincial, Father Horacio de la Costa, last month invited Soviet Embassy officials from 'Washington for lectures on Marxism.

Moscow has just published a Russian translation of French Jesuit Pierre Teilhard de Chardin's "The Phenomenon of Man."

The Vatican Secretariat Non—believers has established Christian Atheist study groups.

This search for understanding through dialogue is carried on without dismantling military alliances or softening the military posture that both sides continue to find necessary to strike in the interest of security. It is being carried on, we might add, in spite of Vietnam, in the hope of discovering enough common belief so that military postures may finally become obsolete.

Rome, in short, has spoken, as our American friend in Washington would like it to speak, decisively, on the way to dialogue and a new social order.

Will the followers of Rome act as decisively?

The Layman's Action

It will do no good for the layman to grumble about "conservatism in high places." The Documents of Vatican II have unequivocally declared that the lay Catholic shares responsibility with his bishop and priests for the conduct of the Church and for the incarnation of the Christian spirit in secular society.

Will the layman act? A world in revolution, and along with it the Filipino nation with a largely Christian soul, awaits that action.

APPENDIX

POLICY DEFECTS CITED
IN LOCAL AUTONOMY ACT

FERDINAND E. MARCOS

(The President's message to the House explaining why he vetoed the Decentralization Bill)

Gentlemen of the Congress:

I have the honor to return herewith, without my signature, the bill (S. No. 1 —— H. No. 3100) entitled:

"AN ACT DECENTRALIZING AND RE-DISTRIBUTING CERTAIN GOVERNMENT POWERS AND RESOURCES TO LOCAL GOVERNMENTS."

After having gone over the various provisions of this bill and studied the comments, opinions and recommendations of competent persons and relevant institutions, both private and governmental, whose views on this vital and far-reaching issue I have sought to arrive at a fair and just conclusion compatible with the national interest, I have found many basic and fundamental policy defects which alone could have justified the veto of this bill.

Lnfirmities

Even if I were inclined to sign the bill notwithstanding its many defects in relation to policy, I have no other alternative but to take note of its constitutional infirmities. It is this constitutional doubt inherent in the bill that constrains me to return this measure. To quote a. constitutional authority:

"But when all the legitimate lights for ascertaining the meaning of the Constitution have been made use of it may still happen that the construction remains a matter of doubt. In such a. case it seems clear that every one called upon to act Where, in his opinion, the proposed action would be of doubtful constitutionality, is bound upon the doubt alone to abstain from acting. Whoever derives power from the Constitution to perform any public function is disloyal to that instrument, and grossly. derelict in duty, if he does that which he is not reasonably satisfied the Constitution permits. Whether the power be legislative, executive, or judicial, there is manifest disregard of constitutional and moral obligation by one who, having taken an oath to observe that instrument, takes part in an action which he cannot say he believes to be no violation of its provisions. A doubt of the constitutionality of any proposed legislative enactment should in any case be reason sufficient for refusing to adopt it, and, if legislators do not act upon this principle, the reasons upon which are based the judicial decisions sustaining legislation in very many cases will cease to be of force." (1 Cooley's Constitutional Limitations (8th ed.) 153.)

Learned framers

The learned framers of our Constitution, some of whom still sit with that august body, have decided upon the establishment in this country of a unitary or centralized system of democratic government under which the President shall exercise general supervision over local governments, rejecting by that token an imperium in impem, or the concept of an autonomous municipal government within a state as detrimental to a strong national government and as not suited to our country's interests.

Thus, under the Constitution, Congress may not grant the President the power of control over political subdivisions. (Mondano v. Silvosa, 51 O.G. 2884; Hebron v. Reyes,_G.R. No. L-9124, July 28, 1958). By the same token neither may it so reduce the general supervisory power of the President over local governments as to virtually remove or nullify it. To quote the late Justice Laurel:

"It is an illusion to think of this. if we bear in mind the fact that these municipalities are public corporations created by the State. A municipality cannot be set up in the position of an important in imperio. The municipality, even if it so desires, cannot completely emancipate itself from the central government. An autonomy, partial, sound and constructive, is the most that it can aspire for."

The authors of the present bill appear to be of the impression, as indicated in the explanatory note, that we have an "overcentralized system of government, a system imposed by the colonial powers." While this might have been true at the time of our independence, it is a fact attested by recent legislation that Congress has already granted greater independence or autonomy to local governments compatible with a unitary or centralized system of government, as provided in the Constitution.

Significant step

Republic Act No. 2264, approved in 1959, in the passage of which I have contributed, marks a significant step towards the establishment of local autonomy. Therein local governments are granted broader taxing powers, more freedom in the preparation of their budgets and the right to choose their own officials. Even the smallest unit of government, the barrios, have to a certain extent been endowed by Congress with self-governing powers. Republic Act No. 2370, approved on June 22, 1968, endowed the barrios with separate legal personalities as quasi-corporations and vested with powers including that of taxation.

On the erroneous assumption that our system of government is still "overcentralized," the present bill declares it to be the policy of the State "to transform local governments gradually into effective instruments through which the people can, in a most genuine fashion, govern themselves and work out their own destinies," and in accordance therewith, seeks to transfer to local governments various powers and functions, essentially national in character, in order to enable them to operate as autonomous, self-government units.

It is evident, therefore, that the bill, if signed into law, would not merely decentralize or redistribute the powers of government but would practically establish or implant in the Philippines that system of local self-government which was precisely rejected by the Constitutional Convention. However desirable, this indeed may not be done without first amending the Constitution.

Bill prejudicial to rice program, public works and infrastructure projects.

Constitutional detects

Apart from the constitutional defects of the bill, there is also the paramount consideration of its implications open the national programs that we have adopted towards the solution of our perennial problem of rice shortage and the corollary problems of road building and construction and development of other infrastructure projects all too vital to the growth of the national economy. It is my strong conviction that the present bill, if allowed to become a law, would prove a serious obstacle to our nationwide efforts to. bring an end to our rice problem and our inadequacies in public works.

The bill clearly deprives the national government of its fundamental function insofar as concerns the implementation of the rice production program as well as the road-building program. The first is fully and the latter partly financed by the general funds. Agricultural" extension work which is essential in rice production is proposed to be transferred to the provinces. Public works expenditure is proposed to be transferred to parties other than those that have prepared and started to implement the program pertaining thereto. If the hill were approved in its present form, the national government cannot after such transfer create any new office or appoint new officers for the functions so transferred, first because of the lack of legal authority and second because of the lack of funds appropriated for the purpose.

National character

Moreover, by removing from the national government and vesting in the provinces the agricultural extension work, a function that is national in character, and thus divorcing it from the over-all national policy, direction and coordination, a precondition which I consider necessary to the success of the rice program, the bill would lead to an almost absurd situation where plans are drawn at the national level and implemented, if at all, at the local level, thus resulting in the bifurcation of what should be complementary efforts of planning and implementation. In addition to this fragmentation of effOrts there is the primary question of funding. Since under the bill the source of the funds for the transferred services, estimated to cost about 'P53 million annually, is the general fund, to that extent therefore the national government will be deprived of the finances necessary to support the rice program envisioned.

It is all too easy to say that the provincial governments can be trusted with the responsibility of carrying out national programs on the local level. But, even if the provincial governments were to be entrusted with the implementation of some national programs, as we have always maintained they should be, as far as the present bill is concerned it does not give the President any power of correction in case of errors or failures of the local government in the discharge of its implementing functions. The Executive cannot create a new office which would take over or supplement the functions of agricultural extension nor that of rural health nor that of public works. The exclusive powers in relation to this are transferred to the provincial governments by this bill. When I consider that what is involved here is the rice problem itself, a problem crucial to our future economic survival that has defied solution for the last fifty years, I do not have any second thoughts in withholding from the local governments the agricultural extension function sought to be transferred by this bill although I am in favor of their performing such function in a manner supplementary to the national government.

Rice production

Hand in hand with the rice production program, and essential to its eventual solution, is the massive public works construction program and other infrastructure projects which the government has initiated and started to implement Irrigation, roads and bridges have already been constructed in many parts of the country as part and parcel of this national program as planned, implemented and coordinated from the national viewpoint.

I am of the firm belief that in order to successfully proeecute our national public works construction program and infrastructure projects, it is essential that the control of planning, coordination and implementation as well as the funding thereof shall remain with the national government. By setting aside and allocating sixty percentum of public works funds available in the general fund for community projects the listing of which shall be prepared upon consultation with the representative of the congressional district concerned, this bill takes away from the national government that very control deemed expedient and indispensable to the implementation of those projects.

In view of the fOregoing objectionable features of the bill and after considerable reflection, I have decided to veto the same. I have however certified to that body a substitute bill without the defects adverted to herein

Land of Bondage – Land of the Free

Raul S. Manglapus was born in Manila. He completed his Bachelor of Arts, summa cum laude. at the Ateneo de Manila in 1939 and pursued his study of law at the University of Santo Tomas, Manila and at Georgetown University, Washington, D.C. From 1948 to 1954 he was Professor of Constitutional Law at the College of Law of the Ateneo de Manila. Manglapus served in the Cabinet in 1954 as Undersecretary of Foreign Affairs, and later in 1957, as Secretary of Foreign Affairs. In 1961 he was elected Senator of the Philippines with the highest number of votes. His term of office ends in 1967, after which he will devote his time to the Christian Social Movement, to the practice of law and to his civic activities and speaking engagements in the Philippines and abroad. He has authored several books and his speeches have been anthologized. This publication gives insight to the brilliant years of his service to the Philippine government.

Over the past two decades, a great social revolution has been sweeping through Asia. First stirred by the ideas and techniques, the philosophy and technology, the systems of government and material goods brought by Western colonizers, and then spurred on by the retreat of the colonizers after the war, the revolution has often taken on violent forms, sweeping away both the colonial masters and the traditional leadership, upsetting the old order, but not yet quite adjusted to the new. Indeed in many cases not yet having devised a new political and social order to replace the old.

In most countries of Asia, the revolution overthrew both colonial master and traditional leader in one blow. In the Philippines, however, the transfer of power from the United States to the traditional landowning elite was gradual and orderly. The sharp thrust of revolution was thus blunted, and the traditional elite remains in power to this day, heating down sporadic outbursts of armed rebellion.

In most countries of Asia, the revolution overthrew both colonial master and traditional leader in one blow. In the Philippines, however, the transfer of power from the United States to the traditional landowning elite was gradual and orderly. The sharp thrust of revolution was thus blunted, and the traditional elite remains in power to this day, beating down sporadic outbursts of armed rebellion.

But in recent years a quiet revolution has been taking shape in the Philippines intended to diffuse political and economic power among the masses. Uniquely in Asia, this revolution is being carried out through the regular democratic institutions. How this is being done can be seen clearly in the pages of this book, in which are reproduced the significant portions of the proceedings in the Philippine Senate on three revolutionary measures meant to redistribute power, currently in the hands of the elite few, among the long-dispossessed many.

These measures would institute land reform, strengthen provincial and city governments and restore a degree of self-government to the Philippine village. All of them were sponsored by Senator Raul S. Manglapus, one of the leaders — and indisputably the most eloquent spokesman — of new Philippine challenge to the rule of its old oligarchy.